THE NOVELS OF GEORGE ELIOT

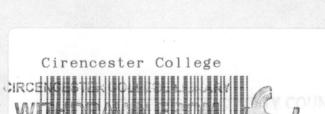

THE NOVELS OF
George Eliot

A STUDY IN FORM

by

BARBARA HARDY

UNIVERSITY OF LONDON
THE ATHLONE PRESS

Published by
THE ATHLONE PRESS
UNIVERSITY OF LONDON
at 4 Gower Street, London WC1

Distributed by
Tiptree Book Services Ltd
Tiptree, Essex

USA and Canada
Humanities Press Inc
New York

First edition 1959
First paperback edition, with corrections 1963
Reprinted 1973

First printed in Great Britain by
WESTERN PRINTING SERVICES LTD, BRISTOL
Reprinted by offset lithography by
THE PITMAN PRESS, BATH

To My Mother and Father

GLADYS AND MAURICE NATHAN

CIRENCESTER SCHOOL

Presented by

POWELL EDUCATIONAL

FOUNDATION

1979

ACKNOWLEDGEMENTS

CHAPTERS Nine and Eleven of the present work have already appeared, more or less as they do here, in the form of articles in *The Review of English Studies* and *The Modern Language Review*. I am grateful to the editors of both journals for their courtesy in permitting me to reprint this material. Perhaps I should add that it is material designed from the outset to form part of this book.

I have to thank the staff of the British Museum Library, and the staff of Birkbeck College Library. The book had its origin in lectures given to Birkbeck students, and I should like to express particular gratitude to the members of a discussion group on *Middlemarch*.

My debt to Professor Gordon S. Haight's edition of *The George Eliot Letters* will be self-evident, and I am grateful to Professor Haight and to Yale University Press for permission to quote from this edition.

To my husband and to Professor Geoffrey Tillotson I am indebted in ways which cannot easily be phrased in the usual formulae. I am very grateful to Joanna Smith for doing much of the typing.

Birkbeck College,   B.H.
University of London,
May 1958

CONTENTS

A NOTE ON REFERENCES

All quotations from George Eliot's novels are taken from the first edition, whether in serial or volume form. For the convenience of most readers I have given references to modern continuous chapter numbering, except in the case of *The Mill on the Floss*, where most later editions still retain the original chapter numbering within books.

SELECT BIBLIOGRAPHY

WORKS BY GEORGE ELIOT

Scenes of Clerical Life. First published in *Blackwood's Edinburgh Magazine* (cited as *Blackwood's*), January–November 1857.

Adam Bede. 1859.

The Lifted Veil. Blackwood's, July 1859.

The Mill on the Floss. 1860.

Silas Marner. 1861.

Romola. First published in *The Cornhill Magazine*, July 1862– August 1863.

Brother Jacob. The Cornhill. 1864.

Felix Holt, the Radical. 18ᶜ 3.

The Spanish Gypsy. A Poem. 1868.

Middlemarch. First published in eight parts, 1871–2.

The Legend of Jubal and other poems. 1874.

Daniel Deronda. First published in eight parts, 1876.

Impressions of Theophrastus Such. 1879.

Early Essays. 1919. Privately printed, Westminster Press.

The George Eliot Letters. Edited by Gordon S. Haight. Vols. i–iii, 1954, vols. iv–vii, 1956 (cited as Haight).

Quarry for Middlemarch. Edited by Anna Theresa Kitchel. 1950.

OTHER WORKS

Eisenstein, S. M.: *The Film Sense.* 1948.
— *Film Form.* 1951.

Empson, W.: *Some Versions of Pastoral.* 1935.

James, Henry: *Daniel Deronda: A Conversation.* This first appeared in *The Atlantic Monthly*, December 1876, and was included in *Partial Portraits*, 1888. It is reprinted by F. R. Leavis in *The Great Tradition.*

— *The Art of the Novel.* With an introduction by R. P. Blackmur, 1934. This is a collection of James's Prefaces to The New York Edition of the Novels and Tales, 1907–9.

Select Bibliography

James, Henry: *The House of Fiction*. Edited by Leon Edel, 1957. This includes the review of *Middlemarch* which James wrote for *The Galaxy*, March, 1873.

Leavis, F. R.: *The Great Tradition*. 1948.

Lubbock, Percy: *The Craft of Fiction*. 1921.

Tillotson, Kathleen: *Novels of the Eighteen-Forties*. 1954.

Willey, Basil: *Nineteenth Century Studies*. 1949.

INTRODUCTION

THIS study is not an attempt at a full critical commentary on George Eliot's art and thought, but is chiefly concerned with her power of form, a striking but relatively disregarded aspect of her work as a novelist. I have however interpreted formal power as widely as possible since it is in this case, as in most others, difficult to abstract strictly formal features like development or contrast or symmetry from such things as plot and character and language.

George Eliot had the special problem of using the novel as a tragic form. She speaks of attempting to write tragedy in the strict sense, and her formal contrivances are often made in the interests of her version of tragedy. She describes herself as urging 'the human sanctities through tragedy—through pity and terror as well as admiration and delights' (Haight, iv, p. 301). Her tragedy sometimes seems to depend more on pity than on any other emotion, presenting ordinary rather than extraordinary heroes, though much less consistently than Mario Praz, in *The Hero in Eclipse in Victorian Fiction*, would have us believe. Even when her protagonist has extraordinary qualities, like Adam Bede or Dorothea Brooke, and demands admiration as well as pity, it is true that her tragedy does not rest on special cases but tries to concern itself with the common human condition. Her novels are social tragedy not merely because she tries to expose the social cause and the social reaction but because she shows tragedy as common experience. Her vision of humanity finds its own appropriate forms: comprehensive rather than selective, tentative rather than dogmatic.

The largeness and comprehensiveness of her novels have meant that she has not been admired as a great formal artist. When critics have turned to questions of narrative form it has been Flaubert or Henry James who have provided the models, certainly not George Eliot. Percy Lubbock, whose *Craft of Fiction* is still one of the most interesting discussions of form in the novel, scarcely mentions George Eliot, though many

Introduction

of the narrative features he discusses are present in her work. But Lubbock seems to inherit Henry James's prejudice against the apparently diffuse and rambling structure of novels with multiple plots, and where he speaks of the 'loose, unstructural form' of *War and Peace*, Henry James speaks, in his Preface to *The Tragic Muse*, of the 'large loose baggy monsters' of *The Newcomes* and *War and Peace*, and describes *Middlemarch*, in a review, as 'a treasure-house of detail, but an indifferent whole'. James was probably more interested in narrative form than any other novelist writing in English, and he is certainly the first English critic to pay sustained attention to the special problems of the novel form. But his concept of form is a very personal and restricted one, based on the tautness of dramatic tension and eschewing multiplicity and even the appearance of accidentality. For all his intelligence, he sometimes equated the multiple plot with accidentality and formal carelessness; George Eliot's view of narrative tension was certainly a looser and more generous one than James's, but she hoped that every detail in *Middlemarch* had its place in the design of the whole. It is the unreliable Pulcheria, in James's *Daniel Deronda: A Conversation*, who says that George Eliot 'has no sense of form'. Theodora, the admirer and defender, can only assent, making the qualification, 'There is something higher than form—there is spirit'. It is my contention that spirit and form are not opposites in George Eliot's novels: the apparently rambling and circumstantial expression of her spirit has its own formal principles.

Adverse comments on her structural power were frequent in contemporary reviews: as George Willis Cooke pointed out in his book, *George Eliot: A Critical Study* (1883), there was an 'almost universal condemnation' of her plots for want of unity and order. Even recent critics have often endorsed this condemnation or—apart from several critics interested in her imagery—have said little about the formal problems. This is not simply a matter of blindness on the part of George Eliot's critics. The problem of narrative form has until quite recently been regarded in a number of simplified ways. Critics with less sense of the subtleties of narrative composition can be pardoned for going even further astray than Henry James. The concept of the ideal narrative form as a simple, single, and lucid story dies hard. Theodore Watts-Dunton, for instance, in his introduction to the World's Classics edition of *Silas Marner*, says: 'As a rule, however, she shows but a slight power over the great art of construction. And this gives an added importance to *Silas Marner*—the one story of hers which can be approached from the artistic point of view, for it has a plot and a very good one.' It is plain that he is following many of George Eliot's earlier critics in thinking of construction as the simple unfolding of an uncomplicated story. If narrative simplicity is our criterion of formal unity and organization, then *Silas Marner* is rare indeed, for George Eliot's forms are almost always highly complicated and intricate organizations, and although *Silas Marner* itself has its own kind of intricacy and design it is certainly simple when we compare it with *Middlemarch* and *Daniel Deronda*.

The rejection of the 'large loose baggy monsters' may be partly explained by James's interest in the dramatic form, but it probably owes something also to his interest in the plastic arts. As Lubbock points out, the criticism of the novel has been invaded by terms from criticism of the other arts, 'words that suppose a visible and measurable object, painted or carved'. The concept of pleasing shapeliness has tended to distract attention from the less obviously discernible 'shape' of long novels. It is easy to see what is meant by the shapeliness of a short or single narrative, where the scope of the human delineation seems to be easily fitted into the curve of beginning, middle, and end. We have to enlarge our concept of narrative shapeliness when we read Tolstoy and Dickens and George Eliot, though this does not mean that their larger and more complex delineation cannot meet the aesthetic demands of unity and order. The novel can gratify the formal pleasure in balance and opposition and unity, and at the same time present its intellectual and moral analysis of men and societies.

The nature and importance of George Eliot's formal power has to some extent been understandably obscured by her power of creating a lively image of man in society. This image is realistic: it gives a full and precisely-documented community, and an overflowing sense of humanity—both in psychological observation and in a Shakespearean sense of character. In many of the novelists of the twentieth century the narrative form—the use of structural rather than human relations of characters, the deliberate and obvious patterning of episodes, the flow of related images—is especially conspicuous because it is often part of an unrealistic delineation. In the novels of James Joyce, Virginia Woolf, or William Faulkner, there is a disruption of the realistic surface of language, characters and chronology, and this usually means that the compositional features are as insistent as they are in a non-representational painting. It is hard to say whether the absence or distortion of conventional narrative makes the pattern plainer, or whether the pattern is pressed into the service of making a distorted human delineation plain and significant. It is probably a little of both. And in addition it may be that the insistent virtuosity of the pattern compensates for the absence of a realistic story and a realistic portrait. The pattern is there in George Eliot's human scene, as it is in Rembrandt's, but in both its presence is less naked and its function less dependent on the reader's immediate recognition than in more stylized and less realistic art. In many later novels it is essential to grasp the formal relations of the characters in order to follow the story and grasp the theme. The relationships of characters may be so isolated or projected against a screen of symbol, as, for instance, with the relationship of Leopold Bloom and Stephen Dedalus, or that of Mrs Dalloway and Septimus Warren, that they appear as formal relationship rather than ordinary human relationship. The importance of Bloom's encounter with Stephen depends largely on this formal reading. We read the encounter in terms of ironical antithesis—the son looking for a father, the father for a son, with the Hamlet-Dedalus-Telemachus echoes pointing the way. We read it in terms of ironical parallelism—two exiles from religion and country and family. It is these formal contrasts and parallels which are prominent in the relationship of the two men, and not the human process and consequence of their brief encounter. It is perhaps often true that the novel, least sensuous of all forms of art, relies on this kind of formal assertiveness to give a satisfaction which may be felt separately and strongly apart from the human material it is shaping. But it would be usually also true that, as in a representational picture with a conspicuously balanced composition, the delight in the unity and variety and symmetry is only a part of the total response.

George Eliot's composition is usually as complex and as subtle as the composition of Henry James or Proust or Joyce, but it is very much less conspicuous because of the engrossing realistic interest of her human and social delineation. In order to recognize this we must put aside the simple notions of the lucid or single well-made story, and recognize that the form of the novel can mean the co-operation of a large number of forms within the novel. The form of the novel must certainly be thought of in terms of its flow and continuity, though this is by no means the only way of approaching narrative form. In the case of novels published serially, as some of George Eliot's were, the organization of the reader's curiosity is, as Mrs Tillotson has pointed out in *The Novels of the Eighteen-forties*, a special problem. We know something of the influence serial publication had on the novels of Dickens. We know that Henry James felt the stimulus and benefit of composing *The Ambassadors* in twelve connected but separately articulated parts. But it would, I think, be difficult to demonstrate that the flow of preparation, tension and curiosity in *Middlemarch* was very different from that of *Felix Holt*, which was not published in parts. There is in fact rather more purely narrative curiosity aroused in *Felix Holt* than in any of George Eliot's novels because from the very beginning we are presented plainly with a mystery—the mystery of Mrs Transome's past. Blackwood[1] received the novel in parts, and was placed in the position of a serial-reader, reacting by guessing and wondering. After reading the first two volumes, where, we might well suppose, the accumulating hints pointed very clearly to Jermyn as Mrs Transome's old lover and even as Harold's father, Blackwood said, rather innocently, 'I am uneasy as to what Mrs Transome has done' (Haight, iv, p. 245). George Eliot let this pass, but on another occasion reacted

[1] Unless otherwise stated the Blackwood referred to is John Blackwood.

sternly to the same kind of speculation. When Alexander Main, her Scottish admirer who compiled the *Wise, Witty and Tender Sayings of George Eliot*, and who was nicknamed 'The Gusher' by Blackwood, began to speculate on the future of Dorothea, George Eliot wrote in rebuke: 'Try to keep from forecast of Dorothea's lot, and that sort of construction beforehand which makes everything that actually happens a disappointment' (Haight, v, p. 261).

As a serial-writer, she was emphatically not interested in keeping the reader guessing,[1] but very much more concerned with balance and continuity. She gave up £3,000 rather than divide *Romola* into sixteen parts, instead of fourteen, for its serial publication in *The Cornhill*. Some alterations were made in *Middlemarch* to meet the practical problems of serial form,[2] but they show her interest in the unity of the novel as a whole rather than in the construction of separate tensions. Lewes wrote to Blackwood a few days before sending him the first part of the manuscript of *Middlemarch*:

> We have added on to the end of part I that portion of part II which closes with the scene at the miserly uncle's—a capital bit to end with; and this new arrangement not only pitches the interest forward into part II, but also equalises quantities better, though making part I rather longer than II which however is desirable. (Haight, v, p. 184)

Joseph Langford, *Blackwood's* London manager, disagreed, and wrote to Blackwood:

> I think she has made a mistake in construction—the part should have ended with Miss Brooke's marriage, whereas after the marriage has been announced she diverts the interest just when it might have been concentrated. She might easily have brought the new people in earlier. (Haight, v, p. 207)

The interest is to be very lengthily diverted from Dorothea, and George Eliot plainly felt that the diversion should begin in the first part. On the other hand, she felt the danger of a too complete diversion, and therefore changed her mind about

---

[1] The probable exception is *Scenes of Clerical Life*: see below, pp. 167–8.
[2] I use 'serial' to describe those novels published in parts as well as her orthodox 'serials'.

the second part, which was originally planned to exclude Dorothea completely. Lewes wrote to William Blackwood:

> We think that the absence of Dodo and her husband from Part II will be felt injuriously and that the part would be greatly strengthened in interest if some of her story be introduced, and to make way for it some scenes must be transposed to Part III. (Haight, v, p. 224)

Chapters xix–xxii were eventually transferred from Book III to Book II—they are the chapters describing the Casaubons' stay in Rome. There was some subsequent discussion about the best conclusion for Book VII. Blackwood suggested that a break might come at the end of chapter lxxiii, which leaves the reader in suspense about the reactions of Rosamond and Mrs Bulstrode to the disgrace which has fallen on both their husbands, but decided in favour of the break coming at the end of chapter lxxi:

> On thinking over the division of the Books I feel that Dorothea's declaration of standing by Lydgate is so good an opening for what is to be expected in the last book that it is the most appropriate finish for Book 7, so I would not mind making one Book thin and the other thick. (Haight, v, pp. 307, 308)

And Lewes wrote back agreeing. Reviewers applauded the happy results of serial form. The reviewer in *The Edinburgh Review* of January 1873, for instance, compared the agitation of interest aroused by *Middlemarch* with that 'with which the Youth of Cambridge tore open the packets of the new volumes of *Clarissa*', though he went on to suggest that the serial form might blind readers to structural defect: 'The arrangement of the groups, their mutual connexion, and their relations in perspective, may provoke criticism which we who are under the immediate influence of the gradually progressive story can hardly appreciate.' This perceptive critic found however in both form and material a mode of deliberately fragmentary representation and an avoidance of 'central effect' comparable with the painting of Turner. Although George Eliot was very much less practically serial-minded than Dickens, the form in which the novel was to be presented to the reader was obviously a determining factor, though she was interested in

7

the flow and continuity of her novels for many other reasons. And the flow of the narrative is itself only a part of the story.

We often speak, with the common-sense of metaphor, of the 'shape' of the novel, meaning something more aesthetically assertive than the necessary manipulation of a well-made story. Pictorial and sculptural analogies of 'shape', or 'moulding' or 'outline' have a certain limited applicability. There are some novels which leave the reader with the final impression of roundedness or smoothness or balance or symmetry or resolved tension, and this kind of metaphorical summary of a response to a novel may be recognizing the similarity of the formal process in all the arts. Our metaphors may indeed have particular descriptive point: there is some sense in thinking of *Anna Karenina* in terms of contrast and counterpoint, or of *Wuthering Heights* in terms of balance and antithesis, or of *The Rainbow* as a growing spiral, or of *Ulysses* as isolated blocks. But it will not do to rest on this kind of analogy because it will probably mean that we are content to equate the form of a novel with the outline of its action, and this would be excessive simplification. To speak of the shapeliness of a novel by Flaubert or Henry James may be entirely accurate but it is rather as if we were to speak of the shape of the human body and think we had said the last word about its structure. The novel may be described in terms of the outline—the disposition of its trunk and limbs—but it must also be recognized as depending on the presence of pattern in every unit, like the pattern within the pattern of a Chinese puzzle or of any bit of matter. The form of the novel may mean the form of everything which contributes to its six hundred pages of story and scenes and events and characters and words and tone. I say 'may mean' advisedly, because there are dead ends when we explore the units of pattern in literature as there are not when we analyse the human body. Some writers—and George Eliot is one—are susceptible to a much more extended formal analysis than others.

George Eliot's organization, like Shakespeare's, extends, for instance, to her imagery. Her irony, her continuity, and her presentation of change and collision, depend to some extent on repetitions, more or less prominent, of phrases and images which may make a casual first appearance. But we need not expect every novelist to use the verbal forms so prominently, and when Mrs Gaskell, for instance, uses recurring images from *The Arabian Nights* in *North and South* it is, I think, rather because of personal predilection or casual association than because these images vibrate recognizably beyond the immediate occasion on which they are used. And the novel, which can say very much more, in quantitative terms, than the lyric poem, very often uses the verbal medium of prose dramatically or reflectively or informatively but without drawing it into the composition and organizing repetition and symmetry and contrast in words as well as in action and in characters. George Eliot's power of composition is a very extensive one and, although she is not generally thought of as a sensuously 'poetic' writer like Melville or Emily Brontë or Lawrence, we lose a great deal, as critics and perhaps as readers too, if we do not see the way in which her words form part of her total pattern. It is only when we recognize the repetitions and formal converse of the imagery in *Middlemarch* and *Daniel Deronda* that we begin to see not only the kind of human generalization she is making but also why certain passages seem to have something we want to describe as resonance and dignity even when the pictorial or musical qualities of the language are perhaps not especially impressive. This formal attentiveness to words may well go beyond the kind of attentiveness we expect to give to the novel, and it is certainly true that it comes out of the unnatural activity of reading novels many times and at varying speeds. Yet the unnaturally attentive reader is doing no more than approach the detailed attentiveness which even the uncreative writer usually gives to his writing, and in the case of novels of the last two centuries there is the further consideration that novels were more likely to be read aloud. George Eliot and Lewes read to each other, Frederic Harrison, commenting on what he called the 'undertones' of her novels, told her that he knew readers of *Felix Holt* who read it aloud and even learnt passages by heart, 'like stanzas of *In Memoriam*', and Henry James's Pulcheria spent six months reading *Daniel Deronda* aloud, always arriving 'by the

9

same train as the new number'. In the case of serially published novels like *Romola* and *Middlemarch*, there was even more encouragement to read slowly and expectantly, on the watch for clues, and with perhaps a final recapitulatory reading when the novel was published in volume form. The reviewer in *Blackwood's*, December 1872, insisted that *Middlemarch* must be read twice; George Eliot may not have written with the serial-reader's guessing habits in mind, but she may well have written in the consciousness of a slower and more attentive reader.

It is surely true that the human delineation is the part of a novel to which the reader gives most scrupulous attention, but here again we lose something if we read the story—and here I would include with the story what George Eliot thought of as the 'aesthetic teaching'—solely in terms of ordinary human relations. Like *King Lear* and *War and Peace* the novels of George Eliot depend on the emphasis of formal relations as well as the ordinary interest of the human relations of loving and hating and betraying and serving and so on. Here the formal element binds, unifies, and makes a moral emphasis. Just as it is possible to see the pattern of continued and varied images making part of the form of the novel, so it is possible—and even more important—to see a pattern of symmetry and contrast and repetition forming the tension and irony of action, and contributing to the definiteness and the mutability of what we call theme or generalization. For the intensive patterning of all the units of the novel in George Eliot is not, as it is in the plays of John Lyly, for instance, something which looks very much like the product of an abstract though delightful interest in pattern *qua* pattern. In these novels the pattern is rather the product of a particular kind of generalizing and qualifying vision of the human lot.

This formal organization of characters, very common in drama and fairly common in the novel, is again not something we find in all novels. Its absence or presence seems to have little to do with meritoriousness. There are minor novelists (Harriet Beecher Stowe, for instance) who use highly patterned characters, and great novelists (Fielding, perhaps) who do not. The conspicuousness of the pattern seems to vary enormously. Dickens's carefully annotated and dramatically high-lighted parallelism of Edith Granger and Alice Marwood in *Dombey and Son* is very different from George Eliot's version of the formal parallel in the doubled situations of Mrs Transome and Esther Lyon, or of Dorothea and Lydgate, or of Gwendolen and Mirah. In George Eliot the formal relations of the characters are usually presented unassertively. They are inferred or collected by the reader in the process of reading rather than followed with the loudly explicit guidance of the author's directions. Similarly her images echo much more quietly than the underlined repetitions and cross-references of the imagery in *The Golden Bowl*. Guidance is there in George Eliot's novels but it is often given unobtrusively.

It is because her organization, though complex and sustained, is so embedded in her narrative that it has usually passed unpraised. This is not just because her dramatic variety is greater than Dickens's, but because the formality of his treatment is made more conspicuous by his mode of characterization. Edith Granger and Alice Marwood, or Nancy and Rose Maylie in *Oliver Twist*, are conspicuous as formal doubles, not just because Dickens takes great pains to show the pairing and to underline it melodramatically, but also because the characters themselves have the simple and striking resemblances and differences of simple and striking stereotypes. George Eliot's dramatic penetration and psychological commentary create much more complex and mobile characters, and so there is always the disguising quality of human fullness and change as well as the formal attitude of similarity and contrast. For rather different reasons, her formal use of imagery is also disguised. Her vocabulary and syntax are very much less eccentric and mannered than James's or Faulkner's, and so are less meticulously inspected by the reader or even perhaps by the attentive critic. But very probably the reasons for the obscured formality are not so widely different: both in language and action, George Eliot's world has a quiet normality, and it is this quietness which, above all, diverts our attention from its complicated artifice.

It is the normal appearance of the world which is perhaps responsible also for the kind of tragedy which emerges from her human delineation. All her formal intricacy, far from providing the assertive geometrical pleasures of Lyly, is working in the interest of a tragic statement. Her characters are so organized that the reader makes the moral generalization in the process of the formal reading, like seeing trees bent out of shape by the prevailing wind. Her prevailing wind is the human egoism which may be damned or redeemed, and we make this generalization not because George Eliot, like Meredith in the introduction to *The Egoist*, explicitly makes it for us, in her own voice, but because the tragic 'flaw' is repeated, in large and in little, throughout her novels. And this kind of formal generalization is not made in character alone, it extends also to action. The diffused exemplariness of the characters who make the moral statement by accreting resemblances or differences is supported also by the same kind of formal placing of events. In actions and scenes as well as words and characters there is almost always more than the realistic sequence and relation, and she uses coincidence in action and plot with the same kind of significant symmetry and antithesis.

This does not mean, as anyone who has read even one novel by George Eliot must know, that the formal statement makes explicit and direct statement redundant. In later novels we are used to the assertions of form acting as stand-in for the absent author[1]—in *Ulysses* or *A Fable*, for instance, the full significance of the characters' relations has to be accumulated formally, and antithesis or resemblance becomes a way of making character act as symbol. But just as Joyce and Faulkner make their formal relations of character clearer by using the ironical backcloth of myth, so George Eliot uses her own commentary. There are places where the modern reader feels that the commentary is excessive or tautological, that it is an addition to the excited inference of generalization from formal relations of characters, events, and images. This is probably a sophisticated back-reading from later experimental novels, for George Eliot is always very much in evidence in her novels, deliberately and in many different ways. However, even contemporary readers sometimes objected to her commentary.

---

[1] There are of course some striking modern examples of the author's presence—in Thomas Mann and André Gide.

Introduction

Some of her reviewers criticized it. Joseph Langford said of *Middlemarch*, 'one thing I do not like is the habit of putting her characters at a distance as if to look at them making remarks on them' (Haight, v, p. 254). But in the later novels in particular, there are many details which are not directly commented on but are left to the reader to supply from the trailing clues of image and coincidence. George Eliot does not insist on the resemblance of Casaubon's will and Featherstone's, but gives the clues in chapter-headings and parallel scenes and verbal echo. She does not directly remind us of Gwendolen's terror when the panel sprang open to show the dead face, but leaves it to us to hear the echo when, at the end of the novel, Gwendolen tells Daniel how she is haunted by Grandcourt's dead face. The oblique statements of formal relation, once recognized, do something to lay the ghost of many assumptions about the 'naïve' method of omniscient commentary, and force us to ask searching questions about a device which is more than an easy narrative convention. If we refrain from pre-judging the convention of the author's direct speech, we may find some interest in following its contribution to the changing pattern of the novel, and follow its own internal changes too, as it moves from pathetic appeal to irony and reflective gravity, as it intercepts the action, supplements character, anticipates, echoes, detaches and generalizes. Once we look at the form of the author's commentary we find that it is composed not of one but of many voices.

I have tried in this book to say something of the kind of tragedy which is embodied in these intricate forms, and this is most easily explained by separating the special kind of understatement which forms the tragic appeal of *Scenes of Clerical Life* from the more orthodox 'heroic' tragedy which we find in most of the novels. The *Scenes* are a rehearsal for the novels that follow: where the same kind of moral generalization is given form by a more elaborate pattern of character, action and image, in so far as this pattern can be extracted from the particulars which make each novel. I have tried to indicate the formal process rather than to track it down exhaustively—the experienced reader will add many more instances for himself.

CHAPTER I

The Unheroic Tragedy

GEORGE ELIOT explained that her attempt at tragedy urged 'the human sanctities . . . through pity and terror as well as admiration and delights' and this insistence is, I think, a more important guide to her changing concept of character than either Mario Praz's 'Hero in eclipse' or E. S. Dallas's earlier 'withering of the hero' in *The Gay Science*. Praz is of course more concerned with generalization than with the scrutiny of particular details of form and language or with the tracing of change in a novelist's method, but his generalization has a certain weakness. It is a formula which puts the emphasis on social status rather than on intelligence, sensibility and articulateness, and by making this emphasis he misses many of the variations both in George Eliot's choice of human material and in her attempt at a new kind of tragedy.

It is roughly true to say, as Praz does, that she was concerned with bourgeois tragedy. But this is only in some of her novels. Her concept of tragedy is a changing one, and even within a single novel her sense of human flux and individuality makes for considerable variety. In the early stories the unheroic hero is presented centrally and emphatically, though perhaps the only certain examples of heroes who may be called entirely unheroic are Amos Barton and Silas Marner, neither of whom appears in a full-length novel. George Eliot gradually moves away from the kind of narrative where the author is the only source of wisdom and sensibility, and moves away at the same time from pathos to tragedy. The humble character who is unusual in tragedy (less because of his social class than because of his limited emotional capacity) gradually makes way for the character with sensibility and intelligence, until in *Middlemarch* and *Daniel Deronda* she creates tragic figures who share and express their author's vision of their *catharsis*. The simple soul is almost always present. George Eliot's analysis

14

of the human lot includes the unheroic tragedy which arouses pity but not admiration, but the unheroic figures are eventually restricted to a marginal position where they act as a commenting chorus or serve to underline the theme, always with insistent vitality and social precision. Mario Praz gives us a strangely compiled list of Wordsworthian characters: it includes Rosamond Vincy and Gwendolen Harleth. I think it would surely be more useful to look for the Wordsworthian material and treatment in figures like Bob Jakin and Henrietta Noble, whose gifts of second-hand books and stolen lumps of sugar demonstrate the main theme of human fellowship in a different key. If we miss the distinction between the heroic sensibility and the unheroic humble figure we miss the point. George Eliot's tragic characters are not so strikingly different from Shakespeare's. The truly unheroic tragic figure is there, in the later books, to universalize the theme, rather than to carry its whole burden.

It is true that in the first novels there is the insistent presence of unheroic tragic characters, and these characters are worth close inspection. Their treatment raises the question of *intensity*, a quality both Lewes and George Eliot emphasized. If the human material is a copy of monotonous or inarticulate suffering, how is it to be used in fiction? George Eliot was willing to play down admiration and delights but what did she attempt to put in their place?

Lewes wrote in the third essay on 'Principles of Success in Literature' (*The Fortnightly Review*), 'The intensity of vision in the artist and of vividness in his creations are the sole tests of his imaginative power.' Imagination seems to have been for Lewes, who owed much to Romantic criticism, an essentially formative power. His 'intensity' seems to be seen as the result of a formal grasp of nature. He anticipates Virginia Woolf's attack on Arnold Bennett in his account of the English and German 'detailism' which loses all form and sharpness in faithful and insignificant accumulation. Mario Praz also uses the word 'intensity' and suggests some ways in which George Eliot, whom he compares to Vermeer, transfigures the ordinary detail. 'Realism' we are told, 'is spiritualized through intensity of vision, attaining, in the highest examples, the

15

quality of inwardness and becoming "intimism"; and since it reproduces the joys of prosperity and peace, it suffuses these paintings with an air of great earthly security: moments of everyday life thus become intimations of eternity.' It is a big 'thus', and one which will not do as an explanation of George Eliot. Praz suggests that it is the cult of association both in George Eliot and Proust which brings about this 'transfiguration'. This may be true in the case of a few emotional crises of pathos or nostalgia, but it scarcely covers the whole range of George Eliot's pathos. Her particular kind of unheroic tragedy depends on intensity, but not—in any ordinary sense —on transfiguration. Amos Barton and Hetty Sorrel are faithful portraits of human inadequacy, not 'transfigurations'.

Before beginning to suggest a few of the ways in which this intensification of ordinary things may work, it is as well to say something about the nature of George Eliot's didactic aim. Whereas Lewes attacks 'detailism' as the negation of truthful intensity, George Eliot attacks sentimentality as the negation of her idea of literary truth. She attacks the falseness of 'mind-and-millinery fiction' with its lulling social lies, but she also attacks the more benevolent distortions of Dickens. It is in her review of Riehl's *Die Bürgerliche Gesellschaft* for *The Westminster Review* (1856) that her aims are most clearly stated. This was the year in which *Amos Barton* was written and was plainly a year of hard critical thinking.

The greatest benefit we owe to the artist, whether painter, poet or novelist is the extension of our sympathies. Appeals founded on generalizations and statistics require a sympathy ready-made, a moral sentiment already in activity; but a picture of human life such as a great artist can give, surprises even the trivial and the selfish into that attention to what is apart from themselves, which may be called the raw material of moral sentiment.

George Eliot did not want to extend her reader's sympathies by injecting her own sympathy into her characters. She is of course showing a certain blindness to the arts of simplification when she speaks of the falsity of Dickens's 'preternaturally virtuous poor children and artisans . . . as noxious as Èugène Sue's idealized proletaires', but her objection is not merely an aesthetic one. What she dislikes is not caricature but sentimental caricature. Like Shaw, she refuses to worship the poor, because she has far too much understanding of the degradations of poverty. Dickens is the kind of social reformer who often chooses to make his plea within his characters, showing them as innocents caught in a social trap, or grotesque representatives of a social evil. George Eliot is the social reformer who places her sympathetic plea outside her characters, showing them realistically as too dumb to plead or too charmless to attract. Dickens showed the social horrors, true, but at times he turns the screw of sympathy—at times effectively— by the appealing beauty and frailty of Little Nell or Oliver Twist or even Jo. George Eliot saw in this method 'the miserable fallacy that high morality and refined sentiment can grow out of harsh social conditions, ignorance and want; or that the working-classes are in a condition to enter at once into a millennial state of altruism, wherein everyone is caring for everyone else, and no-one for himself'.

She began by showing dull or even repulsive people: the novel was to make the most practical kind of extension of life by showing the middle classes how the other half lived. It is not an accident that both in the past and the present George Eliot has repelled readers by the very nature of this extension, by the very stuff of the world she forces upon them. The *Quarterly's* reviewer disliked the uncultured provincials in *The Mill on the Floss* and the petty and trivial inhabitants of Shepperton in the *Scenes*. The rejection of the Jewish parts of *Daniel Deronda* are usually aesthetic rejections, it is true, but sometimes they carry an echo of Gwendolen's casual and 'civilized' anti-Semitism. 'I am sure he had a nose', says Henry James's Pulcheria.

It is not always the humble material itself which makes the reader uneasy. It is often George Eliot's fervent proselytizing on behalf of her characters. If she leaves them untransfigured in charmlessness and dumbness, she speaks on their behalf. Her own direct commentary is an important part of her attempt to intensify the dull material. Its degree of tact varies, but the external appeal by the author is a necessary accompaniment to her underdistanced portrayal of character. The relation between the reader and the characters is in some ways far from intimate, since the characters are neither attractive nor articulate. But in some ways it is over-intimate, for the author continually and energetically cavasses our sympathy for her poor creatures.

'Depend upon it,' she says in one of those addresses to the reader which Blackwood thought might have been more sparingly used, 'you would gain unspeakably if you would learn with me to see some of the poetry and the pathos, the tragedy and the comedy, lying in the experience of a human soul that looks out through dull grey eyes, and that speaks in a voice of quite ordinary tones' (*Amos Barton*, ch. v).[1]

The subject and the theme is this voice of ordinary tones. The direct address is one of George Eliot's favourite methods of thematic intensification. The intensification is made outside the character and the story, in generalization. The sentimental appeal which is within Little Nell is made outside Amos Barton. The effect is not an avoidance of sentimentality, it merely frees the character from making his own appeal.

Fielding too uses unsophisticated and inarticulate characters, but he does not seem especially interested in their lack of sophistication. His emphasis is placed on the scene rather than the sensibility, though when he needs to supplement the voice of Tom or Joseph he too uses his own comment. His attitude to his characters is very different from George Eliot's. He interrupts in order to emphasize his satire, not his sympathy, though his satirical rejection of the reader's expectations may at times result in an oblique appeal for sympathy. But her use of the inarticulate character—and these characters are much more inarticulate than any of Jane Austen's ordinary people—gives rise to the need for this kind of external commentary.

Characters in fiction have tended to grow more self-expressive and more analytical. Arnold's dialogue of the mind with itself becomes the main theme. The inarticulate character has of course survived. He is present in the strong and silent heroes of Hemingway, where sophistication is often implied

[1] It should be mentioned that this direct address is a practical *serial* recapitulation—this is part of the introduction to part ii, *Blackwood's* (Feb., 1857).

in action, or occasionally, as in *The Old Man and the Sea*, completely left out. He remains in the Little Man, who, in Bloom, or Prufrock, or Charlie Chaplin, makes something very close to the kind of appeal which George Eliot was trying to make. In *Adam Bede*, George Eliot is closer to the myth-making of Joyce and Chaplin in the manner in which she gives stature to simplicity. In her first stories she is interested mainly in understatement, in simplicity with no stature. Amos is not generalized as Adam Bede and Bloom are generalized. He remains a particular and pathetic instance of the little man.

He is one of those characters who cannot possibly explain or analyse himself. His appeal depends on his petty sensibilities and his helplessness. George Eliot has to do the analysis and the explanation for him. This analysis is combined very smoothly with the emotional appeal. The appeal is in fact made on behalf of the inarticulateness, so there is an automatic economy.

The filling of the gap between character and creator is not always satisfactory. There seems to be no very good reason why the explanation and analysis should not be provided outside the character, but the appeal for sympathy results in a kind of under-distancing which breaks aesthetic bounds. George Eliot intends it to break bounds, without much doubt, but it is the one recurring narrative device which plainly jars on many modern readers. The example I have given already of the appeal for the dull grey eyes is representative. It is an apostrophe to the reader which makes several mistakes. It is repetitive, exaggerated, over-excited. It is given the appearance of inflation, by not remaining sufficiently particularized: Amos is given little within his character which makes him big enough or exaggerated enough (like Adam or Bloom) to bear the weight of this general statement. This is all very well, we think, moving away as we are beckoned on,[1] cooling as the appeal becomes warmer and more imperative. But the in-intense solicitation is meant to fill the gap not only between writer and character, but between the intelligent man and the

[1] This is not always the reaction of habitual readers of nineteenth-century novels, but it is often the response of the average undergraduate today.

simple man in general. The general claim is made not only on behalf of a particular story but on the behalf of all ordinariness everywhere.

Nevertheless, the method is sometimes successful. It can be used with a cool and restrained irony. It can modulate with more tact and skill from particular to general. It can in fact avoid that exaggeration of the particular case which is one of the things we may mean by sentimentality. Let us look at another instance of the direct address:

> It was happy for the Rev. Amos Barton that he did not, like us, overhear the conversation recorded in the last chapter. Indeed, what mortal is there of us, who would find his satisfaction enhanced by an opportunity of comparing the picture he presents to himself of his own doings, with the picture they make on the mental retina of his neighbours? We are poor plants buoyed up by the air-vessels of our own conceit: alas for us, if we get a few pinches that empty us of that windy self-subsistence! The very capacity for good would go out of us. . . .
> Thank heaven, then, that a little illusion is left to us, to enable us to be useful and agreeable—that we don't know exactly what our friends think of us—that the world is not made of looking-glass, to show us just the figure we are making, and just what is going on behind our backs! By the help of dear friendly illusion, we are able to dream that we are charming—and our faces wear a becoming air of self-possession; we are able to dream that other men admire our talents—and our benignity is undisturbed; we are able to dream that we are doing much good—and we do a little. (ch. ii)

This, it is true, has a certain ejaculatory cosiness but as a running commentary I think it escapes sentimentality and achieves some dignity. When the author's commentary does this its true function is more plainly visible.

This function is a compensation for the characters' lack of articulateness, and indeed for their lack of vitality. Their maker disarmingly draws attention to the poor stuff of which they are made. When her underlining does not make the exaggerated call on our sympathies which makes us retreat, it gives emphasis, stiffening, and the right kind of expansion into the general. The characters are given aesthetic stiffening by being placed in the frame of comment; they are given generalization by being slowly and discreetly placed in relation to the theme, by being temporarily and tentatively presented as social examples.

The movement towards generalization was also slowed down, in this last example, by another formal device—the frame and the chorus. The solid chorus, built up into a realistic portrait of a community by that accurate and detailed professional realism which Lewes demanded in his article 'Realism in Art: Recent German Fiction' in *The Westminster Review* where he insisted that 'the merchant must have an air of the counting-house, an ostler must smell of the stables', is given many crowd scenes in which to display itself. These scenes also make an important contribution to the intensification of theme and character.

The chorus is not given the task of thematic statement, or at least not in these first stories. Its task is more indirect. Apart from its role as background and its equally prominent role as agent—from *Amos Barton* to *Middlemarch* the collective personality of the community acts as a causal agent, making and breaking relations—the chorus has also a formal function. Like the narrator's voice it interrupts the track of the protagonist and is the chief source of that narrative irony which is important in making George Eliot's tragic statement. Because the crowd scenes are segregated from the scenes in which Amos is presented in close-up, we turn with the ironical superiority of the reader's view from misunderstood man to misunderstanding crowd, or from self-approving man to disapproving society. In *Amos Barton* and *Janet's Repentance* the movement is alternating; in *Mr Gilfil's Love-Story* the chorus occupies the frame and the protagonist the inset story. The effect is roughly the same: we move from the shot in the dark to the truth; from the isolated creature to the diffused and comfortable warmth of the crowd; from tension to casual humour. One man's tragedy is everyone else's comedy—in *Scenes of Clerical Life*, in *Silas Marner*, and though less prominently, in most of the later books. There is usually also the moment when one man's tragedy becomes everyone's tragedy: the strength and weakness of the community, its power to destroy with a casual murmur and to heal with the friendly smile, are shown directly, in the course of the story, and built up dramatically in this structure of counterpointed and segregated action. It is rather like the creation of tension and oblique commentary in D. W. Griffith's *Intolerance*.

The chorus provides the formal correlative for the theme of isolation and connection, a theme which had the same kind of interest for George Eliot, the first great agnostic novelist, that it has for later writers like Joyce, E. M. Forster and Virginia Woolf. And the contrast between the crowd's view and the inner truth makes something like the structural irony of the contrast in *War and Peace* between historical forces and the personal life.

The chorus throws the ordinary hero into relief, the relief of the frame and the relief of contrast. The choric comments build up a kind of tension of curiosity, a perpetual stating of the question 'And what was really happening?' which gives an interrogative lift to a flattish story. But it is dangerous to take George Eliot's statement of theme at its face value. The 'dull grey eyes' passage is disingenuous. She does not in fact restrict her material to dull grey eyes and ordinary tones. The ordinariness of man is there, certainly, but it would not be true to say that it is always shown in ordinary action. The *Scenes* are a magnificent example of narrative understatement but, like Germanic epic, they rely on overstatement as well. The eclipsed hero has sometimes to be shown against a dramatically lit background.

George Eliot disliked not only the sentimentality of the silly lady novelists but also their melodrama. She spoke contemptuously of overstatement in which 'very ordinary events of civilized life are exalted into the most awful crises' and of this kind of emotional contrivance her writing is free. But although she did not make mountains out of molehills she still made mountains. There is Milly's death in *Amos Barton*; Tina's attempted murder of her faithless lover in *Mr Gilfil's Love-Story*, and her own death; and the death of Dempster and the death of Tryan, in *Janet's Repentance*. George Eliot's realism is not of the kind which excludes the violent crisis. Unlike Jane Austen, who laughed at Gothic mountain-making by deflating the artificial mountains, she was attacking reticence as well as melodrama, and had to show squalor and violence as well as the dull flow of daily life.

Her treatment of violence is sometimes conventional, as in the treatment of Tryan's death, which is not very different from the sort of pathos Lewes attacked in the German novels. It is a visible bid for tears, coming not quite inevitably and organically out of the action:

> The pale wasted form in the easy-chair (for he sat up to the last) . . . the grey eyes so full even yet of inquiring kindness, as the thin, almost transparent hand was held out to give the pressure of welcome . . . the sweet woman, too, whose dark watchful eyes detected every want. . . . (ch. xxvii)

Here there are too many, and too obvious, bids for pathos. But George Eliot, doing another death scene, really attempting a brutal extension of the reader's experience, can write like Zola. In fact, Dempster's death, with the frantic imagery of *delirium tremens*,[1] is rivalled only by the length of the corresponding scene in *L'Assommoir*. Here is a realistic death-bed:

> Her hair is all serpents . . . they're black serpents . . . they hiss . . . they hiss . . . let me go . . . let me go . . . she wants to drag me with her cold arms . . . her arms are serpents . . . they are great white serpents . . . they'll twine round me . . . she wants to drag me into the cold water . . . her bosom is cold . . . it is black . . . it is all serpents. . . . (ch. xxiii)

Violence is there besides ordinariness, the flats are given a context of excitement, the crises a context of calm and mono-tony. But on the whole, in the *Scenes*, these very violent crises are few, and they do not form part of the thematic emphasis. The true thematic crises are really understated. There is the narrative pivot of *Amos Barton*, the village's sensational exaggeration of the visit of the Countess. The gossip-ing villagers mistake for illicit passion what is at worst some difficulty in putting up with an expensive guest. It is an ironically large gulf between reaction and event, or supposition and truth, and in its effect it is not unlike Catherine Morland's

---

[1] It is something like the extraordinary scene of panoramic delirium in Kingsley's *Alton Locke*.

23

response to Northanger Abbey. This contrast between what
seems and what is makes not only a kind of understatement,
or narrative bathos, but is directly related to the understatement of character. It is because the people are small and dull
that they, like Amos, their best example, are 'more apt to fall
into a blunder than a sin'. The ordinary man's ordinary life is
given further emphasis by the romantic misunderstandings
within the action. The eclipse of the hero is not always recognized by the other characters in the novel.

There is the other kind of understatement in *Amos Barton*,
shown in the death of Milly Barton. This is not an ordinary
understatement. The death is presented lengthily, pathetically,
and fairly conventionally, with one exceptional emphasis.
It is this emphasis which must be completely ignored by anyone capable of describing this part of the story as sentimental.
Milly's death is in the centre of both narrative and theme, one
reason why the story seems to me to be so much better than
the other two, where there is more of a gap between theme and
narrative. Milly's death is Amos's personal crisis but it is also
the climax of the theme of social conflict.

Amos Barton, like Silas Marner, moves from social isolation
to integration, though the heartening irony of the story lies in
the kind of reversal brought by Milly's death. When his one
human relationship snaps he is brought into relation with the
village in which he has been an exile unawares. The unaware-
ness is the essential quality in Amos. Both in his professional
relations, and then in his personal tragedy, he is only partially
responsive. The unresponsiveness is shown, naturally enough,
in the children: 'They cried because mamma was ill and
papa looked so unhappy; but they thought, perhaps next
week things would be as they used to be again' (ch. viii). But
there is parallel, and not the expected contrast, in the adult
reaction described on the next page: 'Amos knelt by the bed
and held her hand in his. He did not believe in his sorrow. It
was a bad dream. He did not know when she was gone.' The
short simple sentences have the moving effect of controlled
inarticulateness. Again, when Amos fears the move from
Shepperton the emphasis is placed on his lack of tragic passion:
'To part from that grave seemed like parting with Milly a

second time; for Amos was one who clung to all the material links between his mind and the past. His imagination was not vivid, and required the stimulus of actual perception.' Later, at the grave, 'He stood a few minutes reading over and over again the words on the tombstone, as if to assure himself that all the happy and unhappy past was a reality.' If the word 'unhappy' were left out this would be a conventional graveside scene, as it is it stands as a pointer to the lack of equipment for tragedy. 'Where we should only see a calamity', Lewes said, 'the poet makes us see a tragedy' ('Principles of Success'). It might be said that George Eliot makes us see a tragedy which is too big for her characters. The claim for sympathy is not made directly by tragic response but has to be made on behalf of the very absence of tragic response. Pity lies in the way the sufferers fail to rise to their tragic occasion. The eclipsed tragic hero is given a special context.

In *Adam Bede* George Eliot is making her ordinary man rather greater in stature. Adam is the generalized ordinary man, and, moreover, the ordinary man of ability, integrity and growing sensibility. He is not made of the same stuff as Amos Barton. But Hetty Sorrel is, as one of George Eliot's reviewers recognized. Reviewing *Daniel Deronda* in *The Edinburgh Review* he wrote of Hetty,

> In most cases, when a human soul, either in history or fiction, is brought face to face with the darker passions and calamities, it is of a nature lofty enough to cope with and combat them; but George Eliot was the first to thrill the spectator with the sight of a helpless, frivolous, childish creature, inadequate even to understand, much less to contend with, those gigantic shadows. (Oct. 1876)

The refusal to make Hetty a tragic heroine, he knows, makes of the tragedy a generalization of humanity as a whole. It 'gains in depth and solemn force from the helpless weakness of the central figure' he says, and this unheroic tragic centre throws its light on the 'whole world of helpless creatures, who are innocent without virtue . . . and whose . . . slight natures lie helpless . . . on the edge of the most fatal whirlpools'.

It was perhaps not strictly true to call Hetty innocent. Compared with Amos, too small even for much egoism, Hetty is much more positively involved in the moral issues of self and selflessness. Of people like Amos George Eliot asked 'Is there not a pathos in their very insignificance—in our comparison of their dim and narrow existence with the glorious possibilities of that human nature which they share?' Hetty's egoism is small because her imagination is small, but her insistent self-regard is strongly emphasized:

They are but dim ill-defined pictures that her narrow bit of an imagination can make of the future; but of every picture she is the central figure, in fine clothes; Captain Donnithorne is very close to her, putting his arm round her, perhaps kissing her, and everybody else is admiring and envying her—especially Mary Burge, whose new print dress looks very contemptible by the side of Hetty's resplendent toilette. (ch. xv)

The egoism of fantasy-life has seldom been more ruthlessly exposed. But George Eliot softens irony to pity when in a later chapter she presents Hetty as the image of agony in a bright day. The external discussion of Hetty's sensibilities suddenly reduces itself to an uncommenting repetition of Hetty's thoughts and acts. Her dream—that little dream—has failed her, even 'the blind vague hope that something would happen to set her free from her terror' (ch. xxxv). She is desperate but unable to imagine or anticipate, unable to look tragedy in the face until it is upon her. She cannot believe in it: 'it is as hard to a boy or girl to believe that a great wretchedness will actually befall them, as to believe that they will die' (ibid).

This is the tragedy of the little soul. Unlike Oedipus and Lear who commit themselves to tragedy with giant fury and endurance, Amos and Hetty hardly recognize tragedy when they meet it. Hetty's desperate journey is given by the faithful stream of her consciousness. There is no more analysis and explanation, only: 'Her poor narrow thoughts, no longer melting into vague hopes, but pressed upon by the chill of definite fear; repeating again and again the same childish, doubtful images of what was to come.'

Hetty plans to kill herself. George Eliot gives us each stumbling movement of panic, of the mind which cannot express or explain its own responses. It is almost—though not quite—a reduction to animal consciousness:

The Unheroic Tragedy

The horror of this cold, and darkness, and solitude—out of all human reach—became greater every long minute: it was almost as if she were dead already, and knew that she was dead, and longed to get back to life again. But no: she was alive still; she had not taken the dreadful leap. She felt a strange contradictory wretchedness and exultation: wretchedness, that she did not dare to face death; exultation that she was still in life—that she might yet know light and warmth again. She walked backwards and forwards to warm herself, beginning to discern something of the objects around her, as her eyes became accustomed to the night: the darker line of the hedge, the rapid motion of some living creature—perhaps a fieldmouse—rushing across the grass. She no longer felt as if the darkness hedged her in: she thought she could walk back across the field, and get over the stile; and then, in the very next field, she thought she remembered there was a hovel of furze near a sheepfold. If she could get into that hovel, she would be warmer; she could pass the night there, for that was what Alick did at Hayslope in lambing-time. (ch. xxxvii)

We are restricted, with a claustrophobic economy, to the slow movements and unforeseen jumps of the narrow mind. Instead of the overstatement of melodrama, we have the understatement of tragedy without a tragic protagonist. Like Hopkins, George Eliot sees a viol which is no bass for tragic tones. She demonstrates its inadequacy by forcing the tragic tones upon it.[1]

The only other understated tragedy is that of Silas Marner, and his reaction is in some ways more stifled than that of Amos, who produces his forced emotional reaction, or of Hetty, who is pressed into an unthinking violence. Silas shares their innocence, but not their egoistic guilt. His tragedy, presented in retrospect, produces an appropriate emotional catalepsy. It is not so much that he does not react tragically as that his tragedy lies in a state of nullity and unreality, where 'the past becomes dreamy because its symbols have all vanished, and the present too is dreamy because it is linked with no memories'. Like Hetty, he lives a reduced life:

His first movement after the shock had been to work in his loom; and he went on with this unremittingly, never asking himself why, now he was come to Raveloe, he worked far on into the night to finish

[1] For further discussion of Hetty, see Chapter VIII below.

27

the tale of Mrs Osgood's table-linen sooner than she expected—without contemplating beforehand the money she would put into his hand for the work. He seemed to weave like the spider, from pure impulse, without reflection. Every man's work, pursued steadily, tends in this way to become an end in itself, and so to bridge over the loveless chasms of his life. Silas's hand satisfied itself with throwing the shuttle and his eye with seeing the little squares in the cloth complete themselves under his effort. Then there were the calls of hunger; and Silas, in his solitude, had to provide his own breakfast, dinner, and supper, to fetch his own water from the well, and put his own kettle on the fire; and all these immediate promptings helped, along with the weaving, to reduce his life to the unquestioning activity of a spinning insect. (ch. ii)

The simple man is not merely incapable of tragic response but is made even more impotent and inarticulate by the tragic blow. This stunned reaction—obviously one which cannot easily be shown in drama—recurs in almost all the later books. Maggie, Dorothea and Gwendolen are creatures of sensibility. They rise to their tragedy, and are even nurtured by it, but they all pass through this period of dulled reaction, when violent crisis makes life seem reduced or unreal. It is not just a matter of writing an unheroic tragedy, it is also a way of avoiding the intensity of selected crisis and showing the tragedy diffusing itself through life.

These are two methods of understatement. There is the insistence on the gap between tragedy and the tragic hero, and there is this refusal to show tragedy only in the peaks of crisis. Nevertheless, it would be inaccurate to suggest that in these ways George Eliot avoids melodrama. There is overstated action as well as understated. I have already mentioned Tryan's death, and there is the more familiar example of Arthur's ride to the scaffold with Hetty's pardon. Where the violence or excitement strikes us as melodramatic or inflated, it is not only because we are repelled by the external and sensational action. It is also because of the existence elsewhere of the decorous and sensitive treatment of the commonplace mind and the commonplace event. The unsuccessful crisis is made particularly conspicuous because of the context of understatement. This kind of melodramatic crisis is not very common. Sometimes it is cut short, and understatement returns in a deliberate and successful version of bathos. Tina seizes the dagger, but she would never have used it. Gwendolen's is the guilty wish, not the guilty act—though the difference between wish and act is not exaggerated. But it is there. The peripheral melodrama in the novels may be a kind of indirect compensation—probably not a deliberate one—for the flats which make the norm of action and conduct. These flats are present in all the novels, with the exception of *Romola*, but they only form the main statement of character in *Scenes of Clerical Life*, a part of *Adam Bede* and *Silas Marner*. George Eliot moved from the ordinary man struggling with tragedy to the extraordinary man and woman struggling with ordinary life. The ordinary man is still present, but on the margin of someone else's excitement.

He recurs, for instance, in the understatement which almost always accompanies the portraits of clergymen. All the novels contain the variations on the theme of clerical life—as it is, and not as it was sentimentalized in what George Eliot called 'white neckcloth novels'. The clergymen are not merely unromantic replies to the curate, whom she dismissed, along with other ladylike sillinesses, as the Orlando of the Evangelical novel. They are also variations on the theme of ordinary life, and their function is a complex one. Like the hostess in Virginia Woolf's novels, the clergyman is presented both as an example and a symbol of social connection and fellowship. The scenes of clerical life create *ex officio* symbols of the making of harmony and relation, though usually with an ironical gloss. For our attention is usually drawn, quietly and sympathetically, to the gap between the professional service and the personal life. This varies in quality and in emphasis. Barton fails professionally, though he has some human contact in his family life. Gilfil, on the other hand, succeeds as a parson, but not in his 'love story'. This is emphasized in the choric framework of the story which presents him as a human being isolated and distant even from the parishioners he serves. His life is observed from two points of view: in what the choric characters say, and less directly in the formal segregation of the frame, which is the present; and also in the inset story, which takes us back to the unknown and unguessable past. Tryan too is a professional success, and is the agent of Janet's social restoration. He is a mentor with many and various descendants: Kemp, Irwine, Savonarola, Farebrother and Gascoigne. The relationship of Tryan and Janet is tinged with a faintly unpleasant suggestion of irrelevant and undesirable romance, which blurs the theme instead of sharpening it. The portrait of Tryan, though humanized to some extent by his confession of human failure (also an inset narrative, though a short one) lacks irony and moving understatement. It is this understatement which makes Amos tragic because of his very inefficiency as hero, and which makes Gilfil tragic because he is on the margin of even his own romance, and that is over and hidden.

The ordinariness is there in the understated events and characters. But it is a lively image of ordinariness, not a flatly realistic presentation. It is enlivened by anti-climax and irony, by isolated melodrama, and by the changing formal contrast between groups and voices. There is also another formal source from which these realistic stories draw their intensity. This is the old dramatic device of repetition. Although the formal structure of the *Scenes*, if we take them as a related whole, is episodic, using successive 'parallel' where later we get counterpoint, there is a similar effect of repetition, especially for the modern reader who usually reads them one after the other. The very repetition of the simple man and his understated tragedy throws a spotlight on the theme. Instead of making for rigidity, it makes for flexibility. The characters have an emphatic resemblance which points its moral while leaving room for variation. We seldom feel in George Eliot that the theme occupies the whole of the character. Amos is nothing but the simple soul though his dullness and unattractiveness come alive in a genuine impression of personality. In Gilfil, we have a variation, for his unattractive ordinariness in old age is the result of a fatal accident. In Janet we are moving towards the less ordinary sensibility. But apart from the central figure there are many portraits of simple souls in these stories. In *Adam Bede* and *Silas Marner* the eclipse of the hero is not the only theme—it is important, but it is only a part of the great and complex mass. What is true of the character is true of the narrative as a whole. We feel the thematic heart of the matter but we do not feel that the whole world of the story is constructed for the simple purpose of demonstrating the theme. Dickens's method of simplification was not George Eliot's. Hers is a method of imaginative presentation which keeps as close as possible to the appearances of nature. In the world of her narratives and in its human units we find the free life of realistic fiction at its best—free even to show the undramatic and unromantic bits of life—but organized by the intense and driving emphasis of formative vision.

CHAPTER II

The Tragic Process: Adam Bede

(i)

IT is true—for what the generalization is worth—that in the nineteenth century the novel becomes the medium of tragedy. The novel has both the space and the time to unfold in great detail the social causes and effects of the tragic subjects of pain and evil, and the individual's responsibility and suffering. George Eliot makes it plain, as we have seen, that she was deliberately setting out to write tragedy, and her novels are tragedies in a strictly technical sense, not because they show pain and evil, crime and punishment, but because they impose a moral pattern which shows the pain as productive. George Eliot's interest lies in modes of suffering which are moral and exemplary, after the manner of Greek or Shakespearean tragedy: the tragic process is a demonstration of human endurance and development.

As early as *Adam Bede* her own definition of the kind of tragedy which appeals 'through pity and terror, rather than through admiration and delights' ceases to be an exactly appropriate description of what we find in her novels. Adam Bede is very much closer to the conventional tragic hero than Amos Barton, both in his stature and his capacity for tragic nurture, and it is in her treatment of Adam's tragedy that we see George Eliot making the modulation from the unheroic pathetic character, the very ordinary man, to an extraordinary hero. In his tragedy admiration is certainly not excluded.

There is still a gap of sensibility and understanding between Adam and his author. His own slow moral summaries are made painfully and unimaginatively, in the terms of his own limited experience, but as the story proceeds the gap narrows. Adam extends his experience, and this extension is the first example of George Eliot's tragic pattern. Adam, like Maggie and Esther and Dorothea and the rest, enlarges his imagination and his

sensibility. It is the egoist's process towards a wider com-
prehension, and it is George Eliot's version of the tragic sensibility growing through pain—not so very different, in spite
of the difference in the *dramatis personae*, from Henry James's
concept of tragic nurture.

In the case of Amos and Hetty and Silas Marner, there is
little or no evolution in the tragedy. We are made to pity
the unheroic figure who is equipped neither to understand
what is happening to him, nor to endure and to grow. Adam
is an active protagonist. He shares the humble social status of
Amos and Hetty, but even his social position is dignified.
In him the life of the good man is very largely identified with
the life of the good workman, and his moral training, his
terminology, and his refuge and strength, are all found in his
carpenter's trade. He is actually more than a mere carpenter,
for George Eliot dignifies his position by making him, like
Robert Evans and Caleb Garth, combine managerial with
manual skill, and he is a pastoral figure of a very special kind.
He is socially inglorious—the social moral of the book demands
it—but far from mute, and he is certainly warmly admired
as well as pitied by his author. He is indeed one of those
characters perpetually accompanied by his author's admiration—an accompaniment which often overreaches itself and
chills the reader. But if we do not always respond as warmly
as his author seems to expect us to, it is not because he is a
static character, nor because his rectitude is a complacent one.

Adam is the idealized artisan. He is some degrees removed
from the Noble Savage, but provides something of the ironical rebuke which the Noble Savage makes to those who are
more sophisticated but less noble—within the novel, to Arthur
Donnithorne in particular. But the idealization is fairly tentative. Adam's moral position is made clear when we first meet
him, in a long address putting spiritual values in their place
and extolling the dignity of labour:

And there's such a thing as being over-speritial; we must have
something beside Gospel i' this world. Look at the canals, an' th'
aqueducs, an' th' coal-pit engines, and Arkwright's mills there at
Cromford; a man must learn summat beside Gospel to make them
things, I reckon. . . . An this is my way o' looking at it: there's the

sperrit o' God in all things and all times—weekday as well as Sunday—and i' the figuring and the mechanics. (ch. i)

This is the new pastoral, with the industrial context there as well as the rural community. Adam himself is the intelligent artisan who is given his skills and his self-expression by Bartle Massey's night-school: the Mechanics' Institute is re-making the pastoral hero.

He also represents his author's glorification of the small but weighty social contribution:

He had no theories about setting the world to rights, but he saw there was a great deal of damage done by building with ill-seasoned timber,—by ignorant men in fine clothes making plans for outhouses and workshops and the like, without knowing the bearings of things,—by slovenly joiners' work, and by hasty con-tracts that could never be fulfilled without ruining somebody; and he resolved, for his part, to set his face against such doings. (ch. xvi)

Heroism is supplanted, in George Eliot, by the diffusion of good works. We see the small beneficent act not only in Adam, but in Bartle Massey, in Dolly Winthrop, in Caleb Garth, and in those characters who never make an appearance but act as ghosts, living in their resonant deeds—the superbly ironical example being Rosamond Vincy's music-master, whose 'hid-den soul' lives on in Rosamond's echoing precision, and forms part of the trap for Lydgate. The 'choir invisible' is not only the Positivist's immortality but a collective heroism. Adam's contribution is seen as part of a communal glory, just as Hetty's suffering is seen as part of a communal disaster.

This does not mean that Adam's abilities are underplayed. When George Eliot insists on his humble origin, it is with a proviso:

Adam, you perceive, was by no means a marvellous man, nor, properly speaking, a genius, yet I will not pretend that his was an ordinary character among workmen; and it would not be at all a safe conclusion that the next best man you may happen to see with a basket of tools over his shoulder and a paper cap on his head has the strong conscience and the strong sense, the blended suscepti-bility and self-command of our friend Adam. He was not an average man. (ch. xix)

This is a long way from Amos or Gilfil or Silas Marner. But although he 'was not an average man', she insists that his achievement is an anonymous one:

He was not an average man. Yet such men as he are reared here and there in every generation of our peasant artisans—with an inheritance of affections nurtured by a simple family life of common need and common industry, and an inheritance of faculties trained in skilful courageous labour: they make their way upward, rarely as geniuses, most commonly as painstaking honest men, with the skill and conscience to do well the tasks that lie before them. Their lives have no discernible echo beyond the neighbourhood where they dwelt, but you are almost sure to find there some good piece of road, some building, some application of mineral produce, with which their names are associated by one or two generations after them. . . . Others there are who die poor, and never put off the workman's coat on weekdays: they have not had the art of getting rich; but they are men of trust, and when they die before the work is all out of them, it is as if some main screw had got loose in a machine. . . . (ch. xix)

Rather oddly, this passage follows an appeal made in the sentimentally pathetic vein of *Amos Barton*. We are asked to sympathize not with 'dull grey eyes' but with 'his athletic body with the broken finger-nails', and the blunderingly soft appeal is only partially toughened by the dry catalogue of his little learning which follows—Adam, like the later heroines, is not idealized in his lack of learning, and the lack is firmly placed amongst his inadequacies. But it is only his exterior which places him with the unattractive Amos: he needs very much less sympathy and demands very much more admiration.

George Eliot insists on showing the social waste. Bartle Massey says to Irwine:

Why, sir, he's the only scholar I've had in this stupid country that ever had the will or the head-piece for mathematics. If he hadn't so much hard work to do, poor fellow, he might have gone into the higher branches, and then this might never have happened—might never have happened. (ch. xl)

The social waste is underlined by the tragedy of Hetty, which 'might never have happened' if Adam's circumstances had been different. But this is not a very prominent social

35

indictment. Adam's wasted talent is blurred by the insistence on his social contribution—he merges into a general achievement, and it is this achievement which George Eliot acclaims, leaving it to Bartle Massey to elaborate the possibilities buried in Adam.

She tells us of Adam's sense and susceptibility, and it is by virtue of these qualities that he is capable of canvassing sympathy on his own behalf. Amos had to weep on Milly's grave in order to convince himself of the intensity of his grief; Hetty Sorrel has to perform the same practical substitution for imagination and sensibility when she thinks of her own death in terms of memory alone: 'She thought of a young woman who had been found against the church wall at Hayslope one Sunday, nearly dead with cold and hunger—a tiny infant in her arms: the woman was rescued and taken to the parish' (ch. xxxvii). The unimaginative mind, like Hetty's and Amos's, is dramatically realized by showing this kind of dependence on practical experience,[1] on exact visual image, and on particulars. It has almost no generalizing power, and George Eliot emphasizes this by relying on this kind of actual memory and visual imagery when she is attempting the dramatic delineation of this limited sensibility. Adam is a little like Amos and Hetty in his constant references to his trade, but the resemblance is only a superficial one. Adam uses his limited language and experience but in the process of generalizing. He has ideals and considerable emotional susceptibility to the world outside himself. His vocabulary is small but its application is large—much larger than Amos's. George Eliot has considerable success with her range of simple characters because she uses simplicity of language and reference in a way which is genuinely dramatic. It is language which is varied and individual, and not a stereotyped laconic or fumbling or simple speech, of the kind we so often find in Hemingway's simple heroes. Adam's growth is the growth of sensibility, rather like Strether's or Maggie Verver's, and he begins with an initial ability to move away from particulars, as Hetty Sorrel does not.

The broken finger-nails are embarrassing perhaps because

[1] See Chapter VIII below.

of their triviality—George Eliot need not apologize for Adam's physical appearance as she does for Amos's because in Adam's case it is very much more accidental. Amos's unattractive appearance and his bad taste in dress and his inadequacy in grammar may be apologetically presented as part of his inferior sensibility—they are appropriate symbols for it. But Adam's sensibility is so effectively shown as a growing and complicated state of mind that the physical detail of the finger-nails, even though it is presented in generalization, seems scarcely relevant.

At the beginning Adam has as much to learn, in his terms, as Lear. His rectitude is unimaginative, and George Eliot begins by making this very clear. The human reaction to his defence of labour is beautifully drawn. The other artisans are certainly not more sensible or more susceptible than Adam, and they are presented in terms of a limited and practical application of personal experience, but the collision of the different points of view makes an approach to generalization and defines Adam's egoism:

'There's reason in what thee say'st, Adam,' observed Seth, gravely. 'But thee know'st thyself as it's hearing the preachers thee find'st so much fault with as has turned many an idle fellow into an industrious 'un.' (ch. i)

Seth is objecting to Adam's scientific secularity, and he too has the ability to generalize. The other responses are more stereotyped. When Adam puts precept into practice and objects because the men down tools as the clock strikes there is a chorus of protest. He says:

'Look there, now! I can't abide to see men throw away their tools i' that way, the minute the clock begins to strike, as if they took no pleasure i' their work, and was afraid o' doing a stroke too much.' (ch. i)[1]

Mun Taft objects:

'Ay, ay, Adam lad, ye talk like a young un. When y'are six an' forty like me, istid o' six an' twenty, ye wonna be so flush o' workin' for nought.'[1]

[1] The very slight gradations of more and less educated vulgar speech are interesting.

Wiry Ben's is a different objection:

'Bodderation, Adam!' exclaimed Wiry Ben; 'Lave a chap aloon, will 'ee. Ye war a-finding faut wi' preachers a while agoo— y'are fond enough o' preachin' yoursen. Ye may like work better nor play, but I like play better nor work; that'll 'commodate ye— it laves ye th' more to do.'

This is a deceptively casual debate which seems at first sight to be filling in background but which is actually sounding the main theme. Adam's suffering comes out of his rigidity. In the main action of the novel it is demonstrated in his attitude to his drunken father, whom he judges and finds wanting, and later in his equally uncompromising belief in Arthur and Hetty. Mun Taft is right, in a sense he cannot anticipate, for time does change Adam's mind. And Wiry Ben's preference for play becomes the moral extremity of Arthur's relation with Hetty, which Adam at first can barely comprehend, and which he is forced not only to comprehend but even to forgive. His unimaginative rigidity, in its way as egoistic as Arthur's self-delusion or Hetty's shallow inability to feel the world outside herself, is stressed by many voices: Mun Taft's and Wiry Ben's, Seth's and Mrs Bede's, and Casson's, when as choric minor character usefully given the surveying point of landlord of the Donnithorne Arms, he gives the crudest outside view, 'He's a little lifted up an' peppery-like.'

(ii)

In Adam, as later in Dorothea, egoism is no less a flaw which tragedy has to mend because it happens to take the form of a vision of duty, and the process of the tragedy is chiefly, though not entirely, the education of Adam's sensibility and imagination beyond this initial egoism. It is the first version of the main theme of all the later novels. It is also George Eliot's first attempt to show a character changing, and in many ways it is very much less successful than the delineation of change in Dorothea and Gwendolen. This is mainly because Adam is intrinsically less complex. To some extent the novel suffers by the restriction of the human material, however subtly this may be treated, and although *Adam Bede* is that very rare thing, a good pastoral or proletarian novel,[1] its human centre would almost certainly fail to bear our concentrated interest. In fact, it does not need to, for variety is provided by Hetty and Arthur, the two other prominent studies in egoism. But the problem of showing a changing character is almost entirely confined to Adam. The changes in Arthur are shown off-stage; the change in Dinah, who has her limitations of sensibility too, is very much smaller; the change in Hetty is no more than the breaking of silence in the prison and the defensive movement towards another human being—though this single act of change is a very moving thing in the context of her moral and physical isolation. But the main theme is demonstrated most elaborately in Adam's tragic growth.

George Eliot tries to show this growth as gradual and continuous. This slow growth embodies her belief that change must not be sudden if it is to be organic and permanent, and her belief—also coming out of her own break with Christianity and its associations—that change must be a change of heart before it is a change of mind.

Adam 'changes' in a series of self-assessments: for all his simplicity, he is always the articulate and reflective hero. He makes his first re-assessment at his father's funeral service, itself a moment of change—loss, end and beginning. George Eliot's describing eye and dramatic presentation takes us round the church, filling in minor figures, lingering within Hetty's disappointment at Arthur's absence—her only response to the funeral service—and then settling on Adam. The transition is quiet, with no assertion of the irony:

> Yet while this selfish tumult was going on in her soul, her eyes were bent down on her prayer-book, and the eyelids with their dark fringe looked as lovely as ever. Adam Bede thought so, as he glanced at her for a moment on rising from his knees.

> But Adam's thoughts of Hetty did not deafen him to the service; they rather blended with all the other deep feelings for which the church service was a channel to him this afternoon, as a certain consciousness of our entire past and our imagined future blends

[1] Compared with a novel like Gissing's *Demos* it is of course idealized rather than realistic.

itself with all our moments of keen sensibility. And to Adam the church service was the best channel he could have found for his mingled regret, yearning, and resignation; its interchange of beseeching cries for help, with outbursts of faith and praise—its recurrent responses and the familiar rhythm of its collects, seemed to speak for him as no other form of worship could have done: as, to those early Christians who had worshipped from their childhood upwards in catacombs, the torchlight and shadows must have seemed nearer the Divine presence than the heathenish daylight of the streets. The secret of our emotions never lies in the bare object, but in its subtle relations to our own past: no wonder the secret escapes the unsympathising observer, who might as well put on his spectacles to discern odours. (ch. xviii)

This scene in the church is characteristic in many ways of George Eliot's treatment of crisis. Adam's response to the ritual underlines the strength of his rootedness—Hetty has no roots—and this scene is not only a crisis for Adam, and an appropriate occasion for looking back and ahead, but it is also one of the communal scenes, like the preaching on the green, in chapter ii, and the Coming of Age of Arthur, which occupies the whole of Book iii. These scenes present the community as something reaching back in time as well as actively joined in social life. This sense of time is very necessary here because George Eliot is going to show Hetty's tragedy, in part coming from her casual unattachment, as a social disaster which shakes the tenacious life of the whole village, sending Arthur into exile and nearly tearing the Poysers and Adam from their strong roots. It is a fine example of the way in which her communal scenes move from the individual to the social impression. The contrast between Adam and Hetty is carefully pointed, of course, and both here and in Arthur's birthday feast there is on the one hand Hetty's self-absorption and on the other Adam's susceptibility to the life around him.

He is on this occasion legitimately self-occupied, but the occupation stretches his complacency, and we see the first stage in his progress:

'Ah, I was always too hard,' Adam said to himself. 'It's a sore fault in me as I'm so hot and out o' patience with people when they do wrong, and my heart gets shut up against 'em, so as I can't

40

bring myself to forgive 'em. I see clear enough there's more pride than love in my soul, for I could sooner make a thousand strokes with th' hammer for my father than bring myself to say a kind word to him. And there went plenty o' pride and temper to the strokes, as the devil *will* be having his finger in what we call our duties as well as our sins. Mayhap the best thing I ever did in my life was only doing what was easiest for myself. It's allays been easier for me to work nor to sit still, but the real tough job for me 'ud be to master my own will and temper, and go right against my own pride. It seems to me now, that if I was to find father at home tonight, I should behave different; but there's no knowing—perhaps nothing 'ud be a lesson to us if it didn't come too late. It's well we should feel as life's a reckoning we can't make twice over; there's no real making amends in this world, any more than you can mend a wrong subtraction by doing your addition right. (ch. xviii)

Adam's self-awareness is echoing some past judgements: 'Ye may like work better nor play' said Wiry Ben, and Adam now admits it, and even looks twice at his motives; 'A bit lifted-up and peppery-like' said Casson, and Adam, 'It's a sore fault in me as I'm so hot and out o' patience . . . '. The confessional's echoes underline the change—the character is moving. And it looks ahead as well as back, both to the occasion when his heart shuts up against Arthur, and to the occasions when he is forced to sit still and wait—while Hetty is in prison—and to master his will and temper—when he meets Arthur after Hetty's trial. There is the growing irony for Adam that 'life's a reckoning we can't make twice over', for with each successive lesson what is learnt comes too late to hold any hope for the past, and even its next application shows the tragic time-lag between principle and practice. But here is the first admission of error, and a fairly sophisticated one, though made in the simple symbols of his simple arithmetic.

The next crisis comes in his relationship with Arthur. George Eliot makes this a personal loss and a social disruption, for Adam is a pastoral figure to whom feudal context is very important, in spite of his respect for the industrial revolution:

The word 'gentleman' had a spell for Adam, and as he often said, he 'couldn't abide a fellow who thought he made himself fine by being coxy to's betters'. I must remind you again that Adam had the blood of the peasant in his veins, and that since he was in his prime half a century ago, you must expect some of his characteristics to be obsolete.

Towards the young squire this instinctive reverence of Adam's was assisted by boyish memories and personal regard. . . . He felt sure it would be a fine day for everybody about Hayslope when the young squire came into the estate—such a generous open-hearted disposition as he had, and an 'uncommon' notion about improvement and repairs, considering he was only just coming of age. (ch. xvi)

Adam sees Arthur rather as Arthur sees himself, and when once more experience comes to change his mind, the crisis is made up of a personal loss of trust and a social disruption. The feudal relation gives way to the fight between two men —the fight was Lewes's suggestion—and then the narrative runs on through Adam's ultimatum to Arthur, Arthur's departure, and Adam's betrothal to Hetty. The third great shock in Adam's tragic process comes with the search for Hetty and his discovery of her crime and imprisonment.

This crisis, like his father's death, forces him to self-assessment: the tragic suffering is an imaginative step in human sympathy, a genuine catharsis within the tragic hero:

Deep, unspeakable suffering may well be called a baptism, a regeneration, the initiation into a new state. The yearning memories, the bitter regret, the agonised sympathy, the struggling appeals to the Invisible Right—all the intense emotions which had filled the days and nights of the past week, and were compressing themselves again like an eager crowd into the hours of this single morning, made Adam look back on all the previous years as if they had been a dim sleepy existence, and he had only now awakened to full consciousness. It seemed to him as if he had always before thought it a light thing that men should suffer; as if all that he had himself endured, and called sorrow before, was only a moment's stroke that had never left a bruise. Doubtless a great anguish may do the work of years, and we may come out from that baptism of fire with a soul full of new awe and new pity. (ch. xlii)

'Awe' and 'pity'—they are the familiar terms of the tragic purgation. Adam's purgation, or baptism, to use the word George Eliot uses so often, comes out of his personal loss and, then, going beyond self-pity, out of the human implications of

Hetty's suffering. Change comes with a leap, but recollecting
all that is past, and Adam's pity and awe moves even beyond
Hetty towards the true tragic generalization which embraces
all poor wretches:

> 'O God,' Adam groaned, as he leaned on the table, and looked
> blankly at the face of the watch, 'and men have suffered like this
> before . . . and poor helpless young things have suffered like her. . . .'
> (ch. xlii)

This is the appropriate purgation for Adam, whose fault, we
have been told much earlier, was a lack of fellow-feeling:

> Whenever Adam was strongly convinced of any proposition, it
> took the form of a principle in his mind: it was knowledge to be
> acted on, as much as the knowledge that damp will cause rust.
> Perhaps here lay the secret of the hardness he had accused himself
> of: he had too little fellow-feeling with the weakness that errs in
> spite of foreseen consequences. Without this fellow-feeling, how
> are we to get enough patience and charity towards our stumbling,
> falling companions in the long and changeful journey? And there
> is but one way in which a strong determined soul can learn it—by
> getting his heartstrings bound round the weak and erring, so that
> he must share not only the outward consequence of their error, but
> their inward suffering. That is a long and hard lesson, and Adam
> had at present only learned the alphabet of it in his father's sudden
> death. . . . (ch. xix)

With Hetty's suffering Adam goes beyond this alphabet, and
the tragic spectacle of her pain makes the repetition, for the
third time, of a crisis which forces fellow-feeling upon a not
very imaginative mind, a mind which fuses principle and action
too readily and too simply. But the novel is of course not
merely the tragic ordeal of Adam Bede, for its complete dramatic survey includes Hetty and Arthur as well, and the
reader is not only in academic possession of Adam's sympathy,
but is given the imaginative sympathy of Hetty's direct
portrayal. This moving focus turns the novel, for all its moral
simplicity, into something closer to *King Lear* or *The Golden
Bowl* than to *The Pilgrim's Progress*.

We follow Adam out of this tragic regeneration into the
peaceful happy ending, and here George Eliot is plainly trying

to avoid a reconciliation which might come too glibly after the slowly unfolded growth of Adam's sensibility. For many readers the glibness is there, but it is worth noticing George Eliot's attempts to qualify it. She does it by a commentary which goes beyond Adam's vision, for his is not the catharsis which, like Dorothea's, seems to make a final leap over the gap between the character's blindness and the author's vision. Adam's simplicity is decorously maintained, and George Eliot inserts her own interpretation, which makes this clear, and which also has the practical effect of combining the jump in time with some illusion of a gradual passage.

Eighteen months pass after Adam's last encounter with Arthur, where he makes his admission, 'I'm hard—it's in my nature', and George Eliot looks back before she establishes the security of Adam's love for Dinah:

> For Adam, though you see him quite master of himself, working hard and delighting in his work after his inborn inalienable nature, had not outlived his sorrow—had not felt it slip from him as a temporary burthen, and leave him the same man again. Do any of us? God forbid. It would be a poor result of all our anguish and our wrestling, if we won nothing but our old selves at the end of it—if we could return to the same blind loves, the same self-confident blame, the same light thoughts of human suffering, the same frivolous gossip over blighted human lives, the same feeble sense of that Unknown towards which we have sent forth irrepressible cries in our loneliness. Let us rather be thankful that our sorrow lives in us as an indestructible force, only changing its form, as forces do, and passing from pain into sympathy—the one poor word which includes all our best insight and our best love. Not that this transformation of pain into sympathy had completely taken place in Adam yet: there was still a great remnant of pain. . . . (ch. l)

This generalization has many functions. It sums up the tragic process: 'our sorrow lives in us as an indestructible force . . . passing from love into sympathy'; and it marks Adam's transition by looking back and ahead, and resting lightly on the present. It also spreads its tentacles inside the novel and beyond it, in the usual manner of George Eliot's general summary. The particular focus here is Adam, and some of the generalization points to him: 'the same blind loves, the same self-confident blame'. But 'the blind loves' point to Arthur and Hetty too, and 'the feeble sense of the Unknown' extends to most of the characters of the novel, as well as to the human condition in general, covered also by the whole range of response to tragedy: 'the same frivolous gossip over blighted human lives'. It is a general vision of limited and selfish sensibility with a movement away from the particular story, though at the same time underlining the irony and unity of the events and the people who have made this particular delineation. Adam's change is set in the context of other changes, though it is his process which carries the main moral burden.

This novel carries an interesting example of the quietness with which George Eliot can present her tragic moral. We are told that a proposition was for Adam a principle, and 'knowledge to be acted on' and both his intelligence and his moral self-confidence are expressed in terms of the images of his trade and his limited theory. 'I've seen pretty clear, ever since I could cast up a sum', he tells Arthur, 'as you can never do what's wrong without breeding sin and trouble more than you can ever see'; and, 'The square o' four is sixteen, and you must lengthen your lever in proportion to your weight, is as true when a man's miserable as when he's happy.' Adam's pride in his work and his belief that 'good carpentry was God's will' is used to show his mind's advantage over the enclosed egoism of Hetty and even of Arthur. Gwendolen's tragic ennui, we are told in *Daniel Deronda*, has no outlet in the joy of work, and for Adam, 'the best o' working is, it gives you a grip hold o' things outside your lot'. But Adam's faith in arithmetical analogy demonstrates his weakness as well as his strength—it is part of his simple and rigid equation of proposition with action, and he comes in the end to revalue even arithmetic. But this revaluation is placed not at the end of the novel, but in an inset towards the beginning, and its simple reversal of Adam's favourite symbol sounds rather less glib and easy in this context. It is an apparently casual movement forward in time, introducing George Eliot talking to Adam ,'in his old age', about Mr Irwine. But the subject of Irwine is not the whole point of Adam's discourse and on re-reading we displace the passage and see it as the final summary of his tragic education—a summary best made after many years, and so well placed in this inserted digression:

'Nay, nay,' said Adam, broadening his chest and throwing himself back in his chair, as if he were ready to meet all inferences, 'nobody has ever heard me say Mr Irwine was much of a preacher. He didn't go into deep speritial experience; and I know there's a deal in a man's inward life as you can't measure by the square, and say, "Do this and that'll follow," and "Do that and this'll follow." There's things go on in the soul, and times when feelings come into you like a rushing mighty wind, as the Scripture says, and part your life in two a'most, so as you look back on yourself as if you was somebody else.' (ch. xvii)

When we read this with the wisdom after the event—perceiving, by the way, that Dinah has had some little influence on Adam's style—we see for the first time that Adam's simple arithmetic can be rejected as an incomplete answer. He is the first elaborate demonstration, as a middle way between an Amos Barton and a Dorothea, of Farebrother's dictum: 'Character is not cut in marble.'

CHAPTER III

The Tragic Process: The Heroines

(i)

FAREBROTHER says to Dorothea, 'Character is not cut in marble—it is not something solid and unalterable. It is something living and changing, and may become diseased as our bodies do' (*Middlemarch*, ch. lxxii). To this we must add two qualifications. One is Dorothea's immediate reply, 'Then it may be rescued and healed'. The other is George Eliot's answer to Novalis's 'Character is destiny'—'But not the whole of our destiny' (*The Mill on the Floss*, bk. vi, ch. vi).

After *Adam Bede*, all the novels, except *Silas Marner*, are primarily concerned with the tragic heroine instead of the hero, and the choice of a heroine has several consequences. The heroines of George Eliot's novels—Maggie Tulliver, Romola, Esther Lyon, Dorothea Brooke, and Gwendolen Harleth—all share the *ex officio* disability of being women. A disability is, as we have seen, something which George Eliot seems to have needed for the compassionate appeal of her tragedies. In Amos it was an unattractive person and little sensibility; in Adam it was social inferiority; in Hetty it was narrow imagination and humble position. With the heroines it almost ceases to be a matter of class—though Maggie is an exception—and becomes a matter of gender. The woman's disability, like the inferior chances of the Poor Man or the Younger Son of folk-tale, provides the handicap. It is a handicap which does not necessarily make the impetus for tragedy, but which plays a large part in determining the quality of the tragic suffering and redemption.

The disability is carefully stressed. George Eliot provides us with a *curriculum vitae* for all her heroines. As usual, her commentary moves from the individual lot to the general condition, and we are told of Maggie:

She was as lonely in her trouble as if she had been the only girl in the civilised world of that day who had come out of her school-

47

life with a soul untrained for inevitable struggles—with no other part of her inherited share in the hard-won treasures of thought, which generations of painful toil have laid up for the race of men, than shreds and patches of feeble literature and false history—with much futile information about Saxon and other kings of doubtful example. (bk. IV, ch. iii)

Romola is an exception, as we should expect of a woman of her time and class. She has been taught by her father and by Calcondila, and although we do not know what the syllabus was, we know that she has both Latin and Greek. When her father says, 'And even in learning thou art not, according to thy measure, contemptible. Something perhaps were to be wished in thy capacity of attention and memory, not incompatible even with the feminine mind,' he adds Calcondila's testimonial, 'thou hast a ready apprehension, and even a wide-glancing intelligence' (ch. v).

Maggie sometimes longs for 'all Scott's novels and all Byron's poems', but she is aware of her reason: they may provide 'absorbing fancies' and 'dull the sensibilities'. She is aware too of their uselessness: they can give her no explanation of her father's pain and her own ennui—an interesting reaction, incidentally, for the consideration of those who would make much of George Eliot's 'debt' to Scott. Maggie's dream of romantic glamour has been partly fed by the Romantics, but she is a little more critical in her reading than Mrs Transome and Esther Lyon are in *Felix Holt*. Mrs Transome is, like Maggie, uneducated, and her *curriculum vitae* is a masterpiece of elliptical caricature and anti-climax:

When she was young she had been thought wonderfully clever and accomplished, and had been rather ambitious of intellectual superiority—had secretly picked out for private reading the lighter parts of dangerous French authors—and in company had been able to talk of Mr Burke's style, or of Chateaubriand's eloquence—had laughed at the Lyrical Ballads and admired Mr Southey's Thalaba. . . . The history of the Jews, she knew, ought to be preferred to any profane history; the Pagans, of course, were vicious, and their religions quite nonsensical, considered as religions—but classical learning came from the Pagans; the Greeks were famous for sculpture; the Italians for painting; the middle ages were dark

and Papistical; but now Christianity went hand in hand with
civilisation, and the providential government of the world, though
a little confused and entangled in foreign countries, in our favoured
land was clearly to be seen to be carried forward on Tory and
Church of England principles, sustained by the succession of the
House of Brunswick, and by sound English divines. For Miss
Lingon had had a superior governess, who held that a woman
should be able to write a good letter, and to express herself with
propriety on general subjects. (ch. ii)

Esther, the possessor of 'one of those exceptional organisations
which are quick and sensitive without being in the least mor-
bid', admires Byron and Chateaubriand, and her susceptibility
to Romantic literature, though presented without the scathing irony of Mrs Transome's *curriculum*, is to some extent made
a touchstone both of her sensibility and her superficiality.
Felix's angry account of Byron (much the same as that of
Sandy Mackaye in Kingsley's *Alton Locke*) as 'A misan-
thropic debauchee whose notion of a hero was that he should
disorder his stomach and despise mankind' is rather more
than the modern reader can take. It is made in this context
of educational satire, and if Felix's literary criticism lacks
the brake of George Eliot's usual irony, its moral import is
as plain as the implications of Mrs Transome's attitude to
Wordsworth.

Dorothea is uneducated, too, but her reading is very different from Mrs Transome's and Esther's:

Dorothea knew many passages of Pascal's *Pensées* and of Jeremy
Taylor[1] by heart; and to her the destinies of mankind, seen by the
light of Christianity, made the solicitudes of feminine fashion
appear an occupation for Bedlam. . . . Her mind was theoretic, and
yearned by its nature after some lofty conception of the world
which might frankly include the parish of Tipton and her own rule
of conduct there. . . . She, the elder of the sisters, was not yet
twenty, and they had both been educated, since they were about
twelve years old and had lost their parents, on plans at once
narrow and promiscuous. . . . (ch. i)

Dorothea's lack of education is carefully exposed. It contributes to her illusions—it combines fatally with her theoretic

---

[1] Adam Bede also read Jeremy Taylor.

mind, her inexperience and youth, and her social ardour. She is as unrealistic as the childish Saint Theresa in her first enterprise, and this childishness is given continued emphasis. Her lack of education is measured against Lydgate's ironical preference for the more harmonious womanly graces of Rosamond, 'the flower of Mrs Lemon's school, the chief school in the county, where the teaching included all that was demanded of the accomplished female—even to extras, such as the getting in and out of a carriage' (ch. xi).

Gwendolen is not unintelligent, but she too is the product of the same kind of sketchy female education, though she is complacent about it:

> With regard to much in her lot hitherto, she held herself rather hardly dealt with, but as to her 'education' she would have admitted that it had left her under no disadvantages. In the schoolroom her quick mind had taken readily that strong starch of unexplained rules and disconnected facts which saves ignorance from any painful sense of limpness; and what remained of all things knowable, she was conscious of being sufficiently acquainted with through novels, plays, and poems. About her French and music, the two justifying accomplishments of a young lady, she felt no ground for uneasiness. . . . (ch. iv)

Gwendolen is not insensitive, though her dread of isolation and space is shown as a rather special kind of susceptibility, but the limits of her taste and imagination are clearly defined in this sense of her educational advantages. She has more polite vulgarity and self-assurance than most of the other heroines, and George Eliot's educational satire moves in two directions at once, sparing neither the institution nor its happy victim. This satire is certainly not restricted to female education: her comments on the defective education of Arthur Donnithorne, Tom Tulliver, Fred Vincy, and even Daniel Deronda, make it plain that her criticism was a more fundamental one. But the reference to women's education is of course persistent. Her view of the social handicap of her sex is very like that of other writers. In *Blackwood's*, for July 1857, for instance, where George Eliot's *Scenes of Clerical Life* were appearing, we find the writer of an article on *Currer Bell* saying much the same sort of thing as George Eliot:

The Heroines

Although her success was extraordinary, her struggles were by no means peculiar; and in the simple facts of her life we have touching evidence of what hundreds of young women have to undergo, who have no proper outlet for their mental activities. If the employments to which women in this country can turn their hands are few enough, how very few are the occupations for educated women! . . . They can become either governesses or authoresses.

When George Eliot's heroines are faced with the problem of a career none of them become authoresses and although some become governesses, George Eliot carefully refrains from showing us a Jane Eyre. Her governesses are ghosts: Miss Merry in *Daniel Deronda* scarcely appears, and Gwendolen is saved from becoming a governess by Grandcourt's offer; Maggie Tulliver has 'a dreary situation in a school', but we do not see her there, and when she becomes daily governess to Dr Kenn's younger children we see nothing of the schoolroom; Esther is a governess but we do not see her at work; Mary Garth, a reluctant teacher, is also saved from going back to teaching. For the most part we see the heroine without an occupation. Tom Tulliver, despite his inappropriate education, can go off and retrieve the family fortunes. Fred Vincy and Daniel Deronda, both initially at a loss in seeking a vocation, and certainly not helped by educational institutions, do eventually find their vocation. The heroine is deprived of their outlet in action and of their opportunities. She may find her vocation in marriage, successfully, like Esther, or almost fatally, like Dorothea. She may be driven into a passive and tormenting ennui, like Maggie and Gwendolen. The tragic ennui, which can be both temptation and punishment, is presented emphatically as a state of isolation. Maggie is cut off 'from her inherited share in the hard-won treasure of thought, which generations of painful toil have laid up for the race of men', and this is of course entails not merely loneliness but also—in every case—the fatal flaw of ignorance. All the heroines are like Maggie, 'quite without knowledge of the irreversible laws within and without'.

This does not mean that George Eliot is writing as a prose-lytizing feminist. We know of her friendship with Barbara

Bodichon, her support for the foundation of Girton and the Elizabeth Garrett Anderson Hospital, and her general sympathy with Victorian feminism, but she played no active part in the movement, and her books make their feminist protest in a very muted way. *Middlemarch* assimilated the earlier project of *Miss Brooke*, and one of the consequences of the assimilation is the way in which Lydgate's tragedy qualifies our response to Dorothea's. Any suggestion of a feminist moral is controlled and extended by the complex plot, which puts Dorothea in her place as an example less of a feminine problem than of the frustrations of the human condition. This is made emphatically plain by George Eliot's revision of the end of the novel. The first edition (1871-2), in parts, had this passage in its penultimate paragraph:

Among the many remarks passed on her mistakes, it was never said in the neighbourhood of Middlemarch that such mistakes could not have happened if the society into which she was born had not smiled on propositions of marriage from a sickly man to a girl less than half his own age—on modes of education which make a woman's knowledge another name for motley ignorance—on rules of conduct which are in flat contradiction with its own loudly-asserted beliefs.

In the edition of 1874 this passage was deleted, and whatever the reasons for the deletion, its effect is undoubtedly that of a clear movement away from the particular case of Dorothea. The precise references in this first version are, in the second, covered by generalization. The last version compresses and summarizes the particular indictment in the words 'the conditions of an imperfect social state, in which great feelings will often take the aspect of error, and great faith the aspect of illusion'. The more general and open statement glances at Lydgate, and at Bulstrode, Casaubon, and all the others, not merely at Dorothea's handicap as a woman.

The heroines have this initial handicap, and it is very carefully pointed by generalized satire as well as by a pathetic individual appeal. They are otherwise very different from Amos Barton and Silas Marner, and have all the conventional equipment for tragic nurture: intelligence, some sensibility, imagination, and the power to speak for themselves. The tragic process of the heroines has one constant theme: they are all, in different ways and in varying degrees, concerned with a problem of sensibility. This is, incidentally, one of the themes which has a Comtean echo, for George Eliot, like Lewes and Comte, and unlike Bentham and Mill, is occupied with the value of feeling and its place in the life of ideas and the human progress. Lewes makes his position clear in the introduction to his exposition of Comte's *Cours de Philosophie Positive*, which he published in 1853 as *Comte's Philosophy of the Sciences*: 'Logic and Sentiment—to use popular generalizations—have been long at war,' and, 'man is moved by his emotions, not by his ideas: using the intellect only as an eye to *see the way*'. George Eliot uses her heroines to demonstrate both the importance of sensibility and the tragic problem of the break between feeling and reason.

Each story is different, in spite of this constant theme. Even within this repeated predicament there is variation: it is neither the same flaw nor the same suffering. The emphasis varies: Maggie has passionate capriciousness and energetic self-abnegation; Romola is calm and passive; Esther has her exaggenerated finicky sensibility—the excessive good taste which makes her shrink from real issues; Dorothea, at war with Esther's kind of propriety, has her blundering and blinding— and, for some readers, endearing—moral ardour; Gwendolen has an arrogant reliance on her own undefined powers, and her strong almost superstitious fears. The process of rescue by the hero is appropriately designed in each case. The hero is not only the male who is superior in education though with the same problems of feeling, but the lover with a particular understanding of the heroine's predicament, and often with an implausibly detached moral view of it. Most of George Eliot's readers would probably agree that she is not unreservedly successful in the way in which she tries to assimilate the moral interpretation of the heroine to the presentation of the human relationship.

(ii)

Perhaps the most successful mentor and rescuer is Philip. He is also, in human terms, the least successful, for his rescue, like his love, is frustrated. His understanding of Maggie is perfectly in character: he is one of George Eliot's male characters who fully convinces us of his humanity as well as his powers of moral criticism. His relation with Maggie has its strong didactic element, and though, practically speaking, it does little for Maggie, it warns and prepares the reader. He sees it all—or nearly all. He recognizes her need, her clamping control of the need, and all the consequent dangers. He sees too—later—that the irony of her temptation by Stephen lies in the very fact of Stephen's 'unworthiness', in spite of the numerous readers, from Leslie Stephen onwards, who have objected to this unworthiness as if it were something George Eliot did not notice, a failure in distance and a piece of bad taste on her part.[1] It is Philip who gives us the clue:

I believed then, as I believe now, that the strong attraction which drew you together proceeded only from one side of your characters, and belonged to that partial, divided action of our nature which makes half the tragedy of the human lot. I have felt the vibration of chords in your nature, that I have continually felt the want of in his. But perhaps I am wrong; perhaps I feel about you as the artist does about the scene over which his soul has brooded with love. . . . (bk. VII, ch. iii)

Philip's character and function have been strangely neglected by George Eliot's critics. This piece of interpretation of Maggie is finely done. It is spoken by the partial voice, and Philip is intelligent enough and detached enough to allow for his own partiality. This allowance is made in terms of his artistic sensibility, and George Eliot, like Henry James, often uses the artist's receptiveness and imagination as a metaphor for the growth of sensibility. Philip paints and sings, and

[1] An earlier and rather more intelligent objection is that of the reviewer in *The Westminster Review*, July 1860, who complained that Maggie's love for Stephen is realistic but not in this novel, since 'Maggie is the representative, after all, of the poetical temperament'. George Eliot plainly wished to show the self-betrayal as well as the strength of the poetical temperament.

The Heroines

Maggie's aesthetic susceptibilities and deprivations are stressed as clues to her conflict and development. But although this commentary on Maggie is particularized—it is Philip's voice we hear—it is reasonable to suggest that it has a weight and a reliability which represent the author's point of view. George Eliot does not talk casually about 'tragedy' and 'human lot'. Philip's point of view is surely neglected when Dr Leavis complains that Maggie's susceptibility to Stephen and her religious exaltation are presented uncritically. Even allowing for Philip's partiality, it is hard to reconcile the passage I have just quoted with Dr Leavis's comment in *The Great Tradition* that 'it is quite plain that George Eliot shares to the full the sense of Stephen's irresistibleness', and it is equally hard not to make some qualification of his comment that the 'soulful side of Maggie' is 'offered by George Eliot herself—and this of course is the main point—with a remarkable absence of criticism'. Philip's voice speaks clearly against Stephen's 'irresistibleness' and the 'soulful side of Maggie'. It might be argued that this voice is not strong enough to bear the choric function, though on the question of Maggie's renunciations his criticism also receives support from the author's commentary. But we cannot claim that Maggie is not criticized. I think most readers would sympathize to some extent with Dr Leavis's reactions to the novel: it is true that this is not the kind of tragedy where the tragic heroine is made to share her author's judgment. But that judgment is passed, even though Maggie dies before she can achieve the maturity which might accept and understand it.

Philip is very much more than a character with this critical function. When he comments on the tragic divided action of Maggie's nature which draws her to Stephen, he is unwittingly commenting also on his own relationship with her. This is shown with complete plausibility. Philip, like Stephen, feeds Maggie's sensibilities—her imagination though not her passion —and answers her childish need to be loved. He tempts her too through pity. And Maggie's inexperience is nowhere more ironically and calmly presented than in George Eliot's account of this love she feels for Philip. He breaks into her dream of renunciation, which is just as romantic as her earlier dream of love and beauty and glamour. He gives her music and books and talk, and a temporary resting-place and peace which she mistakes for love. The friendly and relaxed gentleness of Maggie's relation with Philip meets its contrast in the uneasy embarrassment of the early stages of her relation with Stephen—perhaps George Eliot's only real portrayal of sexual tension. But before Maggie meets Stephen, there are hints that her belief that she loves Philip is another of her illusions: ' And yet, how was it that she was now and then conscious of a certain dim background of relief in the forced separation from Philip? Surely it was only because the sense of a deliverance from concealment was welcome at any cost?' (bk. v, ch. v).

The first part of *The Mill on the Floss* is a perfect piece of preparation: the growth of Maggie, and of her generation, is humanly plausible and formally essential. Every crisis in the slow and spacious childhood scenes has its later counterpart. Irony, narrative unity and psychological conviction seem to spring up easily together. Maggie is absent-minded, and lets Tom's rabbits die. She rushes from shame into dreams made up of love and self-importance. She has a doll as a scapegoat. She pushes Lucy into the mud. She tries to turn one of her dreams into reality by running away to the gipsies, finds the truth unpleasant and goes back gladly. There is no need to labour the later parallels. But although the first part has both symbol and rich human substance George Eliot was herself dissatisfied with the balance of the novel as a whole. She felt that the 'epic breadth' of the first half overbalanced the speed and brevity of the second.

My love of the childhood scenes made me linger over them; so that I could not develop as fully as I wished the concluding 'Book' in which the tragedy occurs, and which I had looked forward to with much attention and premeditation from the beginning. (Haight, iii, p. 374)

There is in fact no obvious reason why the last book should not have been longer and fuller, and George Eliot's obstinate rejection of criticisms of Maggie's relation with Stephen may have resulted in a rationalization. The haste and cursoriness of the last two books is perhaps appropriate. The strong attraction of Maggie and Stephen is shown as violent, rapid, and, in a sense which is entirely reconcilable with its sexual tension, superficial. Certainly it is not very easy to see how either of the last books could have improved had they been treated with the slow and lavish circumstantial detail of the earlier parts. In the last book but one, that dealing with Maggie's passion and her flight with Stephen, speed is essential. In the last book, dealing with her return, her social rejection, her last temptation and her death, the cursoriness is partly the result of a rather hasty introduction of a new character and a new relationship—Dr Kenn and Maggie's friendship with him —and partly the impression given by the flood which comes to answer Maggie's prayer. Even a well-prepared *deus ex machina* like this one may give the appearance of an arbitrary concluding rush. The human mentors and healers do not work alone in *The Mill on the Floss*.

The hero as mentor recurs throughout the novels, beginning with Tryan, in *Janet's Repentance*, and ending with Daniel Deronda. Tryan, Philip, Savonarola, and Daniel, are the mentors whose intellectual direction does not have a romantic happy ending; Felix Holt and Mary Garth proselytize and love successfully. The relationship of the ignorant heroine and the didactic hero has no trace of Comte's anti-feminist condescension to women. Comte saw woman as biologically specialized in vocation in the most limited way, and saw no need for woman's place to leave the home in the Positivist Utopia. George Eliot's continued irony plays significantly on the Maggies and Dorotheas and Gwendolens who have no social medium for their energies. But she too sees women as playing a special role in the growing evolution of thought and affection. Comte puts it this way:

Of the two general attributes which divide Humanity from Animality,—intellect and affection,—one demonstrates the necessary and invariable preponderance of the male sex, whilst the other directly characterizes the indispensable moderating function devolving on women independently even of maternal cares. (op. cit., section IV)

George Eliot says, after a characteristic shift of perspective from Gwendolen Harleth's story to a picture of the cosmic and social energies of which Gwendolen knows nothing:

What in the midst of that mighty drama are girls and their blind visions? They are the Yea or Nay of that good for which men are enduring and fighting. In these delicate vessels is borne onward through the ages the treasure of human affections. (ch. xi)

The last four novels are to some extent concerned with the strength of affection, and its inadequacy.

(iii)

One of the characteristics of this theme of affection is that it is given a formal and fairly elaborate statement. The characters are never left to demonstrate it by action alone. It might be argued that this is true of all the major themes in the novels: the theme of unheroic tragedy is introduced and explained in all the novels where it is important, that is to say, from *Scenes of Clerical Life* to *Silas Marner*; the theme of egoism and altruism, expounded in terms of the slow but sure movement of the 'deeds that determine us', has its formal exposition, dispersed throughout the novels, and in particular, through *Adam Bede* and *Romola*. But there is, I think, this difference: this theme of the divided sensibility is in itself less demonstrable in action, for it is only part of a possible explanation of the characters' conduct. One could extract the passages expounding it from *Felix Holt* and *Daniel Deronda* and not lose much. In *Romola* and *Middlemarch* it is more organic to the structure of character and less of a theoretical excrescence, though perhaps part of the relative failure of *Romola* is attributable to the way in which two of the central characters— Romola and Savonarola—are created in exposition and dialectic rather than—like Tito—in an accumulation of many actions. The exposition and dialectic are in part concerned with the split between heart and mind.

All Romola's ardour had been concentrated in her affections. Her share in her father's learned pursuits had been for her little more than a toil which was borne for his sake; and Tito's airy brilliant faculty had no attraction for her that was not merged in the deeper sympathies that belong to young love and trust. Romola had had contact with no mind that could stir the larger possibilities of her nature; they lay folded and crushed like embryonic wings, making no element in her consciousness beyond an occasional vague uneasiness. (ch. xxvii)

This is pure exposition: one may have drawn various conclusions from Romola's relation with her father and Tito—about her isolation, her nobility, her ardour, her fidelity—but although there is nothing in the action which does not substantiate the exposition, there is not the rush of acquiescence with which we meet—for instance—the comments on the dull provincial life in *The Mill on the Floss* or the summary of Dorothea's small and not ideally beautiful acts. But once the exposition has been made, we have been shown what to look for and we find it. Romola's crushed wings (the image of wings is used frequently in the letters and throughout the novels) unfold when she meets Savonarola. Her untheoretical ardour is stressed because it is there to motivate her relation with Savonarola. He moves her through ardour but also through reason and dogma. He meets her when her wife's ardour has chilled and her new ardour leaps to accept the dogma she had been brought up to reject:

In spite of the wearisome visions and allegories from which she recoiled in disgust when they came as stale repetitions from other lips than his, her strong affinity for his passionate sympathy and the splendour of his aims had lost none of its power. His burning indignation against the abuses and oppression that made the daily story of the Church and of States had kindled the ready fire in her too. His special care for liberty and purity of government in Florence, with his constant reference of this immediate object to the wider end of a universal regeneration, had created in her a new consciousness of the great drama of human existence in which her life was a part; and through her daily helpful contact with the less fortunate of her fellow-citizens this new consciousness became something stronger than a vague sentiment; it grew into a more and more definite motive of self-denying practice. . . . The pressing problem for Romola just then was not to settle questions of controversy, but to keep alive that flame of unselfish emotion by which a life of sadness might still be a life of active love. . . . Romola was so deeply moved by the grand energies of Savonarola's nature, that she found herself listening patiently to all dogmas and prophecies, when they came in the vehicle of his ardent faith and believing utterance. (ch. xliv)

When she breaks with him it is in a revolt of feeling. Her moral progress is based on a paradox: she learns self-denial from Savonarola and then comes to reject what she sees in him as self-interest. She accepts his ideas in the warmth of her ardour, then rejects him in the same passionate loyalty which made her despise Tito's rational defence of his betrayal of Bardo. The relationships are antithetical but they have similarity too. In both there is the same process of ardent awakening, illusion and dissent:

After all has been said that can be said about the widening influence of ideas, it remains true that they would hardly be such strong agents unless they were taken in a solvent of feeling. The great world-struggle of developing thought is continually foreshadowed in the struggle of the affections, seeking a justification for love and hope. (ch. lii)

This is not a simple rejection of theory by feeling. Romola is carefully presented as intellectually capable of seeing what she would rationally reject in Savonarola but not rejecting it until her *feeling* rebels:

If Romola's intellect had been less capable of discerning the complexities in human things, all the early loving associations of her life would have forbidden her to accept implicitly the denunciatory exclusiveness of Savonarola. She had simply felt that his mind had suggested deeper and more efficacious truth to her than any other, and the large breathing room she found in his grand view of human duties had made her patient towards that part of his teaching which she could not absorb, so long as its practical effect came into collision with no strong force in her. But now a sudden insurrection of feeling had brought about that collision. (ch. lii)

And later:

It was inevitable that she should judge the Frate unfairly on a question of individual suffering, at which *she* looked with the eyes of personal tenderness, and *he* with the eyes of theoretic conviction. (ch. lxi)

Yet Romola and Savonarola are both established as creatures of sensibility—any attempt to abstract George Eliot's themes has to take refuge in endless modification. The final irony in this relationship comes when Savonarola too recoils from the Trial by Fire—his mind flooded with passionate sensibility:

> Savonarola's nature was one of those in which opposing tendencies co-exist in almost equal strength: the passionate sensibility which, impatient of definite thought, floods every idea with emotion and tends towards contemplative ecstasy, alternated in him with a keen perception of outward facts and a vigorous personal judgement of men and things. (ch. lxiv)

It is not that Savonarola represents the life of ideas, and Romola the life of the feelings, but rather, ironically, that he gives her the ideal of fellowship which is for her a passionate and practical idea, whereas her particular kind of individual loyalty tears them apart. It is a demonstration of different combinations of the forces of emotion and intellect, and, as the quoted expositions show, a demonstration carried out largely in terms of the author's reflection. One of the deadnesses of *Romola* comes from its life of unrelieved grand crisis which, except perhaps in Tito's case, does not allow motive and action to unfold slowly, and which is explained in exposition rather than revealed in dramatic and varied action.

(iv)

In *Felix Holt* the theme is present in Felix's influence on Esther: he gives her, by love, and by what she calls angry pedagogy, the strong vision which leads her away from the life of her romantic dream, where her ladylike sensibility may be gratified. The theme comes to the surface in a burst of dogma, but in the words of Felix:

> 'My text is something you said the other day. You said you didn't mind about people having right opinions so that they had good taste. Now I want you to see what shallow stuff that is.'
> 'O, I don't doubt it if you say so. I know you are a person of right opinions.'
> 'But by opinions you mean men's thoughts about great subjects, and by taste you mean their thoughts about small ones: dress, behaviour, amusements, ornaments.'
> 'Well—yes—or rather, their sensibilities about those things.'
> 'It comes to the same thing; thoughts, opinions, knowledge, are

only a sensibility to facts and ideas. If I understand a geometrical problem, it is because I have a sensibility to the way in which lines and figures are related to each other; and I want you to see that the creature who has the sensibilities that you call taste, and not the sensibilities that you call opinions, is simply a lower, pettier sort of being.' (ch. x)

Felix offers both love and salvation. Esther's progress from mere 'good taste' towards a wider vision of herself and the world is treated with tragic gravity. But when we compare her progress of the soul with Maggie's or Dorothea's we have to admit different degrees of tragic intensity. Esther's weakness may be felt partly because Felix himself is a lifeless character, except in local flashes, but it is also, I think, because Esther's moral choice does not carry the conviction of a tragic ordeal. George Eliot tries to show Esther's isolation at the moment of choice: if she chooses duty there is no guarantee that she will be choosing love also:

It is not true that love makes all things easy: it makes us choose what is difficult. . . . What if she chose the hardship, and had to bear it alone, with no strength to lean upon—no other better self to make a place for trust and joy? Her past experience saved her from illusions. She knew the dim life of the back street, the contact with sordid vulgarity, the lack of refinement for the senses, the summons to a daily task; and the gain that was to make the life of privation something on which she dreaded to turn her back, as if it were heaven—the presence and love of Felix Holt—was only a quivering hope, not a certainty. It was not in her woman's nature that the hope should not spring within her and make a strong impulse. She knew that he loved her: had he not said how a woman might help a man if she were worthy? and if she proved herself worthy? But still there was the dread that after all she might find herself on the stony road alone,[1] and faint and be weary. (ch. xlix)

George Eliot is doing all she can to free the moral choice from the desires of the heart, but the conflict is confused. We are asked to admire nobility, but this nobility has powerful self-

[1] This is perhaps an echo of Romola on her 'stony road alone'. The novels sometimes pick up images from their predecessors: another more prominent instance is the transference of images of light and pagan gods from Tito to Will Ladislaw.

interest behind it. We may congratulate George Eliot on her honesty—it is true that motives are mixed. It is true also that we are made to feel Esther's isolation, but it is only a temporary impression. Her growth has not only been made with Felix's help but it is made also in order to prove herself worthy. Moral improvement is a fair and common means of promoting one's attractions and justifiable in this context, but the amorous motive weakens the moral choice. And the conclusion confirms our suspicions of complacency: Esther, like Maggie Verver, has too much to gain by her tragic ordeal: 'That young presence, which had flitted like a white new-winged dove over all the saddening relics and new finery of Transome Court, could not find its home there' (ch. 1). The strong image—this time evoking a contrast, not a parallel, with Henry James, is not fully endorsed by the action. Esther is no Milly Theale.

It might be argued that George Eliot always evades the tragic conclusion: Maggie is rescued by death, and by a death which acts as a symbol of reconciliation; Dorothea is rescued by Casaubon's death and by her personal happy ending. But there is in these two cases a very much fuller demonstration of the frustration and loneliness and pain which precedes the tragic conclusion—or evasion. Dorothea's deficiencies as a tragic and noble figure are moreover fully brought out by the final apology for her imperfections. It is only in Esther's case that we are asked to applaud a renunciation and a moral reversal which seem weakened by the absence of pain and moral strength. 'Her woman's passion and her reverence for rarest goodness rushed together in an undivided current', we are told, but the two motives have never been shown as separate. Esther's progress is too painless and her end too complacent.

The image of the current is repeated in *Middlemarch*. In Dorothea, we are told, 'There was a current into which all thought and feeling were apt sooner or later to flow—the reaching forward of the whole consciousness towards the fullest truth, the least partial good' (ch. xx). Dorothea is presented as both 'theoretic' and ardent, and she makes her initial mistake because of her ardour for knowledge. Where Romola found Savonarola, Dorothea finds Casaubon:

The Tragic Process

It would be a great mistake to suppose that Dorothea would have cared about any share in Mr Casaubon's learning as mere accomplishment. . . . All her eagerness for acquirement lay within that full current of sympathetic motive in which her ideas and impulses were habitually swept along. She did not want to deck herself with knowledge—to wear it loose from the nerves and blood that fed her action; and if she had written a book she must have done it as Saint Theresa did, under the command of an authority that constrained her conscience. But something she yearned for by which her life might be filled with action at once rational and ardent; and since the time was gone by for guiding visions and spiritual directors, since prayer heightened yearning but not instruction, what lamp was there but knowledge? Surely learned men kept the only oil; and who more learned than Mr Casaubon? (ch. x)

Casaubon's failure, interestingly enough, lies both in ardour and intellect, George Eliot's concept of knowledge being one of integrated ardour and learning. The integration is there in Lydgate, as far as his science is concerned, but it is imperfectly sustained in his human relations. He is the parallel portrait to Dorothea, and in the carefully woven likeness and antithesis, there is a similar problem:

He carried to his studies in London, Edinburgh, and Paris, the conviction that the medical profession as it might be was the finest in the world; presenting the most perfect interchange between science and art; offering the most direct alliance between intellectual conquest and the social good. Lydgate's nature demanded this combination: he was an emotional creature, with a flesh-and-blood sense of fellowship which withstood all the abstractions of special study. He cared not only for 'cases', but for John and Elizabeth, especially Elizabeth. (ch. xv)

Dorothea is the ardent creature whose intellectual longings are born of intellectual inexperience; Lydgate is the intellectual whose ardour—in spite of experience—is not entirely subject to his judgement: 'That distinction of mind which belonged to his intellectual ardour, did not penetrate his feelings and judgment about furniture, or women, or the desirability of its being known (without his telling) that he was better born than other country surgeons' (ch. xv).

The problem of sensibility finds a vigorous dramatic expression in *Middlemarch*. Here there is not the continual thematic insistence of *Romola*, but instead enough space and time for the minds and feelings of the characters to make themselves freely felt in domestic and social scenes, unclamped by analysis and exposition. The author's commentary is still used extensively but it is so dispersed with dramatic action and with the characters' reflections that it weighs less than the sustained general commentary in *Romola*. The gap between mind and heart which was so important in the lives of Romola and Savonarola is there too, though treated very differently, in the motives of Lydgate and Dorothea.

Dorothea, like Maggie and Esther, makes a tragic error: she is gravely deluded. Her ordeal, like Maggie's though not like Esther's, takes the form of an awakening from the desirable dream to the hard unexpected pressures of life as it is. First comes her marriage with Casaubon, and this turns out to be the exact reversal of all her hopes. Next comes her friendship with Will, passing unsuspectingly into love—and it is true that her innocence is not entirely plausible in this relation. The crisis here comes with her discovery of Will and Rosamond, leading to the scene in her own room, where—as often before—she meets temptation and triumph. After the triumph we have the happy marriage, delicately underplayed—it is true that her life has not been 'ideally beautiful'. This disclaimer is both ironical and literally accurate.

Dorothea is given the ability to see herself—and more or less as her author sees her. This makes her tragic ordeal one which ends in a kind of catharsis within the heroine. Maggie can recognize her predicament, but only in the particular terms of its immediate urgency. Dorothea is made to generalize her own faith, in its power and its inadequacy:

'I have a belief of my own, and it comforts me.'
'What is that?' said Will, rather jealous of the belief.
'That by desiring what is perfectly good, even when we don't know what it is and cannot do what we would, we are part of the divine power against evil—widening the skirts of light and making the struggle with darkness narrower.' (ch. xxxix)

This is fully endorsed by the action, first by her efforts to sympathize with her husband, then by her defence of Lydgate, and last, after her discovery of Will and Rosamond, by her resolute movement away from her private and partial grief:

> And what sort of a crisis might this not be in three lives whose contact with hers laid an obligation on her as if they had been suppliants bearing the sacred branch? The objects of her rescue were not to be sought out by her fancy: they were chosen for her. She yearned toward the perfect Right, that it might make a throne within her, and rule her errant will. 'What should I do—how should I act now, this very day, if I could clutch my own pain, and compel it to silence, and think of those three?' (ch. lxxx)

This is the reversal of her early illusion and confidence when she had sought out 'objects of her rescue', and the climax of all her generous impulses. If we find nobility and innocence exaggerated here we should remember that the Saint Theresa parallel sometimes makes its presence felt.

In *Daniel Deronda* we return to something which at first seems closer to *Felix Holt* than to *Middlemarch*. Gwendolen, like Esther, has her mentor. Daniel preaches his 'transmutation of self' to her, and it is a doctrine of feeling:

> 'To delight in doing things because our fathers did them is good if it shuts out nothing better; it enlarges the range of affection—and affection is the broadest basis of good in life.'
>
> 'Do you think so?' said Gwendolen, with a little surprise. 'I should have thought you cared most about ideas, knowledge, wisdom, and all that.'
>
> 'But to care about *them* is a sort of affection,' said Deronda, smiling at her sudden *naïveté*. 'Call it attachment, interest, willingness to bear a great deal for the sake of being with them and saving them from injury. Of course it makes a difference if the objects of interest are human beings; but generally in all deep affections the objects are a mixture—half persons and half ideas—sentiments and affections flow in together. (ch. xxxv)

Once more, as in *Romola* and *Middlemarch*, the image of the current is used for the whole consciousness, for the uniting of thought and feeling. This is only a small part of Gwendolen's problem, but it is a very large part of Daniel's, whose search for a vocation is a search for the cause which can satisfy the heart and the brain. The problem is there also in the case of Mordecai, who echoes some of Gwendolen's sensibility in a very different world. Gwendolen's peculiar sensibility makes her a haunted woman, and her haunting takes the form of the dead face, seen at the beginning of the book, repeating its terror in her dreams until it fuses with the murderous thought and becomes Grandcourt's face. 'Try to take hold of your sensibility, and use it as if it were a faculty, like vision' Daniel tells her, just as Felix told Esther 'nothing but a good strong terrible vision will save you'.

CHAPTER IV

The Tragic Process: The Egoists

A LL George Eliot's characters are shown as egoists. As she says in *Middlemarch*:

We are all of us born in moral stupidity, taking the world as an udder to feed our supreme selves: Dorothea had early begun to emerge from that stupidity, but yet it had been easier to her to imagine how she would devote herself to Mr Casaubon, and become wise and strong in his strength and wisdom, than to conceive with that distinctness which is no longer reflection but feeling—an idea wrought back to the directness of sense, like the solidity of objects —that he had an equivalent centre of self, whence the lights and shadows must always fall with a certain difference. (ch. xxi)

The process from innocence to experience is this emergence from moral stupidity, and it is, as we have seen, and as George Eliot makes clear in this particular comment on Dorothea, a growth in imagination and in feeling. But just as Shakespeare used *Macbeth* as well as *Lear* to show a tragic pattern, so George Eliot too shows the tragic process as one of deterioration as well as one of hopeful nurture. If there are the egoists who emerge from moral stupidity, like Dorothea, there are also those who never emerge, like Casaubon, and there are those who emerge too late, like Arthur Donnithorne, after egoism has found its tragic conclusion in the betrayal or the destruction of another life.

The unredeemed egoist appears in *Scenes of Clerical Life*, in static portraits like those of Countess Czerlaski and Anthony Wybrow, and in the slightly more mobile portrait of Dempster, Janet's husband in *Janet's Repentance*. Dempster is shown as the product of change, though the change itself is mainly shown in retrospect. Dempster's past is shown in exposition, and also, in tactful detail, in his relation with his mother. There is one scene, for instance, where Dempster and his mother go for a walk in the sunny garden, and the detail is a pointed one:

It was rather sad, and yet pretty, to see that little group passing out of the shadow into the sunshine, and out of the sunshine into the shadow again: sad, because this tenderness of the son for the mother was hardly more than a nucleus of healthy life in an organ hardening by disease, because the man who was linked in this way with an innocent past, had become callous in worldliness, fevered by sensuality, enslaved by chance impulses; pretty, because it showed how hard it is to kill the deep-down fibrous roots of human love and goodness—how the man from whom we make it our pride to shrink, has yet a close brotherhood with us through some of our most sacred feelings. (ch. vii)

This is echoed in the melodramatic image used of the death of Dempster's mother: 'When the earth was thrown on Mamsey's coffin, and the son, in crape scarf and hatband, turned away homeward, his good angel, lingering with outstretched wing on the edge of the grave, cast one despairing look after him, and took flight for ever' (ch. xiii).

This is a crude and externalized study, in comparison with the elaborate portraits of deterioration from *Adam Bede* onwards, though throughout her novels George Eliot resorts, from time to time, to this kind of *fait accompli* in villainy. Dunsey Cass is simple to the point of stereotype; Jermyn is given curt if vivid treatment; Grandcourt is shown as the product and not as the process of deterioration. The success of Grandcourt's portrayal suggests that psychological realism does not depend on character being shown in process. But her imaginative sympathy—a phrase which has almost a technical application to the constant shift of focus in the novels—makes George Eliot sometimes explore this tragic deterioration as elaborately as she explores the growth in sensibility. The two processes are often shown together, causally related, or formally emphatic.

The first lengthy study of the tragic egoist is Arthur Donnithorne in *Adam Bede*. Arthur's sensibility to himself and to the world outside is presented in an ironical juxtaposition of his own view and his author's:

His own approbation was necessary to him, and it was not an approbation to be enjoyed quite gratuitously; it must be won by a fair amount of merit. He had never yet forfeited that approbation,

69

and he had considerable reliance on his own virtues. No young man could confess his faults more candidly; candour was one of his favourite virtues; and how can a man's candour be seen in all its lustre unless he has a few failings to talk of? But he had an agreeable confidence that his faults were all of a generous kind—impetuous, warm-blooded, leonine; never crawling, crafty, reptilian. It was not possible for Arthur Donnithorne to do anything mean, dastardly, or cruel. 'No! I'm a devil of a fellow for getting myself into a hobble, but I always take care the load shall fall on my own shoulders.' Unhappily there is no inherent poetical justice in hobbles, and they will sometimes obstinately refuse to inflict their worst consequences on the prime offender, in spite of his loudly-expressed wish. It was entirely owing to this deficiency in the scheme of things that Arthur had ever brought any one into trouble besides himself. (ch. xii)

The author's irony becomes stronger:

Whether he would have self-mastery enough to be always as harmless and purely beneficent as his good nature led him to desire, was a question that no one had yet decided against him: he was but twenty-one, you remember; and we don't inquire too closely into character in the case of a handsome generous young fellow, who will have property enough to support numerous peccadilloes— who, if he should unfortunately break a man's legs in his rash driving, will be able to pension him handsomely; or if he should happen to spoil a woman's existence for her, will make it up to her with expensive *bons-bons*, packed up and directed by his own hand. (ch. xii)

Those who think that George Eliot's harshest irony in *Adam Bede* is reserved for Hetty Sorrel's beauty should look twice at this passage. Some of these comments are pointed preparation—'candour was one of his favourite virtues', for instance, but this excellent direct hit is followed by generalization and disguise. There is an apparently casual choice of invented examples, and the real clue is next to the false: the broken legs and the expensive *bons-bons* are arbitrary examples, though pointing in the right direction, but the spoiled woman's existence is a precise anticipation. Arthur, like Hetty, is not always presented in the strongly critical context of irony and scorn, and the later account of his torment and temptation is a much freer dramatic commentary, kept within his terms and his sensibility. The third person narrator is barely noticed here:

He was getting in love with Hetty—that was quite plain. He was ready to pitch everything else—no matter where—for the sake of surrendering himself to this delicious feeling which had just disclosed itself. It was no use blinking the fact now—they would get too fond of each other, if he went on taking notice of her—and what would come of it? He should have to go away in a few weeks, and the poor little thing would be miserable. He *must not* see her alone again; he must keep out of her way. What a fool he was for coming back from Gawaine's!

He got up and threw open the windows to let in the soft breath of the afternoon, and the healthy scent of the firs that made a belt round the Hermitage. The soft air did not help his resolutions, as he leaned out and looked into the leafy distance. But he considered his resolution sufficiently fixed: there was no need to debate with himself any longer. He had made up his mind not to meet Hetty again; and now he might give himself up to thinking how immensely agreeable it would be if circumstances were different— how pleasant it would have been to meet her this evening as she came back, and put his arm round her again and look into her sweet face. He wondered if the dear little thing were thinking of him too—twenty to one she was. How beautiful her eyes were with the tear on their lashes! He would like to satisfy his soul for a day with looking at them, and he *must* see her again:—he must see her, simply to remove any false impression from her mind about his manner to her just now. He would behave in a quiet, kind way to her—just to prevent her from going home with her head full of wrong fancies. Yes, that would be the best thing to do after all. (ch. xii)

This is the crisis of commitment, presented through Arthur's wish-fulfilment, Arthur's love, and Arthur's vocabulary. George Eliot has withdrawn her commentary, leaving the innocence of moral certainty to speak for itself, emphasized formally by the division into paragraphs, with the italicized *musts* punctuating the fluent undoing of resolution. Arthur's resolution has a short life, and it is succeeded by shame and irritation. Like Macbeth he throws the shame and fear on to external objects:

As for Arthur, he rushed back through the wood, as if he wanted to put a wide space between himself and Hetty. He would not go to the Hermitage again; he remembered how he had debated with himself there before dinner, and it had all come to nothing—worse than nothing. He walked right on into the Chase, glad to get out of the Grove, which surely was haunted by his evil genius. Those beeches and smooth limes—there was something enervating in the very sight of them; but the strong knotted old oaks had no bending languor in them—the sight of them would give a man some energy. (ch. xiii)

This is Arthur's fetishism, not George Eliot's. When he rides away earlier to put himself out of temptation in the most literal fashion, and later when he rides to settle his conflict by confessing to Irwine, there is the same fatal habit. His good intentions move with energy, like his horse—and Arthur's horse is a strong source of symbol for its rider. He disguises his confession in generalization, and when Irwine becomes suspicious and tries to penetrate the veiled discussion, Arthur evades and lies. His downward slide is sometimes presented directly as in the vacillation and effort and fantasy of the last passage, sometimes in the author's omniscient commentary. Arthur's internal monologue, like Bulstrode's, is not always available for it is not always in existence. George Eliot can seize the silence or the blockage within the mind as an opportunity for her pitying explanation. There is the occasion when Arthur gets up early and orders his horse because in bed 'his yesterdays are too oppressive'. He avoids reflection and throws himself into violent action. George Eliot explains:

Are you inclined to àsk whether this can be the same Arthur who, two months ago, had that freshness of feeling, that delicate honour which shrinks from wounding even a sentiment, and does not contemplate any more positive offence as possible for it?—who thought that his own self-respect was a higher tribunal than any external opinion? The same, I assure you; only under different conditions. Our deeds determine us, as much as we determine our deeds; and until we know what has been or will be the peculiar combination of outward with inward facts, which constitutes a man's critical actions, it will be better not to think ourselves wise about his character. There is a terrible coercion in our deeds which may first turn the honest man into a deceiver, and then reconcile him to the change; for this reason—that the second wrong presents itself to him in the guise of the only practicable right. The

action which before commission has been seen with that blended
common-sense and fresh untarnished feeling which is the healthy
eye of the soul, is looked at afterwards with the lens of apologetic
ingenuity, through which all things that men call beautiful and
ugly are seen to be made up of textures very much alike. Europe
adjusts itself to a *fait accompli*, and so does an individual character,
—until the placid adjustment is disturbed by a convulsive retri-
bution. (ch. xxix)

The violence of 'a terrible coercion' is followed by the dryer
tone of the scientific metaphor and the political comparison.
The voices of character and author alternate, and Arthur's
deterioration is both shown and explained, but the voices
themselves are composed of many tones. This is not just a
simple contrast between the character's text and the author's
marginal annotation—the notes on the character are a part of
the process which convinces us that the moral damnation is
fast and certain and subterranean.

Damnation is not the best word. We are shown irrespon-
sibility and rapidly moving disaster: dishonesty, self-indulgence, betrayal, murder. But there is a kind of redemption
for Arthur, even though this is not presented very forcibly
since in the last part of the novel we are more concerned with
Hetty and Adam. But Arthur is the galloping rider who brings
Hetty's pardon; it is he who begs Adam to stay in Hayslope
with the Poysers; and he is brought into a strong moral relation with Dinah—which is, I think, one of George Eliot's
least convincing attempts to end *Adam Bede* on a note of
moral affirmation. There are one or two moving details which
keep Arthur before us. Perhaps the most successful is the
elliptical return to the little pink silk handkerchief which
Arthur put into the wastepaper basket long ago, to hide it
from Adam after their fight. Once more the two men have met
in the Grove, and once more they have gone to the Hermitage. After Adam leaves Arthur alone, this is the last silent
presentation of remorse and love: 'As soon as the door was
closed behind him, Arthur went to the waste-paper basket
and took out the little pink handkerchief' (ch. xlviii).

Arthur has his appropriate nemesis, again expressed rather
curtly: 'I'm going away for years . . . it cuts off every plan of

happiness I've ever formed . . .' and 'I make no schemes now'. This quiet repudiation of his old dream, which links him with Hetty and with Adam, is to some extent overlaid by his return home, as a sick man, and by his last words to Adam, 'But you told me the truth when you said to me once, "There's a sort of wrong that can never be made up for"', which are almost the last words of the novel, and which underline something already made tragically emphatic. But although there are these uneven movements from quiet gravity to emphatic overstatement, the tragic process is not sentimentalized. Arthur is purged of his dream of becoming the Good Young Squire, just as Hetty is purged of her dream of being a fine lady, and we are left not merely with the mechanical donations of nemesis—happy marriage for Adam and Dinah, exile and fever for Arthur—but with a true and appropriate sense of the excited life falling into dreariness:

'You can't think what an old fellow I feel,' he says; 'I make no schemes now. I'm the best when I've a good day's march or fighting before me.' (ch. l)

It is the equivalent of Adam's discovery that 'there's a great deal . . . as you can't measure by the square'. It is the ironical reversal: it binds the action, shows the tragic cause, and demonstrates—even in Arthur's case—the tragic extension of sensibility, which George Eliot points to in Adam:

The growth of higher feeling within us is like the growth of faculty, bringing with it a sense of added strength: we can no more wish to return to a narrower sympathy, than a painter or a musician can wish to return to his cruder manner, or a philosopher to his less complete formula. (ch. liv)

George Eliot does not always show even this measure of redemption, and part of her pattern of variability is the egoist whose complete deterioration comes out of Arthur's kind of self-blindness. George Eliot is both moving and convincing when she demonstrates her characters' self-deception in terms of their almost innocent attachment to themselves. Even a character like Tito Melema, in *Romola*, for whom there is very little moral sympathy in his conflict or action, shows this dramatically realized self-affection, which is something we feel as a substitute for conflict as well as a diagnosis of villainy. Tito too slides down the egoist's insidious slope of deception and betrayal—of adopted father, father-in-law, wife, and adopted country. The measure of his degeneration is shown in the contrast between his actions and his perseverance in thinking well of himself. Like Arthur, he commits himself when he separates intention from action, though, unlike Arthur, he is very much less interested in self-analysis. He becomes increasingly concerned with consequences alone: there is no single crisis in Tito's career which corresponds to Arthur's sudden shocking realization of what he has done to Adam in seducing Hetty. For Arthur, as for Fred and Rosamond Vincy, the actual shock of seeing someone else's suffering as accusation can give a jolt to a not very energetic imagination. This never happens to Tito, and he dies as he lived, in a desperate hand-to-mouth hope for the future. He is an astonishingly successful piece of ironical portraiture, for at first the reader is put—very fairly—in Romola's position, and sees what it is like to be beguiled by his gentleness, his wit, and his charm. This description, for instance, has no irony, unless we can stretch the word to cover our wiser reaction on a second reading. But it has no reservations, and reads literally as an account of sweetness and softness:

'If you will only let me say, I love you—if you will only think me worth loving a little.'
His speech was the softest murmur, and the dark beautiful face, nearer to hers than it had ever been before, was looking at her with beseeching tenderness. (ch. xii)

There is no duplicity here: Tito is an adventurer, but not in his love for Romola, and her susceptibility to the charm is backed by our own. The reader is placed in Romola's position. George Eliot lets Tito's charm work on us, modified only by dark hints, for a considerable time before she discloses his past and begins to withdraw our sympathy.

Casaubon, like Tito, is unredeemed, though he is not shown as developing, and our sympathy for him depends on the moving point of view which controls the form of the whole novel. There are in *Middlemarch* four parallel portraits of the

75

egoist: Casaubon, Featherstone, Bulstrode and Fred Vincy, and of these it is Fred whose growth is most elaborately shown, for the others are more impressive tragic portraits but not shown in terms of the tragic education. Fred is almost a parody, or at least a gentler version, of the blind absorptions of Casaubon and Bulstrode. He acts within the moral pattern as a control: he succeeds in breaking out of the process of degeneration, and in getting his will clear of his deeds. He manages this mainly because, like Esther, he is helped by the coincidence of love and moral education. He has indeed more mentors than one, for Mary Garth, her father, and Fare-brother, all help to explain Fred to himself and all provide him with a variety of deterrents and incentives. There is also the subtle influence, for the reader, of the contrasting portrait of the other spoilt child, his sister. Rosamond's degree of self-absorption introduces us to Fred in a context where we are prepared for his relative success.

Fred's process is rather like Bulstrode's. He is handicapped by an imaginative failure—the inability to see his acts as affecting other people's lives. As with Arthur and Hetty, the moral defect is presented as a failure in sensibility. Fred has just confessed to the Garths that he cannot meet the bill to which Caleb has put his name:

Curiously enough, his pain in the affair beforehand had consisted almost entirely in the sense that he must seem dishonourable, and sink in the opinion of the Garths: he had not occupied himself with the inconvenience and possible injury that his breach might occasion them, for this exercise of the imagination on other people's needs is not common with hopeful young gentlemen. Indeed we are most of us brought up in the notion that the highest motive for not doing a wrong is something irrespective of the beings who would suffer the wrong.

But at this moment he suddenly saw himself as a pitiful rascal who was robbing two women of their savings. (ch. xxiv)

As for Arthur, it is experience which comes to enlarge Fred's not entirely inactive imagination, though the moral statement and the love-story work together, and Fred's search for an honest vocation is largely determined by Mary's conditions and Featherstone's will. He is one of those characters who are almost entirely shaped by the circumstances of the action, but this does not mean that his process is morally negligible. It contributes to the generalized study of egoism, and even to the tragic process, for it is in part through pain that Fred learns his lesson, though, if we can compare pains, it is of course a less tragically moving experience than Dorothea's or Lydgate's. Fred is a good example of a character whose story is infected by the seriousness of its context. He is not merely part of a pattern of contrasts and opposites which makes a generalization, allowing for the variants, but he is also part of George Eliot's attempt to discriminate different kinds of moral endurance. Fred is not a heroic figure, though there is no need for his author to interpret and apologize as she did for Amos Barton. And in his less culpable egoism he gives us a standard for observing Rosamond and Bulstrode, just as in his less admirable progress, he throws some light on Dorothea.

These correcting studies of the downward path are by no means wholly representative of George Eliot's egoists, but the characters of Bulstrode[1] and Casaubon and Grandcourt have a rather different place in the tragic pattern. They are shown as the result of the process, and they are not followed in their movement out of the state of uncommitted possibility into the egoist's betrayal and murder. I have taken Arthur, Tito and Fred as the most prominent examples of moral failure, and of moral failure shown in terms of development. But the moral failures and the moral successes cannot be considered merely in isolation. The hopeful and the hopeless are part of the same process. George Eliot is resisting a facile optimism by including all the variables, and we read the novel less in units of character, or even in units of human relations, than in a carefully manipulated form in which the sheep and the goats are seen in a special structural relation to each other. This manipulation is a way of stating her moral theme.

[1] I have considered Bulstrode more fully in Chapter VIII.

CHAPTER V

Character and Form

(i)

WE have seen that almost all George Eliot's characters are shown as morally committed, and committed as egoists or altruists. Her *homo duplex* is pulled in two directions by the urge of self-interest and the urge of social impulse. The prominent characters are either proceeding outward, towards Daniel Deronda's 'transmutation of self', or inward, in a slowly hardening egoism which blinds the imagination and moves logically towards the exclusions of betrayal and murder. Since the story and the moral analysis depend on each state being shown as a process, often as an unpredictable process, we are not presented with stereotypes but with characters who appear morally 'iridescent', to use George Eliot's word for Gwendolen. But sooner or later, with only one or two exceptions, the process becomes fixed, though we are often presented with the ironical situation where author and reader recognize the fixed point while the character re-mains beguiled by the hope of change.

This general moral commitment in terms of egoism and its opposite is largely responsible for the pattern of character. In spite of a great range of dramatic variety, and in spite of this moral mixture which suspends the conclusion, the characters are sheep or goats, or shown as becoming sheep or goats, and this means that they take their places in a pattern of correspondence and contrast. The dramatic presentation of individual personality tends to obscure the pattern, but it is as elaborate, though less conspicuous, as the correspondence in a play by Ben Jonson, where the same humour is repeated many times, or as the central antithesis of *King Lear* or Joyce's *Ulysses*. In each case it is the moral classification, as well as the delight in the aesthetic properties of formal relations, which seems to determine the pattern. George Eliot's moral vision is very like Lewes's description of science, 'the systematic classification of experience'. Except—and it is an important exception—that the characters are presented dramatically as well as being allocated to moral categories. They are also presented in the medium of strong sympathy: they are realized dramatically and act and speak for themselves, but running together with the dramatic medium is the personal voice of George Eliot's compassion. When a character stands outside that compassion, as Grandcourt does in *Daniel Deronda*, the bleakness of the withdrawal has its own quality of terror.

It is fairly obvious that the major characters fall into a moral classification, though perhaps slightly less obvious in the case of minor characters. If we consider some of the minor figures who appear to be playing 'character' parts for the purposes of filling in social background or providing comedy, it will often be found that they too are making their contribution to the moral theme. George Eliot, unlike Jane Austen and Dickens, does not usually make the exaggerated feature of the 'character' the moral trait. Mrs Poyser, in *Adam Bede*, is placed on the side of warm human fellowship both in her relations with others and in her judgments, but the prominent features are her sharp tongue, her feminism, and her common-sense. She is constructed rather as a comic personality who is involved in the tragedy, than a conspicuous moral example. Mrs Poyser's satirical powers are often directed, it is true, towards the main theme of the novel: 'For my part, I think he's welly like a cock as thinks the sun's rose o' purpose to hear him crow', she says of Craig the gardener. This is a comic chorus to George Eliot's analysis of Arthur and Hetty, but for one epigram which has this kind of relevance I suspect that there are several which are merely there as jokes or witty shafts in their own right, providing a running patter which is comic and which is also further demonstration of Mrs Poyser's daring, her outspoken shrewdness, her garrulousness and so forth. The same disguised relevance is there in Bartle Massey, the schoolmaster, in the same novel, or in Mrs Arrowpoint in *Daniel Deronda*, or in Celia or Mr Trumbull in *Middlemarch*. Such characters have a variety of functions, but they mostly have a submerged commitment to the main theme.

79

There are other minor characters in whom the moral reflections of the main dilemma is much clearer. There is Bob Jakin, or Dolly Winthrop, or little Henrietta Noble, all with some 'character' interest, in the theatrical sense, but all possessing a very strongly delineated moral feature of benevolence. There is Caleb Garth, very much more prominent both in the story and in the moral scheme, but possessing all kinds of attributes which bring him to life as a character yet have no obvious moral relevance—his simplicity, his slowness, his inadequate speech, his brusqueness, his tremendous enthusiasm, and his great respect for his wife—which can on occasion surprise us by being transformed into unquestioned husbandly authority. Then there are the dramatic failures —charmless characters like Dinah or Felix Holt or Daniel Deronda, who are fairly obviously not read with the affection or admiration which their author hoped for. There may be many reasons for their failure, and George Eliot's dramatic delineation is indeed a subject for a separate study, but I would suggest that one possible reason is the complete moral relevance of such characters. They do not provide us with much more than moral example. There is very little in Dinah or Felix or Daniel which gives us the impression of vitality and personality: almost all the features of these characters— though not quite all—are devoted to the business of providing the moral example. It is not very helpful to throw the problem back on to the old cliché about the dullness of good characters, since Caleb and Mary Garth, for instance, are both animated portraits and highly effective moral examples. But with Caleb and Mary we are conscious both of the exemplariness and of a rich, varied, and mobile personal impression. In most of the major characters this balance of exemplariness and personal liveliness is even more marked.

It is hard to say where moral classification begins and delight in pattern leaves off, for the two seem to go together in George Eliot's presentation of character. The two formal features which are most conspicuous are antithesis, or contrast, on the one hand, and correspondence, or resemblance, on the other. Both work together. They make their first appearance in what may be one of George Eliot's earliest attempts at fiction, the parable entitled *A Little Fable with a Great Moral* included in the collection, *Early Essays by George Eliot*, privately printed in 1919. The story tells us of two hamadryads, Idione and Hiera, who lived by a lake. Idione spent her days looking at her own reflection in the water, Hiera in watching the reflections of the sky and clouds. There is a sense in which both the moral and the pattern of this story lies at the heart of all her books. This is the contrast of the in-turned and the out-turned heart.

(ii)

We first meet the contrasted pair in *Scenes of Clerical Life*: Milly Barton and the Countess Czerlaski, Gilfil and Wybrow, Tryan and Dempster. In *Adam Bede* the pairing is more elaborate, for we have the twin contrasts of Adam and Arthur, Dinah and Hetty. Here there is the contrasted nemesis, as well as the contrasted moral cause. Just as the narcissistic hamadryad was fittingly punished by age, which changed her reflection, and by a lonely death, so Hetty and Arthur are punished by exile. Just as the hamadryad who looked outside herself was rewarded by the stability of what she watched, and never knew that she grew old, so Dinah and Adam are rewarded, at Lewes's suggestion, with each other. The contrast is simple, and it is observable in character and action, and also carefully underlined by commentary and by debate. There are several conversations between Dinah and Hetty which are thinly disguised moral debates. One which is especially prominent is introduced, in the chapter headed 'The Two Bed-Chambers' by a contrast in scene. It is very close to the two hamadryads, for we find Hetty looking into her mirror, while Dinah is looking through her window over the wide fields—this is the first appearance of the gaze through the window at the world outside, which we find significantly placed in *Felix Holt* and *Middlemarch*. The scenes overlap in time, linked by Hetty's dropped looking-glass which startles Dinah, and since they take place in adjoining rooms the concurrence gives a highly formal impression, rather like a divided set in the theatre. The scene ends with Dinah's compassionate promise that she will

help Hetty in any future trouble, a promise which Hetty's
narrow imagination takes literally as a frightening prophecy
—which indeed in a larger sense, going beyond Hetty's fears, it
turns out to be.

There is the same highly formal scene-setting before the
most prominent debate between Adam and Arthur. This comes
immediately after 'The Two Bed-Chambers' and it also has a
clue in the chapter-heading, which is 'Links'. It is a scene with
many functions. It contains the growth of Arthur's misunderstanding about Adam's relation with Mary Burge, which
has been suggested to him by Irwine, and which diverts him
from any hint that Adam loves Hetty; it looks ahead in the
casual talk about Adam's fighting—'I'll never fight any man
again, only when he behaves like a soundrel'; and it presents
the strong moral contrast. Arthur, who on this occasion, and
also later in Irwine's presence, is enjoying the indulgence of
thinking aloud about his conflict, and of generalizing to cover
his particular problem, asks Adam:

'I fancy you would master a wish that you had made up your
mind it was not quite right to indulge, as easily as you would
knock down a drunken fellow who was quarrelsome with you. I
mean, you are never shilly-shally, first making up your mind that
you won't do a thing, and then doing it after all?'

'Well,' said Adam, slowly, after a moment's hesitation—'no. I
don't remember ever being see-saw in that way, when I'd made
my mind up, as you say, that a thing was wrong. It takes the taste
out o' my mouth for things, when I know I should have a heavy
conscience after 'em. I've seen pretty clear, ever since I could cast
up a sum, as you can never do what's wrong without breeding sin
and trouble more than you can ever see. It's like a bit o' bad workmanship—you never see th'end o' the mischief it'll do.'(ch. xvi)

In the end, all four points of view are re-valued, and again
the contrast and parallelism have an emphasis to make. Hetty
and Arthur are both punished, Dinah and Adam are both rewarded, but Dinah and Adam have been pushed by tragedy
from their early position of easy confidence. As George Eliot
says of Dinah, in this last scene in Hetty's bed-chamber:

It is our habit to say that while the lower nature can never understand the higher, the higher nature commands a complete view

of the lower. But I think the higher nature has to learn this com‑
prehension, as we learn the art of vision, by a good deal of hard
experience, often with bruises and gashes incurred in taking things
up by the wrong end, and fancying our space wider than it is.
(ch. xv)

In these two sets of moral contrast there is of course a cer‑
tain social contrast too. The tragedy of *Adam Bede* is mechanic‑
ally dependent on the social gulf separating Adam and Arthur.
It is Arthur's ignorance about Adam's love for Hetty which—
it is implied—makes the seduction possible and also makes
the final disclosures burst with irony on both men. It is this
social gulf, which keeps these two in ignorance about each
other, which gives an edge to the scene of debate. This is not
just a moral contrast but a debate made in an apparently
detached context. The reader, who knows what the characters
do not, is able to appreciate the full irony of the scene. Arthur
is using the very remoteness of Adam as a possibility of
disguised confession and a relief from silence, and Adam
naïvely takes the generalization at its face-value and treats the
discussion as a general discussion, in contrast to Irwine who
quickly suspects the trend of Arthur's tentative examples,
and asks the premature question which makes Arthur retreat
from confession: 'Is it some danger of your own that you are
considering in this philosophical, general way?' The social con‑
trast also cuts across the formal pairing. Hetty's narrow self-
occupation makes it clear that this is no simple social stereotype of the wicked young squire and the village maiden.
Hetty's egoism makes her a moral parallel rather than a social
victim, and the parallelism blurs the social causality.

(iii)

In *The Mill on the Floss* there is much less of this conspicuous
pairing. There is the central contrast of Tom and Maggie, but
here the moral antithesis is always part of the personal relation, and makes its point in the particular context of this relation. There is certainly a careful contrast between Maggie's
imagination and caprice and Tom's less sensitive rectitude,
and it is brought out in their quarrels—in childhood and after
—and in the fairly explicit criticism of social problems of

education and work, for men and for women. It is brought out too in the delicately unobtrusive hints about Tom's love for Lucy, which blur the simplicity of our sympathy for Maggie's generous flaws and our criticism of Tom's less complicated virtues: Tom's conflict is controlled and put aside, and his reserve is strongly if obliquely indicated in the author's refusal to bring it into the open. But the theme is the theme of tragic personal division, and the final resolution in the death which brings them together as life could never do, merely emphasizes their relation as brother and sister. It is this relation, rather than the formal opposition of two ways of life, which is prominent throughout the book, partly because of a relative absence of structural relations to point the moral in the other characters, partly because it is the most personal of George Eliot's novels, too close to her own childhood and to her relation with Isaac to be expanded into a series of generalizations. It is perhaps its intimate connection with her own life which gives it its formal simplicity.

Silas Marner is a much more formal novel, if we consider the relations of the characters. The contrast is simple and rigid. Godfrey does not claim his child, and Silas takes her. Godfrey remains childless. Silas finds all he has lost—love, respect, and a place in the community. At the end, where all is made clear—except that a factory has been built in Chapel Yard, to erase the past which Silas tries to find again—even his gold is returned. Dunsey's body is found, but we know nothing about the end of William Dane. It is a story where the characters are passive, almost as passive as they are in *Amos Barton*, and the weight of the clear central contrast falls rather on accident than on character. Godfrey has done an injustice, Silas is the man to whom injustice has been done. Sarah has left him for William, but Eppie does not leave him for Godfrey. The crossing of rewards and punishments in the incident of the gold coins and the golden hair, and the coincidence of two thefts, leaves us with the gentle irony of a fairy-tale, rather than with the elaborate contrast of two fully-analysed human destinies. It is in the later books, from *Romola* to *Daniel Deronda*, that we return to the complex web of character which we have seen in *Adam Bede*.

Character and Form

In *Romola* there is the moral triangle of Romola, Tito, and
Savonarola, and here the resemblance and the contrast work
together.[1] Romola and Tito are the moral extremes, and their
personal collision—unlike Maggie's with Tom—mostly takes
the form of verbal debate, and is as formal as a Morality Play.
It is formalized even further by the symbols which grow from
casual appearance into a summary of the theme: the vision of
Dino, and its fulfilment in the betrothal procession, the wedding and its 'shower of sweets', and the triptych of *Bacchus
and Ariadne*, which Tito commissions as an image of their
marriage, and as a prison for Dino's crucifix. Tito's growth in
treachery is strong and rapid: he betrays Baldassare, then
Bardo, then Romola, then Florence. It is paralleled by
Romola's sacrifice: for Bardo, for Savonarola, for Tito, for
Florence, and, in the end, for Tessa and Tito's children. But
the opposition is not as simple as it was in *Adam Bede*. The
nature of the egoism and the devotion are analysed, and the
details correspond in each case. Tito's self-persuasion is the
product of a reason which rides down feeling, Romola's education depends on a reason which stiffens sensibility, but which
gives way—and rightly, we are made to feel—in the end. This
contrast is not left to our observation, but is made explicit.
When Tito tells her he has sold Bardo's library, and betrayed
the trust, he uses reason. 'Any rational person looking at the
case from a due distance will see that I have taken the wisest
course', he says, in summary, but Romola has already rejected his reasoning: 'What have I to do with your arguments?
It was a yearning of *his* heart, and therefore it is a yearning of
mine' (ch. xxxii).

There is a later occasion when Romola is shaken by revul-
sion at the sophistries of reason. Savonarola refuses to try to
save her godfather, Bernardo del Nero, who has been con-
demned to death. This time it is Savonarola who reasons, but
Romola repeats her same old plea of the heart's truth: 'God's
kingdom is something wider—else, let me stand outside it with
the beings that I love' (ch. lix). The contrasts cross: Romola

[1] George Eliot wrote to Richard Holt Hutton, 8 August 1863, that
'the great problem of her [Romola's] life, . . . essentially coincides with a
chief problem in Savonarola's' (Haight, iv, p. 97).

learns sacrifice and devotion from Savonarola, but she out-
grows his tutelage, and rejects him, as she rejects Tito, for the
sophistries of his egoism. For part of the book Romola and
Savonarola are presented as parallels, but the pattern changes,
and for a while Savonarola is grouped with Tito. In Savonarola
and in Tito there is the powerful egoism—though much more
complex in Savonarola—and also the submission to expediency.
The parallel is clinched at the moment of Tito's treachery,
when he persuades the Frate to give him the letters to the
ambassador—Tito in fact sends them to the Duke of Milan,
and ruins Savonarola. 'I have not concealed from you, father,'
he says to Savonarola, 'that I am no religious enthusiast;
I have not my wife's ardour.' Savonarola accepts this lack of
religious enthusiasm without dissent, and the irony lies in the
reader's memory of Savonarola's last experience of Romola's
ardour. The irony lies too in the moral grouping of Savonarola
with the man who, also acting from expediency, is about to
betray him. The pattern shifts again—we are not left with this
particular parallel, but with Romola's re-assessment of Savonarola, and this emphasizes the differences of the two men. This
readjustment is finally underlined in her last summarizing
speech to Lillo, Tito's illegitimate son:

There are so many things wrong and difficult in the world, that
no man can be great—he can hardly keep himself from wickedness
—unless he gives up thinking much about pleasures or rewards,
and gets strength to endure what is hard and painful. My father
had the greatness that belongs to integrity; he chose poverty and
obscurity rather than falsehood. And there was Fra Girolamo . . .
he had the greatness which belongs to a life spent in struggling
against powerful wrong, and in trying to raise men to the highest
deeds they are capable of. (Epilogue)

This is the preliminary to the last softened indictment of Tito,
and it is plain that once more he stands apart. This kind of
formal grouping is not a static thing, and we are made to
notice significant temporary resemblances as well as more
constant ones.

There are some striking examples in *Romola* of the way in
which George Eliot reinforces her theme by a different kind of
antithesis—the antithesis of scene. We have already met the

simplest kind of contrasting scene in *Adam Bede*, where the contrast between Hetty and Dinah is pointed by the contrast between the appearance of two bed-chambers, and the gaze into the mirror and out of the window. This scenic contrast is made more obliquely towards the end of *Romola*, in two scenes whose strong contrast is advertised in the chapter-headings. Chapter xliii is called 'The Unseen Madonna'; chapter xliv is called 'The Visible Madonna'. The Unseen Madonna is an image carried in a great procession—one of the many processions in this novel:

> Here was the nucleus of the procession. Behind the relic came the archbishop in gorgeous cope, with canopy held above him; and after him the mysterious hidden Image—hidden first by rich curtains of brocade enclosing an outer painted tabernacle, but within this, by the more ancient tabernacle which had never been opened in the memory of living men, or the fathers of living men. In that inner shrine was the image of the Pitying Mother, found ages ago in the soil of L'Impruneta, uttering a cry as the spade struck it. Hitherto the unseen Image had hardly ever been carried to the Duomo without having rich gifts borne before it. . . .
>
> But today there were no gifts carried before the tabernacle: no donations were to be given today except to the poor. That had been the advice of Fra Girolamo, whose preaching never insisted on gifts to the invisible powers, but only on help to visible need. . . . Not even a torch was carried. Surely the hidden Mother cared less for torches and brocade then for the wail of the hungry people.

The miraculous rescue comes about. Tito—ironically the messenger—brings the news that French galleys bearing corn and men have landed at Leghorn. In the next chapter we have the Visible Madonna: Romola takes Tito's place as messenger and tells the poor the good news, promising to bring them food, and they praise the Virgin and the procession and bless Romola 'in much the same tone'. The engraving in *The Cornhill* shows Romola with the children and is called 'The Visible Madonna'. This contrast is not merely a means for idealizing Romola—though it has that effect, amongst others.[1] It establishes the humane interpretation of Romola's discipleship. This is analysed in detail in this same chapter:

[1] George Eliot told Harrison that the historical accuracy of *Romola* was part of her attempt at idealization (Haight, iv, p. 301).

If she came away from her confessor, Fra Salvestro, or from some contact with the disciples of Savonarola amongst whom she worshipped, with a sickening sense that these people were miserably narrow, and with an almost impetuous reaction towards her old contempt for their superstition—she found herself recovering a firm footing in her works of womanly sympathy.

One chapter-heading does not contradict the other: the antithesis, one of public splendour and ritual with one of simple human love, of miracle—'a rescue which had come from outside the limit of their own power'—with human help, is one which reinterprets rather than contradicts: if the Invisible Madonna gives miraculous help, there is the need for human fellowship too. And on re-reading, the antithesis becomes a thematic emphasis, for it forms part of a chain of similar contrasts: the contrast of Romola and Dino, her brother, and of Romola —rejecting dogma and party in ʋie name of human love—and Savonarola. It also plays an essential part in preparing for Romola's mission in the plague-stricken village, where her human aid is interpreted as miracle. She carries 'the little olive baby on her right arm' and both the acolyte and the priest see her as 'the mild-faced Mother' and the Holy Mother, 'tall as the cypresses, . . . a light about her head'. The final irony is a gentle one, returning to the original contrast between the Visible and the Invisible:

Many legends were afterwards told in that valley about the blessed Lady who came over the sea, but they were legends by which all who heard might know that in times gone by a woman had done beautiful loving deeds there, rescuing those who were ready to perish. (ch. lxviii)

The habit of antithesis, in characters and events, is there from the beginning. Sometimes the antithesis is deceptively simple, like this last example, where the contrast in the title and the scene emerges less as a striking contrast than as a quiet question flowing in the current of the general theme of Romola's religion and her humanism. The chapter-headings here are guides, but not simplified guides: we ask ourselves why the contrast is there, and have to reflect and read carefully, looking for an answer. And the habit of antithesis ranges from such subtle guides to reading to a useful device for local unity, for making transition and symmetrical grouping. The paired scene and the paired chapter are common in George Eliot. 'Inside the Duomo' and 'Outside the Duomo' are twin titles to a mere shift of scene from interior to exterior; 'Check' and 'Counter-Check' to an obvious turn in Tito's fortunes which brings him frustration both in his political intrigue and his attempt to defeat Romola. The antithesis is not always related subtly to theme or character, but is rather the basic device for organizing the narrative movement, a montage building tension, bestowing variety, and only at times acting as a structural correlative for the theme. When we make the irresistible analogy with the art of the film it is interesting to remember that Eisenstein tells us how D. W. Griffith claimed to have been greatly influenced by the cross-cutting of Dickens. There is the story of the making of Griffith's film *After Many Years* (1908), based on *Enoch Arden*. When he proposed to cut from the scene showing the waiting wife to the scene showing Enoch on the desert island, some objection was raised to the 'jumping about'. Griffith is said to have replied, 'Doesn't Dickens write that way?' Eisenstein's detailed analysis of the montage of Dickens in this essay, 'Dickens, Griffith, and the Film Today', published in the collection *Film Form*, is an interesting attempt to analyse the structure of a Victorian novel, and it pays attention to such things as conditions of publication and revision, as well as presenting us with brilliant analogies from Griffith's work. Eisenstein points out that Dickens knew what he was doing in making his cuts and contrasts, and indeed says so in the passage on tragi-comic juxtaposition— 'streaky bacon'—in *Oliver Twist*. Like George Eliot, Dickens used the multiple plot with economy and mounting tension, not as a 'loose baggy monster'.

In *Felix Holt* we proceed by cross-cutting: it is the mode of organizing the small units of the narrative, but it becomes the main structural feature of the novel. We begin with a double introduction, for the novel moves in a narrative tension between two sets of people. First, we are introduced to the Transomes, but this introduction is set within an elaborate frame. We meet Mrs Transome only after the long introductory tour in the stage-coach, which fixes the date of the novel, gives an occasional political reference, sketches the social scene, establishes the author's intimate tone, throws in a few hints about the past, and narrows the focus to Transome Court. We have two chapters devoted to Harold's homecoming, and then in chapter iii there is a second elaborate introduction, geographically more limited than the first, since it concentrates only on the history and situation of the newly enfranchised Treby Magna. At the end of this chapter, paralleling the earlier movement, the focus narrows to Felix Holt. We are given the background to Harold's intention of standing as Radical candidate only after he has brought the political theme into the novel, and this background serves also to introduce Felix. The reviewer in *The Edinburgh Review*, for October 1866, complained that 'the story has the defect of running in two parallel lines with only an occasional and arbitrary connexion', but the parallels are in fact designed to meet.

The introduction is both vague and precise, indicating the theme of social influences, and making anticipations of the plot which are only intelligible on the second reading:

These social changes in Treby parish are comparatively public matters, and this history is chiefly concerned with the private lot of a few men and women; but there is no private life which has not been determined by a wider public life, from the time when the primeval milkmaid had to wander with the wanderings of her clan, because the cow she milked was one of a herd which had made the pastures bare.

A little later comes the groundwork of the elaborate plot of two obscured paternities and an inheritance tangle:

If the mixed political conditions of Treby Magna had not been acted on by the passing of the Reform Bill, Mr Harold Transome would not have presented himself as a candidate for North Loamshire, Treby would not have been a polling-place, Mr Matthew Jermyn would not have been on affable terms with a Dissenting Minister and his flock, and the venerable town would not have been placarded with handbills. (ch. iii)

But this is obscure. It is only an anticipation for the author and its real function is to lead on to the other consequences of the Reform Bill. The two main characters, two sons, two lovers, two Radicals, are brought together:

For example, it was through these conditions that a young man named Felix Holt made a considerable difference in the life of Harold Transome, though nature and fortune seemed to have done what they could to keep the lots of the two men quite aloof from each other. Felix was heir to nothing better than a quack medicine; his mother lived up a back street in Treby Magna. . . . There could hardly have been a lot less like Harold Transome's than this of the quack doctor's son, except in the superficial facts that he called himself a Radical, that he was the only son of his mother, and that he had lately returned to his home with ideas and resolves not a little disturbing to that mother's mind.

But Mrs Holt, unlike Mrs Transome, was much disposed to reveal her troubles. . . .

With chapter iv we begin to see 'that mutual influence of dissimilar destinies' and the action moves towards the meeting of the two stories until they begin to act upon each other and the double plot dissolves into a single plot. It is a double plot for about half the book, and then the relation of Harold and Felix ceases to be chiefly formal and becomes an important element in the plot. But for the first chapters the existence of these two men is joined only in the author's commentary, and kept in the reader's mind by the carefully established contrasts and parallels.

The action divides itself roughly into three connecting episodes in which Harold and Felix exist in opposition. At the beginning there is the parallel but completely separate account of Felix's rebellion against his mother—which brings him into contact with Rufus Lyon and Esther, and of Harold's rebellion against his mother—which brings him into opposition with Matthew Jermyn. Next, there is the account of the election preparations, in which Felix is seen in his attempts to educate the Sproxton miners, and Harold, through his agents, is seen in his more successful attempts to buy them. This section of the story brings Harold and Felix together for the first time, but their encounter is a brief one, and really only emphasizes their moral contrast. Then in the last section, though still without any further bringing together of the two men, they are present in their rivalry for Esther.

The first thing which comes out of the formal relation of

these two characters is the social contrast and completeness. Esther and her father and a few minor characters like Mrs Holt and Job Tudge, represent the vulgar life of the town, in contrast to the wide corridors of Transome Court. The social contrast is not a striking one, since Felix is an educated man, a manual worker only by choice, and Esther indistinguishable from a fine lady. The opposition suggested in the introductory comments is never very realistically displayed. More important is the political contrast. Both men are carefully analysed as Radicals—Harold emerges as an egoist and opportunist, Felix as a conservative idealist. There is the occasional rapport between the actions, as when, for instance, Felix says— referring to Joseph, not Harold: 'O 'yes, your ringed and scented men of the people!—I won't be one of them. Let a man once throttle himself with a satin stock, and he'll get new wants and new motives' (ch. v). He is talking about Harold's social opposite, but the reader, having recently met Harold, makes the connection. Directly and obliquely, the two actions are kept together in the reader's mind.

Although the actions are brought together when Esther goes to Transome Court, there is still an effect of separateness brought about by the change in place and by the fact that Harold and Felix never meet as rivals. This gives the irony to the triangle. There is the additional irony of their carefully contrasted attitudes—this is a moral struggle rather than an amorous one. Harold has dismissed his mother's energy—'Ah, you've had to worry yourself about things that don't properly belong to a woman—my father being weakly. We'll set all that right. You shall have nothing to do but to be grandmamma on satin cushions', and 'a woman ought to be a Tory, and graceful, and handsome, like you.' Felix has said: 'If a woman really believes herself to be a lower kind of being, she should place herself in subjection: she should be ruled by the thoughts of her father or husband. If not, let her show her power of choosing something better' (ch. x). And later: 'You might be that woman I was thinking of a little while ago when I looked at your face: the woman whose beauty makes a great task easier to men instead of turning them away from it' (ch. xxvi).

It is the same moral rivalry that we see in *Adam Bede*, and

the same kind of social contrast too, though the characters
themselves are treated statically and externally compared with
Arthur and Adam. The limitation of time George Eliot imposed on herself in *Felix Holt* seems to have had the result that
her usual interest in character as process had to be subdued
to one full portrait—Esther, and one history implied in
retrospect—Mrs Transome. The narrative irony which played
only a relatively small part in *Adam Bede* is one of the chief
interests in the later part of this novel, where the reader
watches Esther and Harold, with Felix as a kind of ghostly
presence invisible only to Harold. The irony culminates in
Harold's loss of Esther and his gain of the estate, both
brought about by Felix's influence. The parallel is found in
Felix's imprisonment, in its turn brought about by Harold.
And both are kept apart to make the irony intense. Mrs
Transome may be, as Dr Leavis argues, the only really successful character in the book—she is certainly the only one presented with the weight of time behind her, for Esther's transformation is too rapid to compare in complexity with Maggie's
or Dorothea's, but the novel is an interesting experiment in
form and a preparation for the construction of *Middlemarch*
and *Daniel Deronda*.

(iv)

The double plot in *Felix Holt* emphasizes the variability of
human growth, and regeneration and failure are put together
to make a story with two endings. In *Middlemarch* there is
again the multiplication of successes and failures, and the
result is a novel with an extraordinary sense of expanding life.
The double plots of *Felix Holt* or *Wuthering Heights* or *Vanity
Fair* are highly rigid pieces of parallelism compared with
Middlemarch, where the structure has its effect of human
generalization and differentiation, but avoids the stiffness of
symmetry. The four related stories of *Middlemarch* make a
structural equivalent of the novel without heroes. This novel
has its central figures, but the reader is forced to switch attention from each in turn. There is no constant focus, and yet it
is very different from most attempts to shift the point of view.

Its most obvious effect is social breadth, and it is certainly one of the few studies of a community where the community has weight and character. Middlemarch is given its presence in many ways, by an approach to personification, and by a rich variety of crowd scenes—parties, meetings, a funeral, an auction—where there is a rest from the psychological concentration of each of the four main actions. But it is the combined presence of those four actions which gives the community its force and its shaping pressure. The assembly of individuals shows a society. But there is no distant and flickering bird's-eye-view, for the multiplicity of viewpoint has enough space in which to work without sacrificing closeness.

The novel begins for ten chapters as if it were a novel with a central figure. Then we move, rather abruptly, it may seem on first reading, from Dorothea to Lydgate, and we never return to her again with such concentration and such expansiveness. This piece of structural effect may be the result of George Eliot's originally separate conception of *Miss Brooke*, though on the other hand *Miss Brooke's* easy fusion with *Middlemarch* is a practical demonstration of George Eliot's constancy of theme and, more important here, of her urge towards the divided novel.

Dorothea's central position is to some extent weighted by the Prologue and Epilogue, and by her long introductory occupation of the novel. After those chapters she shares the rotation with the other characters. George Eliot and Lewes were aware that readers might be disappointed when the action moves away from Dorothea for so long, but this very disappointment is functional. Dorothea cannot be a Saint Theresa in this society, and the theme of human fellowship must be developed without one engrossing figure. Once the interest and curiosity has been established, by exposition, and revealing action, we move to the story of Lydgate.

The management of transition is worth looking at, especially since it is to some extent determined by the publication in parts. As we have seen from the correspondence with Blackwood, there was the conscious need for representing most of the interests of the four actions in each part. The transition from Dorothea begins in chapter x, which is a crowd-scene introducing Lydgate and Bulstrode and Mr Vincy, as well as making the social expansion from the gentry to the bourgeoisie, and from one main plot-interest to several others. It is a necessary social scene, but carefully related to character and plot:

> In fact, Mrs Cadwallader said that Brooke was beginning to treat the Middlemarchers, and that she preferred the farmers at the tithe-dinner, who drank her health unpretentiously, and were not ashamed of their grandfathers' furniture. For in that part of the country, before Reform had done its notable part in developing the political consciousness, there was a clearer distinction of ranks and a dimmer distinction of parties; so that Mr Brooke's miscellaneous invitations seemed to belong to that general laxity which came from his inordinate travel and habit of taking too much in the form of ideas.' (ch. x)

The dinner-party provides an excellent occasion for choral gossip, mainly about the future bride and bridegroom, Dorothea and Casaubon, and the newcomer, Lydgate. After we have shifted from the choral comment to that part of it which is Lydgate's private point of view, we leave Dorothea: 'Not long after that dinner-party she had become Mrs Casaubon, and was on her way to Rome.'

In the next chapter we go back in time and back to Lydgate. The transition is simple and smooth: 'Lydgate, in fact, was already conscious of being fascinated by a woman strikingly different from Miss Brooke . . .' and, with a few ironical anticipations of future relations, we move to Rosamond, Fred, and to the mention of Mary Garth and the last illness of old Featherstone. Lydgate has been introduced and left in suspense while we move backwards in time to his first meeting with Rosamond. And that first meeting at Stone Court is also the introduction to Bulstrode, who has been— so Featherstone thinks—talking maliciously about Fred. The book ends with all the major characters present, and all interrupted in action.

It is not until the next book that Bulstrode and Lydgate put in a lengthy appearance and the fourfold alternating action begins. The alternation is deliberately ironical—Rosamond's imagination plays with Lydgate (before she has seen him) and she arranges the first meeting. Then we have the drama of

Lydgate's past love for Laure, and his determination that experience shall now guide his relations with women. And so on. As we move from action to action there is a similar effect of irony or contrast, but often merely produced by the mere dismissal of one character or group and the reappearance of another. This is the shared surface of real life—not of course confined to George Eliot: we have a similar tension and stereoscopic realism in *Clarissa* and *Uncle Tom's Cabin* and *Oliver Twist*, though for a comparable multiplicity we should perhaps go to *War and Peace* or *Ulysses*.

This is a diffused structure with no hero or heroine engrossing its centre. In a sense it creates a collective structure for a portrait of society. But it is more than another version of *Vanity Fair*, the other famous 'Novel without a Hero'. Its shifting point of view is the structural equivalent for its theme of illusion, and the insistent rotation, with ironical contrast and comparison, puts each illusion in its place amongst the rest and lets the contradictions stand. Dorothea and Casaubon, Rosamond and Lydgate, Fred and Mary, Bulstrode and Featherstone, all are shown in their private dreams, mostly making their incompatible demands on life. As the novel rotates we change our point of view, and the common illusion of supreme self-importance is exposed. The two marriages are delineated in ironical resemblance and difference, the two men die and the others wait for death, the unspoken dreams clash against each other. The structural movement puts each assertion in its place, and indeed makes it unnecessary for the author to do more than give an occasional jog to the movement. The diffused action is concentrated by this constant contrast and comparison.

Casaubon is at first seen only from the outside. His is a highly satirical portrait composed of a significant physical description, some superb stylistic parodies (the letter to Dorothea and his reflections on the overrated raptures of love) and Dorothea's idealized view: this external and satirical version is underlined by the deflating similes of Celia, Mrs Cadwallader and Sir James Chettam. The clash of his egoism and Dorothea's is established. She casts him for the role of a great teacher, 'It would be like marrying Pascal. I should learn to see the truth by the same light as great men have seen it by. And then 1 should know what to do, when I got older: I should see how it was possible to lead a grand life here—now—in England.' Casaubon, on his side, casts Dorothea for an apparently less arduous role:

The hindrance which courtship occasioned to the progress of his great work—the Key to all Mythologies—naturally made him look forward the more eagerly to the happy termination of courtship. But he had deliberately incurred the hindrance, having made up his mind that it was now time for him to adorn his life with the graces of female companionship, to irradiate the gloom which fatigue was apt to hang over the intervals of studious labour with the play of female fancy, and to secure in this, his culminating age, the solace of female tendance for his declining years. (ch. vii)

There is satire on both sides, but for some time it is only Dorothea who is shown with sympathy as well as irony. Dorothea's own responsibility is not underplayed. This is the tragic crossing and uncrossing of motives and desires which we find in Hardy's fatal marriages. George Eliot shows convincingly Dorothea's ardour and Casaubon's chill, but this prepares the way for what must be a rare movement of sympathy towards an entirely unlovable character. There is damning irony: 'He assented to her expressions of devout feeling, and usually with an appropriate quotation; he allowed himself to say that he had gone through some spiritual conflicts in his youth', but this kind of irony is shattered by George Eliot's sudden refusal to sustain the convention of external report:

Suppose we turn from outside estimates of a man, to wonder, with keener interest, what is the report of his own consciousness about his doings or capacity: with what hindrance he is carrying on his daily labours; what fading of hopes, or what deeper fixity of self-delusion the years are marking off within him; and with what spirit he wrestles against universal pressure, which will one day be too heavy for him, and bring his heart to its final pause. (ch. x)

Or there is the surge of sympathy in this form of abrupt interruption:

One morning, some weeks after her arrival at Lowick, Dorothea —but why always Dorothea? Was her point of view the only possible one with regard to this marriage? I protest against all our

interest, all our effort at understanding being given to the young
skins that look blooming in spite of trouble. . . . Mr Casaubon had
an intense consciousness within him, and was spiritually a-hun-
gered like the rest of us. (ch. xxix)

Here the break comes even more raggedly in the middle of a
sentence, and it is in the interests of the kind of direct appeal
made on behalf of Amos Barton. It is an appeal to the conventional reader who must reconsider his reading habits, but
it is also a plea to the reader as a human being.

The multiple action is not hinged merely by these functional transitions. The main source of the concentration of
Middlemarch, the book which even in this decade has been
said to lack 'architecture', is the correspondence of one plot
with another. These are not tenuously related parts, but different versions of the same story. There are four pairs, linked
by love and marriage: the Casaubons, the Lydgates, the Bul-
strodes, and Fred and Mary. The correspondence is one of
moral implication but George Eliot often uses a relatively trivial coincidence to draw our attention to the greater coincidence, or to put us into her habit of seeing the similarities of
'human lots'. She uses the trivial fact that Casaubon is court-
ing Dorothea at the same time that Lydgate is getting to
know Rosamond in order to point to other similarities and
other differences:

He had seen Miss Vincy above his horizon almost as long as it
had taken Mr Casaubon to become engaged and married: but this
learned gentleman was possessed of a fortune. (ch. xi)

The problems of money is one of the several themes which
run through the contrasts and likeness of these marriages. But
the important cross-reference is that of moral situation. Each
is a marriage of opposites and a moral battlefield where there
can be no truce. Rosamond defeats Lydgate, Mrs Bulstrode
forgives and loves Bulstrode, Dorothea attempts to love and
understand but eventually has to escape Casaubon's 'dead
hand', and Mary Garth, with some help from Ibsen's 'helpers
and servers'—Farebrother, Caleb Garth, and Featherstone's
'dead hand',—succeeds in rescuing Fred.

The Morality Play beneath the full rich novel is laid bare by the structural relations. Dorothea's virtue is exposed and defined by the comparison with Lydgate, with Caleb, and with Mary; though it is also exposed and defined by its opposites: Rosamond, Bulstrode, and Casaubon. In Dorothea's relation with Casaubon the human action overlays this kind of formal contrast, but not entirely. The necessary formal reading of the novel as a whole has some influence on our reading of the separate parts, and having observed the parallelism and contrast which binds the units together, we acquire the trained eye which picks out the Morality Play in the domestic scene. Dorothea waits for Casaubon after he has rebuffed her:

> She hesitated, fearing to offend him by obtruding herself; for her ardour, continually repulsed, served, with her intense memory, to heighten her dread, as thwarted energy subsides into a shudder; and she wandered slowly round the nearer clumps of trees until she saw him advancing. Then she went towards him, and might have represented a heaven-sent angel coming with a promise that the short hours remaining should yet be filled with that faithful love which clings the closer to a comprehended grief. His glance in reply to hers was so chill that she felt her timidity increased; yet she turned and passed her hand through his arm.
>
> Mr Casaubon kept his hands behind him and allowed her pliant arm to cling with difficulty against his rigid arm.
>
> There was something horrible to Dorothea in the sensation which this unresponsive hardness inflicted on her. That is a strong word, but not too strong: it is in these acts called trivialities that the seeds of joy are for ever wasted. (ch. xlii)

She goes to her room, and in 'the miserable light' sees clearly 'her own and her husband's solitude—how they walked apart so that she was obliged to survey him', and lets 'her resentment govern her'. Then she recoils and makes a characteristic second attempt, going once more to wait for him. He comes out of the library, and this time speaks, 'with a gentle surprise in his tone':

> 'Come, my dear, come. You are young, and need not to extend your life by watching.'

When the kind quiet melancholy of that speech fell on Dorothea's ears, she felt something like the thankfulness that might well up in us if we had narrowly escaped hurting a lamed creature. She put her hand into her husband's, and they went along the broad corridor together. (ch. xlii)

Here there is the moral contrast of rigidity and chill, pliancy and warmth, and it is a contrast made more apparent by being repeated in the same kind of contrast between a similar pair of opposites, Rosamond and Lydgate. But within the immediate response to such scenes the Morality contrast is subdued to the dramatic moment: we see the moral opposites, lit by other contrast, and by the formality of images like the 'heaven-sent angel', and by the swift movement of generalization—'it is in these acts'—but what is most prominent is the particular human relationship, its domestic conflict, its temporary peace and resolution. So with Dorothea's approach to Rosamond. When the two women meet on the morning after Dorothea has found Rosamond with Will, there is the full irony of the meeting of opposites. It is the moral humour which determines the meeting: Rosamond's egoism has made the deceptive scene, Dorothea's refusal to stay in her private grief and jealousy has brought her back to Rosamond. But the moral opposition is only a part of the scene. Dorothea has come out of a private and self-absorbing despair; Rosamond is for the moment forced to forget herself—in her way—and tell Dorothea that Will does not love her but Dorothea herself. The excitement of the crisis is only in part the characteristic moral collision, for it is in part the human unpredictability that George Eliot sets free to determine the action.

There is something else which gives this kind of moral antithesis its humanity. The characters are mixed, and even Dorothea has her bitter jealousy, even Rosamond her temporary vision of what it feels like to be someone else. But, even allowing for George Eliot's deference to the mixture which modifies the moral pattern, there is the further tentativeness especially characteristic of *Middlemarch*. The moral issue is shown without complacency. Dorothea is much less and much more than a moral example—unlike Dinah and Felix and Daniel Deronda—and her warm impulse is shown with tact and truth, as a gesture rather than a converting influence. Dinah and Felix and Daniel represent the same urge away

from self, but, with very few exceptions, their words and
actions have a vast converting influence. These characters
have the simplicity and great stature of abstractions in a
Morality Play, and something of their magical power.

It is otherwise with Dorothea. When Casaubon rebuffs her
she subdues her pride and goes to wait for him. He is touched
—to 'kind quiet melancholy', but their marriage is still a
divided one and the division grows after his death. She is the
only one in Middlemarch who tells Lydgate that she believes
in him, but he does not accept her advice when she begs him
to stay. She subdues her scorn and goes back a second time to
help Rosamond, and Rosamond performs her one unselfish
act of confession and self-humiliation, but lives on to become
Lydgate's 'basil plant'. The moral pattern in *Middlemarch* is
blurred by its human truth. Dorothea's influence is exactly
what George Eliot says it is at the end of the novel, 'the effect
of her being on those around her was incalculably diffusive'.
Her generous warmth has no more than a brief effect on the
others, and they go on in their chill, not radically changed.
This tentativeness in Dorothea is something Dr Leavis seems
to overlook when he says of *Middlemarch* that 'the situations
offered by way of "objective correlative" have the daydream
relation to experience; they are generated by a need to soar
above the indocile facts and conditions of the real world'. It
is true that much of the imagery has this daydream quality,
and that Dorothea is often presented in terms of adjectives
and descriptions of 'exalting potency'. But I find this exalting
potency more characteristic of George Eliot's treatment of
love than of her treatment of moral situations. The action
and situations of *Middlemarch* seem to be making a brave
attempt to face this indocile world, and not to soar above it.
Dorothea is idealized in her relationship with Will, and perhaps at times elsewhere, but many of her actions are not
idealized but shown as decidedly unspectacular. It is a novel
where there are no moral miracles.

Dorothea's influence is shown as fragmentary, diffused, and
even temporary. The form in which we read her story is appropriate: we assemble our impression of her influence from fragmentary episodes, often from her brief appearance in other

people's stories, and always interrupted by other lives. She does not play a central part, and her coming and going as a minor character or a spectator in the other actions helps to underline the final tentative verdict. But this piecemeal reading extends to all the characters: it is a characteristic of the form of this novel, and has various effects.

George Eliot makes her structural relations of character plain: even the reader who may not formulate the pattern of the novel, must presumably notice some of the more obvious resemblances and differences between the four pairs of men and women. But there are hints carefully placed for the reader who may be too absorbed in reading the story to observe the pattern. These hints are of various kinds. One characteristic kind of hint comes in the passages of general comment which we skip at our peril. In her generalization we frequently find her giving anonymous and typical examples to reinforce a particular moral commentary, and if we read carefully we often find that the anonymous example in the list may crop up, sooner or later, in the course of the action. I have mentioned one example from *Adam Bede*, where the final summary of Adam's tragic lesson points, without naming, to the particular blind hates and loves which have made up the story, and sets them in the context of the general human condition. Here the anonymous example is given in a concluding modulation from the world of the novel to the fuller human context, but it can also work throughout as a clue to deliberate contrast or parallel. *Middlemarch* is full of examples of this kind of generalization and they are excellent proof—if we need it— of the deliberateness of the contrast and also of the attentive reading expected by the author.

Here, for instance, is Mrs Bulstrode's moment of decision, when she learns of her husband's past crime and present disgrace:

> She locked herself in her room. She needed time to get used to her maimed consciousness, her poor lopped life, before she could walk steadily to the place allotted her. . . .
> The man whose prosperity she had shared through nearly half a life, and who had unvaryingly cherished her—now that punishment had befallen him it was not possible to her in any sense to forsake

him. There is a forsaking which still sits at the same board and lies on the same couch with the forsaken soul, withering it the more by unloving proximity. (ch. lxxiv)

In the next chapter the anonymous example of this unloving proximity comes to life. Lydgate, though innocent—or almost innocent—is involved in Bulstrode's shame. He too has a wife:

> But Rosamond went home with a sense of justified repugnance towards her husband. What had he really done—how had he really acted? She did not know. Why had he not told her everything? He did not speak to her on the subject, and of course she could not speak to him. It came into her mind once that she would ask her father to let her go home again; but dwelling on that prospect made it seem utter dreariness to her: a married woman gone back to live with her parents—life seemed to have no meaning for her in such a position: she could not contemplate herself in it. (ch. lxxv)

Lydgate waits for her to speak to him, as Bulstrode dared not hope for his wife to speak. The anonymous image in the preceding chapter fits her perfectly. Hers is the silence and hers the withering by 'unloving proximity'.

It is impossible to attempt a full analysis of George Eliot's structural relations: her characters are not only fully clothed with their particular interests, but move in a very intricate pattern, where sometimes a chain of likeness and unlikeness seems to be making the generalization clear. Mrs Bulstrode and Rosamond are placed in formal proximity, and the image gives us a clue. But Mrs Bulstrode and Dorothea are also put forward for comparison, not in an exactly answering situation, for Dorothea responds in sympathy not on one occasion only but to Casaubon, to Lydgate and to Rosamond. When she gets ready to go to Rosamond on the morning after her night of despair and jealousy, there is another clue to our reading, which points the parallel between her and Mrs Bulstrode:

> 'And I want you to bring me my new dress; and most likely I shall want my new bonnet today.'
> ... Tantripp went away wondering at this strange contrariness in her young mistress—that just the morning when she had more of a widow's face than ever, she should have asked for her lighter

mourning which she had waived before. Tantripp would never have found the clue to this mystery. Dorothea wished to acknowledge that she had not the less an active life before her because she had buried a private joy; and the tradition that fresh garments belonged to all initiation, haunting her mind, made her grasp after even that slight outward help towards calm resolve. For the resolve was not easy. (ch. lxxx)

This is a clear echo of Mrs Bulstrode's earlier act. It is a superficial reversal, since Mrs Bulstrode puts on mourning, but the resemblance is the important thing. This is Mrs Bulstrode's initiation:

When she had resolved to go down, she prepared herself by some little acts which might seem mere folly to a hard onlooker; they were her way of expressing to all spectators visible or invisible that she had begun a new life in which she embraced humiliation. She took off all her ornaments and put on a plain black gown, and instead of wearing her much-adorned cap and large bows of hair, she brushed her hair down and put on a plain bonnet-cap, which made her look suddenly like an early Methodist. (ch. lxxiv)

Each act is imbedded in character. Dorothea's stern attitude to her mourning, and her dislike of fine dress in general, and Mrs Bulstrode's love of finery, have been lightly but firmly established in several earlier scenes. The climax of such preparation is the emphatic parallel of these sacramental scenes. This is a correspondence of detail which makes us see the characters in the full implications of their moral resemblance.

The clue may be an anonymous example, or a detail like this. It is sometimes a verbal echo, as it is in another episode in the changing pattern of likeness and unlikeness where Rosamond and Dorothea are brought into clear formal contrast. Lydgate and Dorothea are discussing Casaubon's illness, and Dorothea appeals to him, 'You know all about life and death. Advise me. Think what I can do.' Three books later, the words echo in Lydgate's mind, as he is shown in the process of revaluing his wisdom:

He had shut his eyes in the last instant of reverie while he heard Dorothea saying, 'Advise me—think what I can do—he has been

104

all his life labouring and looking forward. He minds about nothing else—and I mind about nothing else.'

That voice of deep-souled womanhood had remained within him ... the tones were a music from which he was falling away—he had really fallen into a momentary doze, when Rosamond said in her silvery neutral way, 'Here is your tea, Tertius'. (ch. lviii)

The echo is made in the context of contrast: Lydgate looks at his two loves, Laure and Rosamond, and is only checked in the act of generalization by the memory of Dorothea. But the echo is picked up again on the next page, after the almost casual contrast of Dorothea's voice with Rosamond's 'silvery neutral way'. He tells Rosamond about their difficulties, and there is a twisting irony here. He is tempted to ask her for help because his memory of Dorothea corrects the hasty generalization about female insensibility. Dorothea is unlike Laure and Rosamond, perhaps there is hope. 'You must help me' he says to his wife, and this is her response:

'What can *I* do, Tertius?' said Rosamond, turning her eyes on him again. That little speech of four words, like so many others in all languages, is capable by varied vocal inflexions of expressing all states of mind from helpless dimness to exhaustive argumentative perception, from the completest self-devoting fellowship to the most neutral aloofness. Rosamond's thin utterance threw into the words 'What can *I* do?' as much neutrality as they could hold. (ch. lviii)

This small echoing phrase is most elaborately placed in the full context of the novel: it is repeated carefully.[1] In the revised edition of 1874 the question-mark after the second 'What can *I* do' in the last passage, was altered to an exclamation mark, showing how conspicuous a detail this was for the author. There is a deliberate attempt to make the reader hear the two voices, one deep and the other thin and silvery. These clues are not casually planted, and the phrase is to return again in Dorothea's last vigil. She comes to say 'What should I do—how should I act now . . .?' (ch. lxxx)

---

[1] It is also put into the mouth of Fred, two chapters earlier, when Caleb Garth despairs of his handwriting, but this is probably *not* part of the echoing, though Fred's 'vocal inflexions' certainly express 'help less dimness'.

This carefully woven pattern extends even to minor characters, for this is a novel where, as far as possible, all the characters are carefully weighted with an implied full existence. It is impossible to separate vision and technical device. The grotesque Rigg Featherstone, for instance, is not merely a character introduced as the unexpected heir, the joke up the old man's sleeve produced after death to frustrate the waiting mourners, and the functional link between Raffles, his stepfather, and Bulstrode. As Coleridge said of the Fool in *King Lear*, this character is brought into the main interest of the story. This story is not merely the usual battlefield of egoism and love, but shows the particular ruling passion of men seeking their vocation. All the characters, including Dorothea, are included in the overture to Lydgate's story, where George Eliot laments that we are 'comparatively uninterested in that other kind of "makdom and fairnesse" which must be wooed with industrious thought and patient renunciation of small desires'. Bulstrode is given dimension and sympathy by being brought into direct connection with this important theme: if he could have had his time over again, 'why, then he would choose to be a missionary'. So with a minor character like Rigg:

> From his earliest employment as an errand-boy in a seaport, he had looked through the windows of the money-changers as other boys look through the windows of the pastry-cooks; the fascination had wrought itself gradually into a deep special passion. . . . The one joy after which his soul thirsted was to have a money-changer's shop on a much frequented quay. (ch. liii)

This is a good example of George Eliot's method of involving even her minor characters: Rigg's ambition is necessary to the plot because it removes him from Middlemarch, leaving Stone Court free, first for Bulstrode, then for Fred. He frustrates Featherstone's grasping dead hand, just as Dorothea frustrates Casaubon's, and Rigg is no mere figure of parody. But George Eliot puts as much imaginative sympathy into this brief glimpse at Rigg's ruling passion as she puts into the long and moving account of Lydgate's love for medicine. It is not merely the act of parallelism which is important, but the quality of the attentiveness. She can use less sympathetic and serious mirrors, of course. There are many lighter instances of this diffused theme of vocation: Mrs Garth, who is unable to understand why anyone could not want to be a teacher, holding her 'Lindley Murray above the waves', Mr Brooke with his extensive list of discarded projects, ending with his political ambition, and little Henrietta Noble and her comfits for the children—the last also a gentle echo of Dorothea's small tentative gestures. The parallel may be made in a different key, but it is never a merely mechanical echo. It is indeed this ability to express the energy of even a minor figure like Rigg which makes this formal pattern say insistently that human beings are very like each other. Human substance is placed before us, and we are not asked to make a quantitative accretion of similar cases but to feel that Rigg's excited vision is of a piece with Dorothea's and Lydgate's. We extract not a theme, not a related subject, but a continuity of passion. Both the ruling passion of man's work, and the slightly more particularized Saint Theresa theme, are generalizations which are forced upon the reader by this deeply felt recurrence. And in *Middlemarch* it is a recurrence which helps to animate the portrait of a society. The community is brought to life not merely by social background—the railway and the Reform Bill—not even by the social influences—the cholera, the hospital and the bank—but because there is this recurrence and difference which make the pattern. We cannot look at one character or one of the four main actions without seeing the 'sameness of the human lot', in love, in marriage, in economic problems, in work, and in the moral process of growing away from self. 'While I tell the truth about loobies', George Eliot says as she concludes her account of the reading of Featherstone's will, 'my readers' imagination need not be entirely excluded from an occupation with lords.' This is more than an arch irony or an apology for humble material It is a reading direction.

There are even plainer reading directions to be found in the titles of the books of *Middlemarch*.[1] Book I is called 'Miss

---

[1] Professor Haight also makes this point in the introduction to his Riverside Edition of *Middlemarch*.

Brooke', and it is almost exclusively Dorothea's, merely diverted from her story just before the end so that the multiple form should begin to make itself felt in the first instalment. But almost all succeeding books have titles which make direct reference to the parallels and contrasts. Book II is called 'Old and Young', and draws our attention to the relation of Fred to his parents and old Featherstone, and to Dorothea's relation with Casaubon, for the age disparity is insisted on —in Sir James Chettam's disgust, for instance, or in Casaubon's irritation when Mr Brooke with cheerful tactlessness calls Ladislaw Casaubon's nephew instead of cousin. 'Waiting for Death' includes two groups of waiting mourners, and two sick men. There are 'Three Love Problems'. 'The Dead Hand' seems to refer directly to Casaubon but it echoes the phrase used of Featherstone. 'Two Temptations' are Bulstrode's and Lydgate's. And 'Sunset and Sunrise' holds a happy ending for some and not for others, failu and success, reward and punishment. These subordinate titles would of course, as a consequence of publication in parts, have the greater prominence of separate titles on individual title-pages.

(v)

The rotating pattern of *Middlemarch* arouses little in the way of preference for one part rather than another, at least in most readers: all parts are equally arresting and convincing. But in *Daniel Deronda* we come up against a special formal problem. Its symmetrical structure is weak in a way in which the form of *Middlemarch* was not, and the evidence for the weakness is to be found in a very common preference for one part, for the story of Gwendolen Harleth. To some extent this is a problem for readers of *Felix Holt* also but the preference there amounts to a more specialized interest in the character of Mrs Transome rather than a preference for a whole zone of action. George Eliot most certainly did not anticipate the Gentile preference for the Gentile part of the story, and when she first came across it in Blackwood's very gentle hints, it dismayed her. It is perhaps unfair to describe this in terms of a racial prejudice, though it may not always be a purely literary selection. But for most readers there is the strong feeling that the Jewish characters, Daniel, Mirah, and Mordecai, are inadequately realized as dramatic portraits. One reason for the failure may well lie in the author's warm sympathy for the Jews which overreaches itself in dramatic expression.

Daniel affords the interesting problem of a failure in dramatic distance. He is more conventionally heroic than any other of George Eliot's characters, except perhaps for Romola, who is equally a failure as a dramatic realization. Daniel's appearance is grand and noble, described with some subtle anticipatory hints in terms of a Titian portrait. Admirable also are his ability, his mind, and his unswerving moral rectitude and sense of human fellowship. He is the altruist whose generous impulse has not grown out of moral stupidity, and is not changed and chastized in the process of the narrative. There are moving passages describing his isolation and his sense of destiny but they are not sustained throughout a convincing and moving portrait of a man being shaped by life. His moral rectitude makes too glib a human example, his high and mysterious destiny adds a symbolic dimension but not a human facet. The best word for him is the one Henry James's Constantius uses of Deronda's mother—'unvivified'. This is the common and conventional reaction to Daniel Deronda, and although I think he is very much more successful than the sentimentalized figures of most of the other Jews, there is little doubt that he is a static and symbolic construction rather than a dramatic character. But George Eliot seems to have been aware of the possible difficulties in creating such a character, and many of our objections to him are cleverly—if not altogether successfully—anticipated within the novel. This anticipation is there, for instance, in Hans Meyrick's assumption 'that for any danger or rivalry in relation to Mirah, Deronda was as much out of the question as the angel Gabriel' and the angel Gabriel is an interesting choice of comparison, since Daniel is later spoken of as 'a terrible-browed angel' in his power over Gwendolen. It is there also within Daniel's personal conflict:

He was conscious of that peculiar irritation which will sometimes befall the man whom others are inclined to trust as a mentor—the irritation of perceiving that he is supposed to be entirely off the same plane of desire and temptation as those who confess to him. (ch. xxxvii)

This is reinforced a little later in the same chapter when Daniel objects to being compared with the Bouddha who gives himself to the starving tiger, though he defends the myth, while objecting to its literal application, in the words which have a special resonance throughout the novel:

'It is like a passionate word,' he said; 'the exaggeration is a flash of fervour. It is an extreme image of what is happening everyday—the transmutation of self.'

But the difficulty is that Daniel's definition of the myth fits Daniel: he is an extreme image of the novel's theme. He lacks the mixed and tentative errors and successes of Adam and Dorothea—characters who share his rectitude but not his woodenness. This may be partly because his tragic lesson is learnt too early—before the novel begins—and retailed to the reader only in exposition, and partly because he is only shown in actions and relationships which have a strict relevance to the moral theme. This complete moral relevance is probably, as I have already suggested, at the bottom of our discomfort about Felix and Mirah and Mordecai: they are not endowed with the rich and various liveliness which make characters like Dorothea and Lydgate contribute to the main theme, without being simply and wholly stamped and shaped by it. This does make for a genuine difficulty in discussing the form of the novel. It does not seem sufficiently serious to talk in terms of extracting the convincing parts because Gwendolen's story is as inseparable from Daniel's as Mrs Transome's is from Esther's. Perhaps all we can do is to recognize the unbalance and make some allowance for it. Certainly Daniel and Mirah are given their appearance of mobility in retrospect: Gwendolen too is given her origin and her environment retrospectively, but her flashback is very much more dramatic and less expository in treatment than Daniel's. To some extent, the tragic impact of the novel is weakened by our preference— a preference certainly not intended by the author—for one part of the action.

Character and Form

One of the few contemporary critics who paid attention to George Eliot's formal powers was the Jewish critic, David Kaufmann, who most certainly showed no preference for the Gentile portion. In his short book, *George Eliot and Judaism* (1877), Kaufmann pays great attention to the structural unity, saying, 'An examination of that part of *Daniel Deronda* which relates specially to the Jews and Judaism is inseparable from an aesthetic estimate of it as a whole'. Kaufmann insists that Daniel must be seen as the centre of both actions: 'Two lines which cut one another at a common point of intersection make a mathematical figure, it is true; but they cannot form the subject of a work of art.' We should compare this with the belief of Henry James's Pulcheria that the function of Daniel is to have Gwendolen fall in love with him.

Kaufmann's reading is an interesting example of the naturally partial view correcting the unbalance—the Jewish preference seems to have given his response a push in the right direction, and George Eliot wrote to thank him for 'the perfect response to the artist's intention'. This perfect response was not the reviewers' response, and even Blackwood had grave reservations about the Jewish portions, which of course explains why George Eliot laments, in this same letter, 'her unsatisfied hunger for certain signs of sympathetic discernment'. Amongst Kaufmann's signs of discernment she singles out his 'clear perception of the relation between the presentation of the Jewish elements and those of English social life', making it plain, once more, that the patterning was, to some extent at least, a deliberate process, Kaufmann's reading lays more stress on the element of contrast than on anything else, and points to such things as the contrast of Gwendolen with Mirah, Grandcourt with Deronda, and the less conspicuous contrast of Jewish and Gentile family life. He may sometimes exaggerate the Jewish-Gentile contrast, as in his insistence on Hans Meyrick's shallowness, for instance, but he qualifies his interpretation with the admission that Judaism is not presented as the only source of high-mindedness.

The novel depends on the central contrast of character— the contrast of Gwendolen Harleth and Daniel Deronda. Like the contrast of Casaubon with Dorothea, or Rosamond with

Lydgate, this is a moral opposition in a human relation. This relation depends on an increasing irony, for Daniel preaches to Gwendolen the lesson of the transmutation of self, but its logical end, for him, is the Zionist vocation which keeps them irrevocably apart. This is why the prior discovery of Mirah—Gwendolen's rival and moral opposite—is organic to the theme and not a piece of plot-making. But the contrast between the two women, accentuated by their separation—like Harold Transome and Felix, they have a subterranean rivalry, meeting only twice—is part of the elaborate social antithesis. Gwendolen's casual anti-Semitism is established in two sentences, one at the beginning when, thinking of selling her necklace, she assumes the avarice of 'Jew-dealers', one at the end where she assures Daniel that it does not matter that he is a Jew. This gives a special irony to her dependence on her Jewish mentor. She is firmly placed in the worldly and frivolous Gentile life, with Grandcourt, the Mallingers, the Arrowpoints, and even the Gascoignes in their version of a scene of clerical life. The complex plot is not merely a division into two actions but a division into two separate worlds, and Gwendolen's dependence on Daniel and her gradual recognition of the limits of worldliness increase as he moves gradually and irrevocably towards his Jewish world. Mirah is part of his Jewish destiny, and George Eliot takes care not to complicate Daniel's career by making him meet Gwendolen first—and, it might be argued, thereby loses the opportunity of putting her hero into a situation of genuine conflict instead of a mere situation of bewilderment and mystery.

The racial antithesis shapes the novel, but there is more in its pattern than antithesis. The contrast is once more carefully controlled by exceptional cases: if there is the devoted clannishness of the Cohen family, so is there a similar devoted clannishness in the Meyricks, and the characteristic benevolence of each family is given a parallel demonstration: the Cohens shelter Mordecai, the Meyricks shelter Mirah. If there are the worldly Gentiles, there are also the worldly Jews. Gwendolen's mother and her uncle, Gascoigne, and the Arrowpoints, have a tacit worldliness which regards marriage as a commercial transaction, but the really barefaced transaction of a human bargain is Lapidoth's attempt to sell his daughter to the count. If Jewish life is shown as devoted and closely united—sheltering the outcast stranger and father— so it is also shown as an imprisoning tradition for Alcharisi, who casts off her race and her religion and her son. But, most important, there is the central significance of what George Eliot explained to Blackwood, when she sent him the first parts of the novel, was to be the redemption of Gwendolen. Gwendolen's tragic process in sensibility and love is a more complex version of the progress of Adam Bede, and it is the central theme which widens the Judaist subject just as the story of Lydgate widened the subject of woman's lot in *Middlemarch*. Daniel is certainly inseparable from the progress of Gwendolen, but he is her opposite and her parallel as well as her mentor. At times their difference is emphasized, it is true, but they are not wholly different. Part of the total effect of the novel is the treatment of the isolated figure. Daniel and Mirah are both Ishmaels, exiled from race and family, wandering and seeking, but at the end of the novel they are neatly restored to their lost world and the solitary figure is Gwendolen, left in the shock of a tragic isolation which breaks on the reader as well as the heroine when the diverging actions separate and leave Gwendolen without Daniel.

This is the pattern: it works as a formal mnemonic, for author and for reader, and such a mnemonic is of special importance in a long novel, and of even greater importance in a novel published in parts. Serial publication has of course advantages as well as disadvantages, and if it is more diffi- cult to read with continuity, the very breaking into parts may encourage slow and repeated reading. The pattern is there because it is the pattern produced by the author's recognition of the 'sameness of the human lot', and it makes its moral generalization while allowing for human variety. The sense of variety is not just the product of alternating parallels with contrasts. It is a matter of giving dramatic vitality to these committed characters. Black in one part of the canvas draws our attention to black in another part; black also makes prominent its opposite, white. But the analogy with painting breaks down because the black and white of George Eliot's moral colours are present only as a nucleus in the complex character. The character is endowed also with personality and with the illusion of movement. It is only a part of the characters that can properly be described as thematic, and this careful grouping of sameness and difference makes the kind of thematic statement which can be made by caricature, but which George Eliot chooses to combine with full and mobile *dramatis personae*. She insisted that 'aesthetic teaching' must not lapse anywhere 'from the picture to the diagram', but the diagram is there, within the picture, made by the careful symmetry and contrast of this pattern of characters. 'The breathing, individual forms' are, as she put it in the same letter, grouped, 'in the needful relations so that the presentation will lay hold on the emotions as human experience' (Haight, iv, p. 301).

CHAPTER VI

Plot and Form

(i)

GEORGE ELIOT'S insistent use of the structural relations of the characters can be seen as a way of classifying humanity. Her classifying division into egoist and altruist is varied from novel to novel. There are other themes interwoven with this main theme: men and women looking for their place in society, men and women trying to shape society, and men and women in love. George Eliot sees a divided world, and the moral view directs the form in which the characters are presented.

But it is possible to see her formative power as something more like deliberate contrivance—a building of a pattern which is the appropriate context for her moral vision rather than the natural consequence of that vision. We have already observed this kind of contrivance at work: the contrast between Dorothea and Rosamond may depend on a vision of the human extremes of warmth and chill, selflessness and selfishness, but the repetition of 'What can I do?' is the novelist's way of drawing our attention to these moral extremes. This kind of repeated phrase, like the repeated event such as the sacramental change of clothing which brackets Dorothea and Mrs Bulstrode, is only a small part of an elaborate formal fantasy where the action itself is organized in a pattern of contrast and coincidence. As Henry James's Theodora says of George Eliot, 'The mass is for each detail and each detail is for the mass'. The placing of detail is at times conscious and at times perhaps not. The imagination seems to organize its material by repetition and opposition, and it is not always possible to determine what is deliberated and what is not. As Freud has shown, even dreams 'use' symmetry and antithesis.

If we can speak of fantasy in George Eliot, it is in a special sense. Her fantastic events are usually, though not always,

115

made of normal human material. The coincidences and repetitions are unlike the coincidences and repetitions in a fairy-tale because they involve no supernatural machinery. There may be the occasional intervention of the novelist as *deus ex machina*, as at the end of *The Mill on the Floss* or *Silas Marner*, but for the most part the characters are shown in the free and active process of making themselves, though always in the context of social influences and human collision or collaboration. Her novels very seldom make their impression by wildness or inconsequentiality, and the sanity of her characters and of her moral view is so strong and usually so acceptable that her fantasy is seldom felt as improbable or imposed. Even where she uses coincidence in the ordinary narrative conventions of discovery and accident, it is hardly ever interpreted as a version of Fate, as it usually is in Hardy, but merely as a narrative means to a moral end. I am here thinking of such coincidences as the discovery of Eppie in Silas Marner's cottage, or the discovery of Esther Lyon's claim to the Transome estate, or Raffles's discovery of Bulstrode's name on the piece of paper wedged in his brandy-flask. George Eliot makes fairly lavish use of this kind of coincidence, but it seldom affects our sense of the responsibility of her characters. There is no President of the Immortals sporting with Esther or Bulstrode, but a novelist working within a convention of a certain allowance of contrivance, arranging events so that they will force her characters to demonstrate their moral direction. This ordinary kind of coincidence is much less prominent in these novels than the kind of coincidence which is used as a mirror, to emphasize and to generalize, just as the characters themselves mirror each other.

At its simplest this coincidence takes the form of a repeated situation. There are many examples of a close repetition which gives us the impression that life is really presenting the character with a second chance. Fedalma, in *The Spanish Gypsy*, is given a series of repeated temptations, and so is Maggie Tulliver. What we notice is the repetition, and not—as in classical temptations—the variations. Maggie is tempted by Philip, first resists and refuses, and then succumbs. Then

116

comes the stronger temptation by Stephen. Both are temptations to betray a loyalty, and a loyalty rooted in the family and her childhood. And both men tempt Maggie through her need for love and her artistic sensibility. Philip's voice, then Stephen's, in deeper tones, speak to her in the music which is one of the recurring images of the novel. Thomas a Kempis speaks to her in 'a strain of solemn music'. Philip sings *sotto voce*, and—after she has said 'I wanted voices to be fuller and deeper'—'Love in her eyes sits playing', in the Red Deeps. Long after, in Lucy's drawing-room, he sings 'Ah, perchè non posso odiarti' from Bellini's *Sonnambula*. Stephen's deeper voice sings Purcell, and it is Purcell which vibrates in her, 'with its wild passion and fancy'. This in its turn carries an echo of an earlier phrase, for we have seen Maggie's disenchantment expressed in terms of an absence of music: 'There was no music for her any more—no piano, no harmonized voices, no delicious stringed instruments, with their passionate cries of imprisoned spirits sending a strange vibration through her frame' (bk. IV, ch. iii).

But the common symbol does not provide the whole of the repetition here. The second temptation follows the same course as the first, and this is where repetition makes itself strongly felt. With Stephen as with Philip she resists, then capitulates, then resists again and renounces him. But within the temptation by Stephen comes the most prominent repetition. She gives him up, but there is a second trial, and it intensifies both her despair and her resolution, and is followed by her prayer and the answering flood. She has tried to adjust herself to a life without Stephen and also without her old ties, and seems to have failed. At this point comes Stephen's letter repeating his arguments and his desire:

At the entrance of the chill dark cavern, we turn, with unworn courage from the warm light; but how, when we have trodden far in the damp darkness, and have begun to be faint and weary—how if there is a sudden opening above us, and we are invited back again to the life-nourishing day? The leap of natural longing from under the pressure of pain is so strong, that all less immediate motives are likely to be forgotten—till the pain has been escaped from. (bk. VII, ch. v)

117

The process is repeated: just as Maggie went on the river with Stephen, and then turned back, so after the second temptation, she first gives in and writes 'Come!' But once more resistance succeeds capitulation, and 'the long past came back to her'. Once more she refuses.

The recoil is more than a mere elaboration, for it tests Maggie's original weakness. First she characteristically commits herself without thought (as when she ran away to the gipsies) and then after the rash adventure, she forces herself to renunciation and return. What is demonstrated is Philip's prophecy when he told her that renunciation is more than negation. If there were only a single rejection of Stephen there would be less tragedy and less triumph, so Maggie is made to renounce, feel temptation again, and then renounce again. Only then does George Eliot produce the other coincidence of the flood in immediate answer to Maggie's prayer.

Something similar happens in *Romola*, where there is a much nicer moral issue. The rights and wrongs of Romola's first flight from Tito are more ambiguous than the moral issue in earlier books. She leaves him, then she is converted by Savonarola's view of human duty, which her mind accepts in a 'solvent of feeling', and she goes back. Towards the end of the novel the situation is repeated. Once more she leaves Tito, and this time, with a fine irony, she is leaving Savonarola too, whom she rejects as another force of selfish betrayal, for Savonarola is an ambivalent moral quantity, at one time reinforcing Romola's altruism, at another running parallel to Tito. But then comes the second return, after she drifts in her boat[1] (like Maggie) and finds the plague-stricken village. What sends her back this time is the practice of human fellowship, while before it had been Savonarola's injunction. In the plague-stricken valley,

> She had simply lived, with so energetic an impulse to share the life around her, to answer the call of need and do the work which cried aloud to be done, that the reasons for living, enduring, labouring, never took the form of argument. . . .

The experience was like a new baptism to Romola. (ch. lxix)

[1] George Eliot wrote to Sara Hennell, 23 August 1863, 'the "Drifting Away" and the Village with the Plague belonged to my earliest vision of

Plot and Form

Even the rejection of Savonarola is modified, and the moral summary which concludes the novel brings together his history and Tito's. As in *The Mill on the Floss*, there is a temporary twist in the heroine's progress, not there for the narrative purpose of making us doubt the end but in order to make more emphatic the moral direction which has been taken. Whatever happens, and the events are made very carefully to repeat themselves, the character responds ultimately in the same way.

There is another kind of coincidence in *Romola*, rather like the most famous coincidence of all, the gold hair of Eppie which comes to Silas Marner after the gold coins are lost, or the other less obvious coincidence in the same story of the two stolen bags of money and the two thieves. In *Romola* the central coincidence is an extension in fantasy of the kind of coincidence which merely depends on characters behaving consistently. It is a coincidence in situation, a literary example of Freud's repetition-compulsion.

When Tito comes to Florence he thinks he is escaping from his foster-father, Baldassare, whom he has left and betrayed. And there is of course the normal kind of coincidence when Baldassare comes to Florence as a prisoner, stumbles against Tito as he escapes, happens to shelter in Tessa's house, and at last happens to be by the riverside when Tito is cast ashore by the current. But there is a more sinister coincidence. Tito is accepted by Bardo as a son, and for the second time he betrays a foster-father. So far, another manipulated proof of the maxim that our deeds determine us. But there is also the gratuitous coincidence that Bardo too has a son who has left him, and—in his father's view—has betrayed him. The mere presence of two old men betrayed by their sons would in itself amount to the kind of generalization through accumulation which we find in *King Lear* or (more crudely handled) in *The Spanish Tragedy* and *A Warning to Fair Women*, but in *Romola* there is the additional coincidence that the betrayed fathers are both betrayed by the same man. It is mere consistency of egoism and reasoned infidelity in Tito, but for Bardo it is a fantastic trap.

the story and were by deliberate forecast adopted as romantic and symbolical elements' (Haight, iv, p. 104).

This kind of situation is highly productive of irony: 'Romola, has this young man the same complexion as thy brother—fair and pale?' 'No, father' (ch. vi).

And later: 'But *you* have come to me, Tito—not quite too late. . . . When you are working by my side I seem to have found a son again' (ch. xii). The coincidence extends even to detail. Bardo is blind, Baldassare's loss of memory has blinded his scholar's eye. Both fathers are antiquaries and scholars: Tito breaks off his work with Bardo, sells Baldassare's rings, sells Bardo's library and denies Baldassare's scholarship. This is much more elaborate than the two thefts in *Silas Marner*, the one of which Silas is accused, the other where he is robbed and himself does the accusing. This is an almost unobtrusive coincidence, like the final irony of *Romola*, when Tito's children are rescued and fostered by Romola as Tito was by Baldassare.

Felix Holt is as dependent on coincidence in the ordinary sense as any of Hardy's novels, but the coincidence which is there for the purpose of plot mechanics (and which George Eliot was afraid to extend by accepting Frederic Harrison's suggestion that Esther's claim to the Transome estate should be through her mother as well as her father) is thrown into the background by the coincidences which are there for irony and generalization. Apart from the coincidences of character, there is the central coincidence which we have already noticed:

> There could hardly have been a lot less like Harold Transome's than this of the quack doctor's son, except in the superficial facts that he called himself a Radical, that he was the only son of his mother, and that he had lately returned to his home with ideas and resolves not a little disturbing to that mother's mind. (ch. iii)

Here the coincidence is partly a device for greater unity, and partly a further emphasis of the contrast in character, and in politics. It is in the last two novels that this kind of coincidence is most elaborately used.

(ii)

Perhaps the most interesting coincidence in *Middlemarch* is that of the two deaths, of Featherstone and Casaubon. George Eliot makes it plain that the parallels are deliberate by calling the book which describes the last illness of both, 'Waiting for Death' and by calling the book which includes the account of Casaubon's death, 'The Dead Hand', which is an echo of a phrase used of Featherstone:

> In chuckling over the vexations he could inflict by the rigid clutch of his dead hand, he inevitably mingled his consciousness with that livid stagnant presence, and so far as he was preoccupied with a future life, it was with one of gratification inside his coffin. Thus old Featherstone was imaginative, after his fashion. (ch. xxxiv)

Mr Casaubon's meditations are less crudely formulated than Featherstone's but they amount to much the same:

> The probability of a transient earthly bliss for other persons, when he should himself have entered into glory, had not a potently sweetening effect. If the truth should be that some undetermining disease was at work within him, there might be large opportunity for some people to be the happier when he was gone; and if one of those people should be Will Ladislaw, Mr Casaubon objected so strongly that it seemed as if the annoyance would make part of his disembodied existence. (ch. xlii)

Both try to clutch the living in a dead hand (Casaubon's dead grasp is called 'the cold grasp'), and both fail: Dorothea gives up her fortune and Rigg sells his father's house to Bulstrode.

The chief irony which comes out of the coincidence is an elaborate one. It underlines the psychological resemblance by a resemblance of situation. Dorothea watches Featherstone's funeral, and as she looks down from the high window the scene takes on a solemn significance: there is the social irony of the high window and 'the belts of thicker life below', but there are other reasons for the scene's importance. Although Dorothea is apparently a spectator she is involved:

> This scene of old Featherstone's funeral . . . aloof as it seemed to be from the tenor of her life, always afterwards came back to her at the touch of certain sensitive points in memory, just as the vision of St Peter's at Rome was inwoven with moods of despondency.

There is the anticipating irony which is only complete after Casaubon's death:

'How piteous!' said Dorothea. 'This funeral seems to me the most dismal thing I ever saw. It is a blot on the morning. I cannot bear to think that any one should die and leave no love behind.'

She was going to say more, but she saw her husband enter and seat himself a little in the background. The difference his presence made to her was not always a happy one: she felt that he often inwardly objected to her speech. (ch. xxxiv)

Then Mr Brooke mentions his fatal generosity of asking Ladislaw to Freshitt, and the storm gathers. It is the coincidence which makes the irony, and it depends on George Eliot's version of parody. The Featherstone episodes are a grotesque comedy acting as a kind of distorting mirror to the story of Dorothea and Casaubon, and the reader sees both the resemblances and the difference.

The central coincidence of the dead hand clutching the living is intensified by minor coincidences: Lydgate is the doctor in each case; both Dorothea and Mary are roused in the night as they wait for death, to be asked to do the impossible, to give the blank promise to carry out Casaubon's wishes after death, to burn Featherstone's will; each clutching dead hand seems to hold the living for a while, but is shaken off by accident and by human energy.

There is another mirroring coincidence in the portrayal of Dorothea, one of the mirrors which the character recognizes as such. This kind of recognition is almost always placed in an emotional crisis: George Eliot shows in her characters, as we have seen in Adam, that movement towards generalization which can accompany the intensity of grief. In Dorothea, as in Adam, grief can generalize in its obsession, seeing the world in its own image, as Lear sees all grief in terms of filial ingratitude, but it can also, almost in the same act of imagination, move outside itself in sympathy, as Lear sees he has taken too little care of human misery. This double vision is shown here in a quieter and more normal world. Dorothea's mirror is the miniature of Ladislaw's grandmother:

At last she saw something which had gathered new breadth and meaning: it was the miniature of Mr Casaubon's aunt Julia, who had made the unfortunate marriage—of Will Ladislaw's grandmother. Dorothea could fancy that it was alive now—the delicate

woman's face which yet had a headstrong look, a peculiarity difficult to interpret. Was it only her friends who thought her marriage
unfortunate? or did she herself find it out to be a mistake, and taste
the salt bitterness of her tears in the merciful silence of the night?
What breadths of experience Dorothea seemed to have passed over
since she first looked at this miniature! She felt a new companionship with it, as if it had an ear for her and could see how she was
looking at it. Here was a woman who had known some difficulty
about marriage. (ch. xxviii)

It is delicately done. The mirror is partly created by Dorothea's imagination. Dorothea asks her question which is not
answered. This parallel case has a peculiar intensity because
this is Casaubon's aunt and Will's grandmother, and is used
to prepare us for the future. It is indeed a face like Will's and
in order to bring us back to Dorothea's case there is a blurring
and a transformation: 'Nay, the colours deepened, the lips and
chin seemed to get larger, the hair and eyes seemed to be
sending out light, the face was masculine. . . .'

History repeats itself for Lydgate too, and within his own
life. He needs no distant mirror to see Rosamond, for he has
already seen Laure, his first love. The repetition is one which
demonstrates his fatal 'spots of commonness', and after
George Eliot tells us the story of his ardour for science she
uses the flashback to show his one deviation, his love for Laure:

As to women, he had once already been drawn headlong by
impetuous folly, which he meant to be final, since marriage at some
distant period would of course not be impetuous. For those who
want to be acquainted with Lydgate it will be good to know what
was that case of impetuous folly, for it may stand as an example of
that fitful swerving of passion to which he was prone. . . . (ch. xv)

There follows the story of Laure, who killed her husband because he wearied her: 'he was too fond: he would live in Paris,
and not in my country'. The parallel with Rosamond need not
be elaborated. It is there to demonstrate the flaw in the man,
and to that extent plausible enough. But the repetition is more
than the compulsion of character: it is a coincidence of a more
sinister kind. Rosamond feels that Middlemarch is not her
country, and is impatient with Lydgate because he wants
to stay there. He sees the repetition for himself, like a man

caught twice in the same trap: 'His mind glancing back to Laure while he looked at Rosamond, he said inwardly, "Would *she* kill me because I wearied her?" and then, "It is the way with all women"' (ch. lviii). She does not need to kill him, and the seal is set on the coincidence by the last words spoken by Lydgate: 'He once called her his basil plant; and when she asked for an explanation, said that basil was a plant which had flourished wonderfully on a murdered man's brains' (Finale). The image is the last ironical comment on the images of flowers first associated with their love, and perhaps even with the names of Laure and Rosamond, in a novel where women's names are not without significance.

(iii)

In *Daniel Deronda* the growth of coincidence into symbol becomes more elaborate. The repetitions are multiplied, and in a context which is very different from the ordinary world of *Middlemarch*. Daniel Deronda's character is itself scarcely realistic. It is he who is the discoverer, ironically, since he is himself lost and exiled. He finds Mirah and Mordecai, and stands as a deliverer to them, and also, in a smaller way, to Hans and his family, and lastly to Gwendolen, whose rescue he sees as a much more difficult one ' than that of the wanderer by the river'. The theme of the lost and the found spreads through the book. Daniel is aware of coincidence when he finds Mirah:

> Deronda of late, in his solitary excursions, had been occupied chiefly with uncertainties about his own course; but those uncertainties, being much at their leisure, were wont to have such wide-sweeping connections with all life and history that the new image of helpless sorrow easily blent itself with what seemed to him the strong array of reasons why he should shrink from getting into that routine of the world which makes men apologise for all its wrong-doing. . . . (ch. xvii)

And later, when he speaks to her: 'The agitating impression this forsaken girl was making on him stirred a fibre that lay close to his deepest interest in the fates of women—"perhaps my mother was like this one"' (ch. xvii).

Plot and Form

The connection becomes closer when Daniel applies Mirah's fear of finding her father to his own feeling about meeting his unknown mother, and there are eventually to be for the reader more connections than are ever present for the characters themselves. Lapidoth took Mirah from her mother, and she is exiled and groping her way back to her Judaism; Alcharisi gives Deronda to Sir Hugo, and he too is rootless, and wandering, and at last found. But although he is in the isolated position of the character who only sees a part of the truth about his situation, he sees a certain parallel: 'How could he be slow to understand feelings which now seemed nearer than ever to his own? for the words of his mother's letter implied that his filial relation was not to be freed from painful conditions' (ch. 1). The coincidence of Daniel's position and that of Lydia Glasher's son acts as a moral warning to Gwendolen. Her inadequate imagination clothes itself in individual cases, but even this particularized sympathy is the beginning of a growth away from self-interest. She hears the gossip about Daniel being Sir Hugo's illegitimate son at the time when her mind is occupied with Lydia Glasher and her dispossessed boy:

An image which had immediately risen in Gwendolen's mind was that of the unknown mother—no doubt a dark-eyed woman—probably sad. Hardly any face could be less like Deronda's than that represented as Sir Hugo's in a crayon portrait at Diplow. A dark-eyed beautiful woman, no longer young, had become 'stuff o' the conscience' to Gwendolen. (ch. xxix)

She begins to generalize, 'Mamma, have men generally children before they are married?' and her conscience works in its own peculiar way:

Gwendolen lay struggling with the reasons against that marriage —reasons which pressed upon her newly now that they were unexpectedly mirrored in the story of a man whose slight relations with her had, by some hidden affinity, bitten themselves into the most permanent layers of feeling.

And a little later in the same chapter: 'What she had now heard about Deronda seemed to her imagination to throw him into one group with Mrs Glasher and her children.' This moral coincidence comes up again when she asks Deronda for help,

'But you have not wronged any one. . . . It is only others who have wronged *you*.'

Mirah mirrors his mother for Daniel, and Daniel mirrors Lydia's son for Gwendolen. The resemblances accumulate in a chain.[1] Mirah also is in a position like Gwendolen's, but she resists being sold to her Count. Gwendolen is told by Klesmer that 'A mountebank's child who helps her father to earn shillings when she is six years old' would have a better chance of becoming a singer, and this prepares for the scene when she goes to hear Mirah sing and she and Klesmer remember how she had once hoped to sing as Mirah is singing. When Deronda tells her about Mirah she is bitter because Mirah is like her in suffering but unlike in her reaction to suffering. Even Catherine Arrowpoint, giving up wealth for love, has a mirroring function: someone says when Sir Hugo tells Gwendolen about the marriage of Catherine and Klesmer, 'It's a sort of troubadour story . . . I'm glad to find a little romance left among us. I think our young people now are getting too worldly wise.' Here the point is made by difference not similarity.

Music itself takes on a symbolic status. Klesmer speaks of its breadth, and indirectly condemns Gwendolen's narrowness by the music she sings, and Alcharisi's desire 'to live a large life . . . and be carried along in a great current' has something in common with Daniel's reply to Gwendolen's ennui and disgust. She has said that her life is 'like a dance set beforehand', and he says: 'I take what you said of music for a small example —it answers for all larger things—you will not cultivate it for the sake of a private joy in it' (ch. xxxvi).

Music is the linking coincidence for Gwendolen, Mirah, Klesmer, Daniel, and Alcharisi. Alcharisi points to several coincidences: like Alcharisi, Mirah sings, but she is 'not one who must have a path of her own'; she is said to draw Daniel after her just as Alcharisi drew her husband, but 'the other way'; she too is a Jew cut off from her religion—'Ah! like you. She is attached to the Judaism she knows nothing of. . . . That is poetry—fit to last through an opera night' (ch. liii). Alcharisi

[1] The resemblances here too are sometimes emphasized by the book-titles, viz. 'Maidens Choosing', 'Revelations', and 'Fruit and Seed'.

sees the parallels, but once more the function of her interpretation is carefully placed in character—the limitations of her 'fit to last through an opera night' has a special irony. The scene itself is a fine example of the effectiveness of George Eliot's structural cutting: Daniel's arrival at Genoa has been followed by the ironically contrasting scene in London where Mirah is jealously lamenting Daniel's Gentile connections. This geographical leap is followed by another scene in Genoa, and this is the scene where Daniel discloses his love for Mirah. There is the usual pressure of the contrasted points of view, and a clearly drawn frame of irony for the major coincidence that Daniel, like Mirah and Mordecai, is a Jew.

There is the other central coincidence which is stressed at this point in the story, that Daniel is fulfilling his grandfather's wish—in spite of Alcharisi's attempt to frustrate it. Alcharisi's vain attempts to circumvent fate, like Oedipus's, produce an impression of inevitability. We are prepared both for the fulfilment of the grandfather's wish and for the fulfilment of Mordecai's vision. Daniel is shown as solitary and restless, dissatisfied with English education and English politics, ardent but uncertain. Daniel—like a later Ishmael, Leopold Bloom—is both solitary and social, and the moment of discovery is both a joy and a shock:

He beheld the world changed for him by the certitude of ties that altered the poise of hopes and fears, and gave him a new sense of fellowship, as if under cover of the night he had joined the wrong band of wanderers, and found with the rise of morning that the tents of his kindred were grouped far off. He had a quivering imaginative sense of close relation to the grandfather who had been animated by strong impulses and beloved thoughts, which were now perhaps being roused from their slumber within himself. And through all this passionate meditation Mordecai and Mirah were always present, as beings who clasped hands with him in sympathetic silence. (ch. lv)

Again the placing of the crisis is important: the Grandcourts too are at Genoa, and Gwendolen's appeal is strong. This discovery about his race is immediately followed by the discovery that Grandcourt has been drowned: Daniel's new sense of fellowship has been found just before Gwendolen, of the wrong band of wanderers but not knowing it, makes her greatest demand on him. This placing—or timing—of Daniel's crisis and Gwendolen's has such a powerfully ironical impression that we scarcely notice that it depends on the relatively flimsy coincidence that all these characters meet conveniently in Genoa. One reason why George Eliot's coincidences of plot are so much less obtrusive than Hardy's is, I suggest, this double working of the realistic coincidence and the other kind of coincidence which approaches moral fantasy. The sense of fate in *Daniel Deronda* does not rely on plot coincidence, but uses it as a basis for something else—this, as Coleridge said of Shakespeare, is expectation rather than surprise.

George Eliot seems always to be planning with this expectation in mind. It is her factual realism which holds her fantasy solidly in place. The imagery of loneliness and exile permeates the account of Daniel's progress, and we are prepared for the part he plays in Mordecai's life and for his final discovery of family and nation. On his side, Mordecai too is given some plausible preparation and analysis, for he is presented as a man whose visual habits might be taken as a psychological explanation for his prophetic vision. But there is a gap between the explanations and the fantasy—for George Eliot allows reality to conform exactly to vision, and at last Mordecai sees Daniel, as he has dreamed, from Blackfriars Bridge.

> Mordecai's mind wrought so constantly in images, that his coherent trains of thought often resembled the significant dreams attributed to sleepers by waking persons in their most inventive moments; nay, they often resembled genuine dreams in their way of breaking off the passage from the known to the unknown. Thus, for a long while, he habitually thought of the Being answering to his need as one distantly approaching or turning his back towards him, darkly painted against a golden sky. (ch. xxxviii)

Later in this chapter we find that Daniel is identified with this Messianic hope:

> It was Deronda now who was seen in the often painful night-watches, when we are all liable to be held with the clutch of a single thought—whose figure, never with its back turned, was seen in moments of soothed reverie or soothed dozing, painted on that

golden sky which was the doubly blessed symbol of advancing day and of approaching rest.

Kaufmann points out the esoteric character of the symbol of the sunset as a beginning, the Jewish Sabbath beginning at evening. But the imagery has many implications, and in the details of Mordecai's vision the symbolism of river and bridge, sunset and wide sky, are repeated and combined. Mordecai sees the bridge as 'the meeting-place for the spiritual messengers', the river as an image of changing life, and the sunset as rest and beginning—these are all associations made explicit, for Mordecai sees in terms of symbols as well as in visual images:

He yearned with a poet's yearning for the wide sky, the far-reaching vista of bridges, the tender and fluctuating lights on the water which seems to breathe with a life that can shiver and mourn, be comforted and rejoice. (ch. xxxviii)

Daniel fulfils his vision: 'The prefigured friend had come from the golden background, and had signalled to him: this actually was: the rest was to be' (ch. xl). The river has been significant for Daniel too, as the scene of his rescue of Mirah, and—an important link with Mordecai—as a symbol of his characteristic rejoicing in wide space and life outside himself. Daniel is indeed eventually brought into close rapport with Mordecai's prophetic vision, partly because he comes to shed his rational aloofness, but also because he is endowed, after the discovery of his nation, with a curious sense of hereditary vision. In a passage already quoted he has been spoken of as feeling that his grandfather's impulses and thoughts were 'perhaps being roused from their slumber within himself'. This is too metaphorical to be taken literally, but a later passage makes it quite clear that Daniel is being presented as the inheritor of a vision. His isolation and restlessness are given the status of Mordecai's visions, partly in terms of some kind of folk-memory. There is a prominent image very like the earlier one of the band of wanderers. Daniel says to Mordecai:

It is through your inspiration that I have discerned what may be my life's task. It is you who have given shape to what, I believe, was an inherited yearning—the effect of brooding, passionate thoughts in many ancestors—thoughts that seem to have been intensely present in my grandfather. Suppose the stolen offspring of some mountain tribe brought up in a city of the plain, or one with an inherited genius for painting, and born blind—the ancestral life would lie within them as a dim longing for unknown objects and sensations, and the spell-bound habit of their inherited frames would be like a cunningly-wrought musical instrument, never played on, but quivering throughout in uneasy mysterious moanings of its intricate structure that, under the right touch, gives music. Something like that, I think, has been my experience. (ch. lxiii)

It can hardly be claimed that Daniel's history has fully endorsed these powerful images. If it had he must have been a more interesting character. But there has been enough indication of his loneliness and his generous ardour to give some context for this moving rhetoric. And George Eliot says at the beginning that he is not an Ishmaelite—even the negative here defines his character in specifically Jewish terms.

Gwendolen's history is given a certain curious unity by this kind of coincidence. A strong source of imagery, chiefly of imagery presented as characteristic of Gwendolen's mental state, is the picture of the dead face and the fleeing figure, disclosed twice to Gwendolen's terror. The dead face returns in her dreams and at last becomes identified with a real face, that of the drowned Grandcourt. This identification is made in the same blend of scientific explanation and genuine fantasy which we met in the treatment of Mordecai's vision and Daniel's sense of exile. The echoes of the dead face usually turn up in passages describing intense fear or despair or even actual delirium. This is the broken speech of her delirium after Grandcourt's death:

'All sorts of contrivances in my mind—but all so difficult. And I fought against them—I was terrified at them—I saw his dead face'—here her voice sank almost to a whisper close to Deronda's ear—'ever so long ago I saw it; and I wished him to be dead.' (ch. lvi)

This is part of Gwendolen's superstitious fears, and part too of the hinted theme of Grandcourt's curse. Lush's first fears for Grandcourt seem, in their context exaggerated: 'He struck Lush rather newly as something like a man who was *fey*—led on by an ominous calamity. . . . Having protested against the marriage, Lush had a second-sight for its evil consequences'[1] (ch. xxviii). But the levity of this anticipation vanishes when Grandcourt finds Gwendolen shrieking with the diamonds around her: 'In some form or other the Furies had crossed his threshold' (ch. xxxi). It is picked up, though again vaguely, when Gwendolen's 'fear of him, mingling with the vague foreboding of some retributive calamity which hung about her neck, had reached a superstitious point' (ch. xxxv). And again:

The thought of his dying would not subsist: it turned as with a dream-change into the terror that she should die with his throttling fingers on her neck avenging that thought. Fantasies moved within her like ghosts. . . . (ch. xlviii)

The vision of her past wrong-doing, and what it had brought on her, came with a pale ghastly illumination over every imagined deed. . . .

. . . The palsy of a new terror—a white dead face from which she was for ever trying to flee and for ever held back. (ch. liv)

When Gwendolen is at the tiller in the last scene with Grandcourt there is a passage which repeats and gathers together all the past fears:

She was not afraid of any outward dangers—she was afraid of her own wishes, which were taking shapes possible and impossible, like a cloud of demon-faces. She was afraid of her own hatred, which under the cold iron touch that had compelled her today had gathered a fierce intensity. . . . She clung to the thought of Deronda: she persuaded herself that he would not go away while she was there—he knew that she needed help. The sense that he was there would save her from acting out the evil within. And yet quick, quick, came images, plans of evil that would come again and seize her in the night, like furies preparing the deed that they would straightway avenge.[2] (ch. liv)

---

[1] In *The Heart of Midlothian* Scott defines *fey* as 'a Scottish expression, meaning the state of those who are driven on to their impending fate by the strong impulse of some irresistible necessity'.

[2] George Eliot frequently uses the significant childhood incident to sharpen her delineation. The young Arthur Donnithorne kicks over the gardener's broth, and offers his pencil-case and knife in recompense; the young Gwendolen strangles her sister's canary.

This not only takes us back to the earlier entry of the Furies with 'the poisoned diamonds' but if we know the novel well, re-echoes the 'Quick, quick' of Gwendolen's frantic thoughts before she accepted Grandcourt: 'Quick, quick, like pictures in a book beaten open with a sense of hurry, came back vividly, yet in fragments, all that she had gone through in relation to Grandcourt . . .' (ch. xxvi). The first impression of the dead face, and Lush's fears that Grandcourt is fey, give substance to the repeated hints of fears and dreams which culminate in Grandcourt's death. The inevitable Furies,[1] the fear, and the pallid dead face, are all anticipated in the prefatory motto to the novel:

> Let thy chief terror be of thine own soul:
> There, 'mid the throng of hurrying desires
> That trample o'er the dead to seize their spoil,
> Lurks vengeance, footless, irresistible
> As exhalations laden with slow death,
> And o'er the fairest troop of captured joys
> Breathes pallid pestilence.

This points ahead to Gwendolen and to Grandcourt.

These fears and dreams join too with Daniel's premonition —it is a book in which nearly everyone has premonitions—of Gwendolen's need and his failure. Again, there are scattered hints throughout the book, many of them images which take colour from and anticipate Grandcourt's death by drowning and Deronda's final voyage:

It was as if he saw her drowning while his limbs were bound. (ch. xxxvi)

It was as if he had a vision of himself besought with outstretched arms and cries, while he was caught by the waves and compelled to mount the vessel bound for a far-off coast. (ch. xlv)

Words seemed to have no more rescue in them than if he had been beholding a vessel in peril of wreck—the poor ship with its many-lived anguish beaten by the inescapable storm. (ch. xlviii)

As if it had been the retreating cry of a creature snatched and carried out of his reach by swift horsemen or swifter waves. . . . (ch. l)

Then there is the coincidence of the repeated theme of gamb-

---

[1] Gwendolen's Furies are replaced by the 'severe angel'—Deronda.

ling. The roulette table is our introduction to Gwendolen, **and** Daniel's imagination interprets it in two ways: as narrowness, in contrast to the breadth he loves, and as selfishness. He sees the gamblers: 'As if they had all eaten of some root that for the time compelled the brains of each to the same narrow monotony of action' (ch. i). And later he tells Gwendolen:

It is a besotting kind of taste, likely to turn into a disease. And, besides, there is something revolting to me in raking a heap of money together, and internally chuckling over it, when others are feeling the loss of it. I should even call it base, if it were more than an exceptional lapse. There are enough inevitable turns of fortune which force us to see that our gain is another's loss:—that is one of the ugly aspects of life. (ch. xxix)

His words become a kind of moral password for Gwendolen, and she uses them several times: 'Suppose I had gambled again, and lost the necklace again . . .?' and two sentences later: 'You wanted me not to do that—not to make my gain out of another's loss in that way—and I have done a great deal worse' (ch. xxvi). Then, at the end: 'I wanted to make my gain out of another's loss—you remember?—it was like roulette—and the money burnt into me. And I could not complain. It was as if I had prayed that another should lose and I should win. And I had won' (ch. lvi). She comes to find her marriage with Grandcourt a very special kind of loss, 'not simply a *minus* but a terrible *plus* that had never entered into her reckoning' (ch. xlviii).

There is an analogue which makes the gambling symbol stronger. Lapidoth, Mirah's father, also plays roulette, and he is an actual example of Daniel's metaphor. In him the taste for gambling has turned into a disease. He acts as a grotesque example justifying Daniel's use of gambling as a symbol of egoism. But he is not the only gambler who underlines Gwendolen's personal symbol. There is also the equation of gambling and financial speculation. This is a further moral extension, and a neat irony. Gwendolen's family is ruined by a gambler like herself. The difference is merely one of degree:

Gwendolen, we have seen, passed her time abroad in the new excitement of gambling, and in imagining herself an empress of luck, having brought from her late experience a vague impression that in this confused world it signified nothing what any one did, so that they amused themselves. We have seen, too, that certain persons, mysteriously symbolised as Grapnell and Co., having also thought of reigning in the realm of luck, and being also bent on amusing themselves, no matter how, had brought about a painful change in her family circumstances. . . . (ch. xv)

This ironical translation of Fortune's wheel as roulette—a remaking of the symbol—gives the reader a parallel which Gwendolen is incapable of observing. The extent of her obtuseness is a measure of her egoism. She has just observed that if she had known that the family fortune was lost she would have brought home her winnings, and goes on:

'You said in your letter it was Mr Lassmann's fault we had lost our money. Has he run away with it all?'
'No, dear, you don't understand. There were great speculations: he meant to gain. It was all about mines and things of that sort. He risked too much.'
'I don't call that Providence: it was his improvidence with our money, and he ought to be punished. (ch. xxi)

This is highly explicit, no more mysterious than the 'symbolism' of the name of Grapnell, and it gives to Daniel's moral attacks on gambling something more than the puritanical dislike which he is made to share with his author. The generalization is made good by the analogues, and the social status of the last example of speculation makes a link between individual and public morality.[1] Gambling is very much more than a private shorthand symbol for Gwendolen and Daniel. Its significance changes and intensifies as the action moves on, covering selfish disregard, misplaced security in Luck, robbery, worldly values, and blind submission to the future. We begin with coincidence and end with a generalization and a symbol.

[1] George Eliot makes a similar comparison in *Middlemarch* between Lydgate's attempt at 'Medical Reform' and the political interest in the Reform Bill.

CHAPTER VII

Possibilities

(i)

ALTHOUGH George Eliot's use of coincidence shows her occupied with personal destiny as something fixed and determined, she has, as we have just seen, a certain interest in the 'external' social or accidental causes of action. She follows the quotation from Novalis—'Character is destiny'—with an instance of the delicate poise of destiny:

Hamlet, Prince of Denmark, was speculative and irresolute, and we have a great tragedy in consequence. But if his father had lived to a good old age, and his uncle had died an early death, we can conceive Hamlet's having married Ophelia, and got through life with a reputation of sanity notwithstanding many soliloquies, and some moody sarcasms towards the fair daughter of Polonius, to say nothing of the frankest incivility to his father-in-law. (*The Mill on the Floss*, bk VI, ch. vi)

I am going to suggest that George Eliot would have written *Hamlet* with this alternative life in mind, having a ghostly presence within the actuality of event, and playing some part in the final impression. Professor Haight's edition of the letters has some revealing details of George Eliot's workmanship. There seems to have been a stage in the imagining, or even in the writing, of the novels, in which her imagination played with possibility. After this preliminary period, which she describes as the 'simmering', the imaginative decision passed into the 'irrevocable' stage. At one time, for instance, as we can see from the letters she wrote asking Frederic Harrison for legal advice about the plot of *Daniel Deronda* (Haight, vi, p. 100), she was playing with the possibility of giving Gwendolen a son. The kind of change which would have been made in *Daniel Deronda* if this possibility had become a fact is extensive: Gwendolen's relation to Grandcourt might conceivably have been shown as much the same, though surely without Gwendolen's final isolation, but her dependence on

Deronda, on which the final irony of structure seems to turn, must have been cancelled or modified in some radical way. There is nothing very startling in this method of trial and rejection in the inventive process, but it has a special interest in George Eliot because it draws attention to an interesting characteristic of her imaginative method. There is something very like the actual appearance of alternative destiny within the 'irrevocable' and finished book. There is a strong and deliberate suggestion of the possible lives her characters might have lived.

Sometimes the hinted possible world is there to give the sense of immediacy in crisis, as it is in Gwendolen Harleth's 'alternate dip of counterbalancing thoughts begotten of counterbalancing desires' before she accepts Grandcourt. Sometimes it seems to be there to underline the fragility of destiny, or its opposite, the fixity of moral tradition. At all times it results in a tremendous increase in realism, and the constant sense of alternatives and possibilities is a rare and difficult thing to combine with the unity and definiteness of this kind of moral novel. Her characters are sometimes haunted —or their author is haunted on their behalf—by the vision of possibilities from which they are redeemed, or seduced, or diverted, and the strength of the possibility is usually in contrast with their apparently determined process. The characters often walk on a razor-edge of action which has the appearance of a moral necessity achieved at great and rare peril. Both the necessary action and the possible one are a part of the purpose of the novels.

In a sense, all her novels overlap with each other in a way which shows them to be explorations of what she calls 'the sameness of the human lot'. The recurrence of the moral situation is less striking than its versatility, and yet we can see a constant process of attempted and rejected variants bearing some resemblance to each other. Arthur Donni-thorne's degeneration takes the same course of self-persuasion and determining action as Tito's, but one has a kind of re-demption, the other none. Dorothea is a more complicated Esther, Gwendolen a less successful Esther, and so on, though with the proviso that each version is clothed in a new per-

sonality, and it is only a new trial when we are considering the
moral implications and not the individuality in which they are
clothed. But it is because the moral is constant that the story of
Miss Brooke could be fused with *Middlemarch,* and it is
because the moral is constant that we find this process of re-
writing one novel in the next eventually catching up with itself and resulting in her special use of double plot within the
novel. William Empson suggests in *Some Versions of Pastoral*
that the double plot of *Wuthering Heights* is a device for telling
the same story twice, with different endings, and this is exactly
the sort of thing achieved by George Eliot.

Perhaps the best example comes in *Felix Holt,* where Mrs
Transome and Esther are carefully drawn in parallel, not
merely for the usual purposes of generalization and thematic
precision, but for the purposes of a curious causal relation. To
begin with, there are carefully underlined resemblances in
their presentation. Mrs Transome has 'a high-born imperious
air' and Esther 'had too many airs and graces, and held her
head much too high'. Mr Transome 'shrank like a timid
animal' when his wife appeared and Mr Lyon found himself
'in timorous subjection' to Esther's wishes. Both women are
fastidious, accomplished, clever. Mrs Transome 'had secretly
picked out for private reading the lighter parts of dangerous
French authors—and in company had been able to talk of
Mr Burke's style, or of Chateaubriand's eloquence—had
laughed at the Lyrical Ballads and admired Mr Southey's
Thalaba'. Esther makes her first appearance to defend Byron:
'I have a great admiration for Byron' she says, when Felix has
knocked the book down and picked it up to abuse it. Felix's
denunciation of the Byronic heroes as 'the most paltry pup-
pets that were ever pulled by the strings of lust and pride'
echoes Mrs Transome's reading list, 'She was interested in
stories of illicit passion'. The insistent details make a kind of
fluidity in the novel—the relationship of the characters chal-
lenges us to see them temporarily as doubles. But it is there for a
decided moral emphasis: Esther escapes the temptation of her
romantic dreams of love and this decomposition of character
underlines the narrowness of her escape. There, but for the
angry pedagogy of Felix, went another Mrs Transome. There

is also the human generalization and change: life repeats itself but with a difference. Where there was tragedy there is redemption, and the second chance is shown in another generation, rather as it is in *The Winter's Tale*. This gives a kind of human optimism rising above any one individual failure. We do not have to make this deduction from the formal parallel alone. The characters make it for themselves. Mrs Transome has a generalization which brackets her life with Esther's:

> 'I wish it were true, Denner,' said Mrs Transome, energetically. 'I wish he were in love with her, so that she could master him, and make him do what she pleased.'
> 'Then it is not true—what they say?'
> 'Not true that she will ever master him. No woman ever will. He will make her fond of him, and afraid of him. That's one of the things you have never gone through, Denner. A woman's love is always freezing into fear. She wants everything, she is secure of nothing. This girl has a fine spirit—plenty of fire and pride and wit. Men like such captives, as they like horses that champ the bit and paw the ground: they feel more triumph in their mastery.' (ch. xxxix)

This is actually more than a generalization. Harold, who might have made Esther's love 'freeze into fear', is the son of Jermyn —the man who mastered Mrs Transome—and heredity becomes an agent in the action. Esther's own consciousness of the parallel hastens her renunciation of what Mrs Transome chose. She is haunted by Mrs Transome's portrait:

> Pretty as this room was, she did not like it. Mrs Transome's full-length portrait, being the only picture there, urged itself too strongly on her attention: the youthful brilliancy it represented saddened Esther by its inevitable association with what she daily saw had come instead of it—a joyless, embittered age. . . . Even the flowers and the pure sunshine and the sweet waters of Paradise would have been spoiled for a young heart if the bowered walks had been haunted by an Eve gone grey with the bitter memories of an Adam who had complained, 'The woman . . . she gave me of the tree, and I did eat.' (ch. xlix)

And later:

> With a terrible prescience which a multitude of impressions during her stay at Transome Court had contributed to form, she

saw herself in a silken bondage that arrested all motive, and was nothing better than a well-cushioned despair. To be restless amidst ease, to be languid among all appliances for pleasure, was a possibility that seemed to haunt the rooms of this house, and wander with her under the oaks and elms of the park. (ch. xlix)

There are many other instances of this use of the parallels of character. There is the coincidence of Gwendolen's ambition and Mirah's achievement, partly visible to Gwendolen as she goes to hear Mirah sing:

While turning her glance towards Mirah she did not neglect to exchange a bow and smile with Klesmer as she passed. The smile seemed to each a lightning-flash back on that morning when it had been her ambition to stand as the 'little Jewess' was standing, and survey a grand audience from the higher rank of her talent—instead of which she was one of the ordinary crowd in silk and gems, whose utmost performance it must be to admire or find fault. (ch. xlv)

Gwendolen and Klesmer's recognition of the smaller irony encourages the reader to see it in full. Mirah and Gwendolen each sing, one a professional, the other an ill-taught amateur. Each has the opportunity to sell herself, but Mirah flees from her Count, who, accidentally or deliberately, seems to bear some resemblance to Grandcourt not only in his title, but in appearance, for he 'was neither very young nor very old: his hair and eyes were pale; he was tall and walked heavily and his face was heavy and grave'. There is the rather different social possibility in the parallel of Dorothea and Lydgate, so alike in mind and ardour, but—significantly—a woman without a vocation and a man with one. Here the moral is underlined further by the likeness in their lots; each chooses badly in marriage, and there is even a close repetition of scenes which echoes from one life to the other. The words 'chill' and 'yoke' are used of both marriages.

(ii)

This is not the only way of suggesting the possible and plausible life that might have been lived but was not. There is also George Eliot's special treatment of crisis and decision. She somehow manages to give an impression of inevitability which is not rigid and not artificial. Her characters 'make a moral tradition' for themselves, and their deeds determine them, but since the characters are morally 'iridescent' there is a certain stage when the determination is held in suspense. She obviously needs a strong suggestion of plausible alternatives at these moral crossroads where redemption and damnation are equally—or almost equally—likely. There are many examples, but perhaps the most striking are Maggie's, Tito's, Will Ladislaw's, and Gwendolen's.

Maggie's vision of possibility is conveyed in the imagery of the river: its enchantment, its power, its isolation, its languor. When she listens to Stephen singing, she is 'borne along by a wave too strong for her' and the metaphor comes true when she is really borne on the river with Stephen in the chapter 'Borne Along by the Tide':

Thought did not belong to that enchanted haze in which they were enveloped—it belonged to the past and the future that lay outside the haze.

Maggie listened—passing from her startled wonderment to the yearning after that belief, that the tide was doing it all—that she might glide along with the swift, silent stream, and not struggle any more.

They glided along in this way, both resting in that silence as in a haven.

Then, finally, comes the irony of Stephen's certainty:

The leap had been taken now: he had been tortured by scruples, he had fought fiercely with overmastering inclination, he had hesitated; but repentance was impossible. He murmured forth in fragmentary sentences his happiness—his adoration—his tenderness—his belief that their life together must be heaven. . . . Such things, uttered in low broken tones by the one voice that has first stirred the fibre of young passion, have only a feeble effect—on experienced minds at a distance from them. To poor Maggie they were very near: they were like nectar held close to thirsty lips: there was, there *must* be, then, a life for mortals here below which was not hard and chill—in which affection would no longer be self-sacrifice. Stephen's passionate words made the vision of such a life more fully present to her than it had ever been before; and the vision for the time excluded all realities. . . . (bk. VI, ch. xiii)

Possibilities

This part of Maggie's fantasy-life is presented strongly, and it comes back twice, with the pressure of a possibility, after she has left Stephen. It is a vision which is strictly in character. It develops all the qualities we have been shown in the earlier parts of the book—her romantic dreaming, her need of love, even her absentmindedness. But the strength of the vision is needed to show the conflict, and perhaps also to be echoed ironically at the end when her dreamy vision of effortless gliding with the stream turns out to be true, though in a different sense. Once more she is carried by the river, but does more than drift, and 'more and more strongly the energies seemed to come and put themselves forth'.

Tito's crisis of decision is the opposite of Maggie's. There is again not really any strong likelihood that Tito will free himself from the 'moral tradition'—he has already betrayed Baldassare. But there is a point where possibility suggests itself: the possibility of undoing what he has done. His subsequent failure reinforces the theme of the deeds that determine us:

> A new possibility had risen before him, which might dissolve at once the wretched conditions of fear and suppression that were marring his life. Destiny had brought within his reach an opportunity of retrieving that moment on the steps of the Duomo, when the Past had grasped him with living quivering hands, and he had disowned it. A few steps, and he might be face to face with his father, with no witness by; he might seek forgiveness and reconciliation. . . .

The moral scheme does not permit a change of heart, and one vision of possibility, based on expediency alone, is succeeded by another:

> But with this possibility of relief, by an easy spring, from present evil, there rose the other possibility, that the fierce-hearted man might refuse to be propitiated. Well—and if he did, things would only be as they had been before; for there would be *no witness by*. (ch. xxxiv)

Where the vision of possibility—like Maggie's or Tito's—is the imaginative trial of something out of keeping with the moral tradition of the character it has of course the obvious effect of insisting on the irrevocability of that tradition. But

I think it also adds a dimension to the reader's imaginative experience of the character's complexity. This is particularly true of Gwendolen's moment of choice, where she waits for Grandcourt's offer of marriage, determined to refuse. Here there is, at first reading, no sense of moral inevitability: Gwendolen's first symbolic gamble, and the subsequent exposition of her character, have remained open. It is a genuine moment of indecision which is so strong that even when one has read the book many times there remains within the wisdom which knows the event the innocence of the first reading.

The tension is introduced by the chapter-motto of chapter xxvii, which reads as irony only when we move on to the next chapter:

> He brings white asses laden with the freight
> Of Tyrian vessels, purple, gold, and balm,
> To bribe my will: I'll bid them chase him forth,
> Nor let him breathe the taint of his surmise
> On my secure resolve.

It is a slightly deceptive use of the motto, unlike the usual function of moral summary or forecast. The moment of choice is preceded and accompanied by George Eliot's close tracking of Gwendolen's oscillating reflection, and there are one or two hints that her earlier decision is weakening. But until Grandcourt begins to speak her mind is apparently made up. She is going to refuse him:

> She had never meant to form a new determination; she had only been considering what might be thought or said. If anything could have induced her to change, it would have been the prospect of making all things easy for 'poor mamma': that, she admitted, was a temptation. But no! she was going to refuse him. Meanwhile, the thought that he was coming to be refused was inspiriting. . . . (ch. xxvii)

That vision of possibility is gradually dissipated: Grandcourt asks her questions she cannot answer, because she is beginning, significantly, to be impossibly literal-minded and reflects that she cannot say 'yes' or 'no' when he asks if she is 'reckless about him'. After the next question 'Is there any man who stands between us?' she feels herself 'against a net'. This feeling of helplessness is the shifting-point. Suddenly comes another possibility. He speaks of riding away, and her reaction surprises her:

> Almost to her own astonishment, Gwendolen felt a sudden alarm at the image of Grandcourt finally riding away. What would be left her then? Nothing but the former dreariness. She liked him to be there. She snatched at the subject that would defer any decisive answer. (ch. xxvii)

The deferred answer—the evasive reference to her mother's losses—is the beginning of her capitulation. And as the veiled motto to this chapter has explained:

> Desire has trimmed the sails, and Circumstance
> Brings but the breeze to fill them.

It is a scene which manages to convince by its immediacy that this is indecision, 'the alternate dip of counterbalancing thoughts begotten of counterbalancing desires'. In George Eliot's moral scheme Gwendolen has to commit herself and choose.

This kind of possibility must be present whenever a novelist succeeds in dramatizing the tension of conflict and choice. But George Eliot also presents us with a rarer vision of possible worlds. In *Middlemarch*, for instance, we feel the pressure of an enormous number of human beings, similar and dissimilar, modifying the doctrines of the novelist as well as contributing to them. George Eliot has a simple and not very varied moral scheme but her novels are never schematic or rigid in their generalizations about human beings. The human examples are always variations of the theme rather than examples which fit it perfectly. The result is an impression of expansiveness which gives new life to the old cliché of the novelist's imagined 'world': this is like a world because of its flux and its size. This sense of expansion and movement—life going on beyond this particular selection of life, implied in all the characters, in their convincing shadows which establish them all as human centres—this depends to some extent on actuality blurring into unacted possibility.

A simple example of this pressure of possibility is found in the relations of Dorothea and Lydgate. Some readers—encouraged no doubt by the serial habit of guessing what is to follow—found some hint of a lovers' ending for these two. The reviewer in *The Edinburgh Review* for January, 1873, expected the 'real hero' to marry the 'real heroine'. The guess may have been encouraged by the initial pointed exclusion of Dorothea from Lydgate's desires:

'She is a good creature—that fine girl—but a little too earnest,' he thought. 'It is troublesome to talk to such women. They are always wanting reasons, yet they are too ignorant to understand the merits of any question, and usually fall back on their own moral sense to settle things after their own taste.' (ch. x)

This possibility, if it is felt at all, is there as a faint stirring of irony asserting itself whenever Lydgate is made to reassess his first intellectual rejection of Dorothea or to make the contrast between the woman he wanted and the woman he did not want. It is certainly not felt at all on Dorothea's side. Both Dorothea and Lydgate are committed by their disastrous desires before they meet, but Dorothea plays a larger part in his reflections than he does in hers.

The romantic possibility for Dorothea might be expected to arise in her early relation with Will, but in fact there is instead a marked and sometimes irritatingly innocent absence of the kind of speculative fantasy which might well mark such a relationship. Will, it is true, has 'dreamy visions of possibilities' but these are left vague, and George Eliot emphasizes that the precise fantasy about the future is Casaubon's, while Will takes a romantic delight in the very hopelessness of his love:

It may seem strange, but it is the fact, that the ordinary vulgar vision of which Mr Casaubon suspected him—namely, that Dorothea might become a widow, and that the interest he had established in her mind might turn to acceptance of him as a husband—had no tempting, arresting power over him; he did not live in the scenery of such an event, and follow it out, as we all do with that imagined 'otherwise' which is our practical heaven. (ch. xlvii)

Dorothea, in spite of her short-sighted abstraction from the present in dreams of 'things as they had been and were going to be', has 'no visions of their ever coming into closer union'. The innocence of this relation may be exaggerated by the sexless glamour George Eliot often casts over love, but it is presented in striking contrast to Rosamond's vulgar little dreams of uncommitted adultery. Will has certainly no room in his dreamy visions for Rosamond, but the reader's knowledge of her fantasy-life supplies an ironical supplement to their relationship.

And when he is cut off from Dorothea Will moves into a curious imagined relation with Rosamond. It is perhaps one of the best examples of what George Eliot said she wanted to show in *Middlemarch* as the slow movement of ordinary causes.

She often shows temptation as a casual almost undesired drift towards the strongest current. Fred's drift back to gambling is like this, and so in a sense, though it is also characteristic of the man, is Lydgate's drift towards the engulfing Rosamond. At one stage in *Middlemarch* both Lydgate and Ladislaw are held in moral suspense, and it is then that they come for the first time into a formally emphatic relation. Lydgate is poised between two ways, the way of redemption which means staying in Middlemarch, and the other way of capitulation, which means Rosamond's victory and departure from Middlemarch. Ladislaw, though with less prominent urgency, since his presence in the book is considerably less concentrated and sustained than Lydgate's, is also torn between staying and going. His departure is brought into direct contact with Lydgate's.

This pressure of possibility begins in the scene with Rosamond, after Dorothea's departure, when for the first time her egoism is bitten into by Will's 'I would rather touch her hand if it were dead, than I would touch any other woman's living'. Then Will's anger goes beyond his fear of what may have happened to Dorothea's faith in him, and this is where the vision of possibility comes in:

The vindictive fire was still burning in him, and he could utter no word of retraction; but it was still in his mind that having come back to this hearth where he had enjoyed a caressing friendship he had found calamity seated there—he had had suddenly revealed to him a trouble that lay outside the home as well as within it. And

what seemed a foreboding was pressing upon him with slow pincers[1]:
—that his life might come to be enslaved by this helpless woman
who had thrown herself upon him in the dreary sadness of her
heart. But he was in gloomy rebellion against the fact that his
quick apprehensiveness foreshadowed to him. . . . (ch. lxxviii)

This crisis is complicated because it is Lydgate's crisis too.
In an earlier scene with Rosamond he has failed in his effort to
'bring her to feel with some solemnity that here was a slander
which must be met and not run away from' and he has also
said to Dorothea 'I have not taken a bribe yet. But there is a
pale shade of bribery which is sometimes called prosperity.'
And there is the additional irony that Dorothea's discovery of
Will and Rosamond is brought about by her promise to help
Lydgate.

The next step brings the possibility of a linked future for the
two men:

When Lydgate spoke with desperate resignation of going to
settle in London, and said with a faint smile, 'We shall have you
again, old fellow,' Will felt inexpressibly mournful, and said
nothing. Rosamond had that morning entreated him to urge this
step on Lydgate; and it seemed to Will as if he were beholding in a
magic panorama a future where he himself was sliding into that
pleasureless yielding to the small solicitations of circumstance,
which is a commoner history of perdition than any single moment-
ous bargain.

We are on a perilous margin when we begin to look passively
at our future selves, and see our own figures led with dull consent
into insipid misdoing and shabby achievement. Poor Lydgate was
inwardly groaning on that margin, and Will was arriving at it.
(ch. lxxix)

The possibilities cross. But it is only Lydgate who is led
into the shabby achievement. The crisis gives Will's character
a measure of realistic toughening which counteracts the glamour
and innocence with which the imagery endows him. Once
more fate is seen as fragile, success as variable. The rigid moral
process is there, but so is the precariousness of chance. The

---

[1] Another echo in imagery: the 'pincers' are used of Rosamond's
power over Lydgate (chs. lxv, lxxviii). For further discussion see Chapter
XI.

elaborate pattern of reflecting mirrors is given a further recession. The real event is not only mirrored and modified in other real events but in the flickering reflection of possibilities.

These converging possibilities are present in other situations in *Middlemarch*, and with the same kind of expansive suggestiveness. There is the 'imagined otherwise' of that other set of characters, Mary, Fred, and Mr Farebrother. The happy success, both romantic and moral, which Fred and Mary achieve, is preserved from glibness by Farebrother's wry vision of possibility. As Mrs Garth says, 'she might have had a man who is worth twenty Fred Vincys', and that possibility has its brief presence in Mary's vision of the future.

'Fred has lost all his other expectations; he must keep this,' Mary said to herself, with a smile curling her lips. It was impossible to help fleeting visions of another kind—new dignities and an acknowledged value of which she had often felt the absence. But these things with Fred outside them, Fred forsaken and looking sad for the want of her, could never tempt her deliberate thought. (ch. lvii)

The possibility is strengthened when Fred begins to slide back into his old ways. Farebrother's warning words have a double irony in the context of our knowledge of Mary's fleeting visions:

'But relations of this sort, even when they are of long standing, are always liable to change. I can easily conceive that you might act in a way to loosen the tie she feels towards you—it must be remembered that she is only conditionally bound to you—and that in that case, another man, who may flatter himself that he has a hold on her regard, might succeed in winning that firm place in her love as well as respect which you had let slip. I can easily conceive such a result,' repeated Mr Farebrother, emphatically. 'There is a companionship of ready sympathy, which might get the advantage even over the longest associations.' (ch. lxvi)

The unplayed possibilities emerge everywhere in *Middlemarch*. There are the possibilities which Featherstone dangled before his prospective heirs, which certainly played a large part in Fred's life. There is Dorothea's decision to accept Casaubon's blank cheque for the future—it is cancelled only because she finds Casaubon is dead before she can accept. And there is the backward glance cast by Bulstrode, whose 'imagined otherwise' was having his time again—'And yet— if he could be back in that far-off spot with his youthful poverty—why, then he would choose to be a missionary' (ch. lxi). This persistent vision of possibilities plays an extensive part because it becomes part of the theme. Like the image of the mirror,[1] it is one of George Eliot's ways of showing the nature of illusion and the colliding multiplicity of human points of view.

The world of unrealized possibility is most prominent in *Daniel Deronda*. It first shows itself in a new way, in the actual repetition of choice. In *The Mill on the Floss* and *Romola* the heroine's choice is repeated, the decision is repeated with the opportunity, and the result is a reiteration of the moral purpose. Gwendolen, unlike Maggie and Romola, is a very uncertain character, and indeed the very shape of the novel emphasizes the uncertainty. The novel turns back on itself after first showing us Gwendolen—Gwendolen in her egoism, Gwendolen gambling, and Gwendolen raising the questions in Daniel's mind 'Was she beautiful or not beautiful?... Was the good or the evil genius dominant . . .?' This means that her first act of renunciation comes in flashback after the reckless and uncertain mood of the first scene has been established, and there is no surprise when the second temptation, or what is really the second presentation of the same temptation, made in the changed circumstances of poverty and disenchantment and humiliation, brings the new result. But the contradiction between the two moral decisions introduces the variety of possibility in Gwendolen's progress.

The central unacted possibility lies in the relation of Gwendolen and Daniel. This is another consequence of the turn in the novel. We are first presented to Gwendolen and Daniel in a promising romantic situation: he sees her gamble and asks his questions, then steps into her life by sending back the necklace she has pawned. Then the novel turns back in time and shows their separate worlds, and their firmly committed lives in those separate worlds. But the first encounter acts as a

[1] See Chapter XI below.

stímulus to expectation, and it is not only the reader who feels the pressure of possibility. The possible relations of Gwendolen and Daniel are discussed with varying degrees of seriousness by Sir Hugo and Hans Meyrick, and also in a way which recalls Will's sharp vision of a future altered by Rosamund, by Daniel himself. The part the vision plays in Gwendolen's mind is even more prominent, and makes a special irony emerge from the double action.

The ambiguity of Daniel's place in her life begins perhaps when Gwendolen asks Mr Vandernoodt—a useful functional character who turns up later in Sir Hugo's house-party and gives Daniel some necessary information about Grandcourt's past—to introduce Daniel to her. The first flicker of other possibilities comes—though not till the second reading—when we read: 'But Gwendolen did not make Deronda's acquaintance on this occasion. Mr Vandernoodt did not succeed in bringing him up to her that evening, and when she re-entered her own room she found a letter recalling her home' (ch. i).

She is not yet committed, but after fourteen chapters in which we go back to the beginning of Gwendolen's acquaintance with Grandcourt, we turn to Daniel. The double plot, as in *Middlemarch*, can hold characters in convenient suspension, and here the reader is put in the same position as Gwendolen: interest is aroused and information is withheld. But after the fourteen chapters the reader's position shifts to something approaching the omniscient author's. We share the direct impact of her ambiguous interest but then receive our fuller knowledge, from which Gwendolen herself is excluded:

'You won't run after the pretty gambler, then?' said Sir Hugo, putting down his glasses.
'Decidedly not.'
This answer was perfectly truthful; nevertheless it had passed through Deronda's mind that under other circumstances he should have given way to the interest this girl had raised in him, and tried to know more of her. But his history had given him a strong bias in another direction. He felt himself in no sense free. (ch. xv)

With an easy transition the two actions then begin their movement in counterpoint. Having followed Gwendolen for fourteen chapters, we return to Leubronn and Deronda, accompanying Grandcourt as he follows Gwendolen. Daniel's flashback emerges as the parallel of Gwendolen's and with the parallel comes the slowly growing irony. It is another way of giving full expression to the theme of isolation which she had expressed in *Middlemarch*, and it is also the emphatic expression of Daniel's destined vocation. The pull which the two actions exercise on each other intensifies the fantasy with which George Eliot presents, in images and premonitions, the destiny of Daniel Deronda.

The misinterpretation of Daniel's interest in Gwendolen runs like a thread through the book, sometimes there as a piece of comic ignorance on the part of Sir Hugo or Hans, sometimes making the further ironies of Mirah's and Grandcourt's jealousy. It is not until Grandcourt's death that Gwendolen's vision of Daniel's relation to her becomes tragically prominent. It is not Gwendolen alone who has this vision at this point in the story. The crudest reaction is Sir Hugo's— he has earlier warned Daniel against 'playing with fire', and he comes to hope that 'the lofty and inscrutable Dan' should have no scheme 'in his head, which would prove to be dearer to him than the lovely Mrs Grandcourt'. 'To him it was as pretty a story as need be that this fine creature and his favourite Dan should have turned out to be formed for each other, and that the unsuitable husband should have made his exit in such excellent time' (ch. lxiv). Then there is Daniel's sense of commitment:

We do not argue the existence of the anger or the scorn that thrills through us in a voice; we simply feel it, and it admits of no disproof. Deronda felt this woman's destiny hanging on his over a precipice of despair. Any one who knows him cannot wonder at his inward confession, that if all this had happened little more than a year ago, he would hardly have asked himself whether he loved her: the impetuous determining influence which would have moved him would have been to save her from sorrow, to shelter her life for evermore from the dangers of loneliness, and carry out to the last the rescue he had begun in that monitory redemption of the necklace. But now, love and duty had thrown other bonds around him, and that impulse could no longer determine his life; still, it was present in him as a compassionate yearning, a painful quivering at the very imagination of having again and again to meet the appeal of her eyes and words. (ch. lxv)

He goes to her when she asks for him and says, 'Think that a severe angel, seeing you along the road of error, grasped you by the wrist, and showed you the horror of the life you must avoid', and Gwendolen, like Maggie or Romola or even Fred Vincy, has the sensation of a new beginning. Her vision of Daniel's place in her future is managed with extraordinary tact:

But the new existence seemed inseparable from Deronda: the hope seemed to make his presence permanent. It was not her thought, that he loved her and would cling to her—a thought would have tottered with improbability: it was her spiritual breath. For the first time since that terrible moment on the sea a flush rose and spread over her cheek, brow, and neck, deepened an instant or two, and then gradually disappeared.

And a little later in the same chapter:

She was in that state of unconscious reliance and expectation which is a common experience with us when we are preoccupied with our own trouble or our own purposes. We diffuse our feeling over others, and count on their acting from our motives. Her imagination had not been turned to a future union with Deronda by any other than the spiritual tie which had been continually strengthening; but also it had not been turned towards a future separation from him. Love-making and marriage—how could they now be the imagery in which poor Gwendolen's deepest attachment could spontaneously clothe itself? (ch. lxv)

With the end of the novel the two actions come together in collision, and Gwendolen for the first time shares the reader's view of Daniel's separate world.

There are many ironies confirmed and brought together by Gwendolen's final exclusion. There is first George Eliot's rejection of the ending she had used in the two preceding novels —the combination of a happy ending and a moral victory. Esther and Fred Vincy confirm their moral progress by marrying their mentors. Gwendolen is left alone, and for her the loneliness seems to be the only appropriate state. It is rather like the storm for Lear—we are conscious of the tragic reversal of power, warmth, ceremony, illusion, and love. For Gwendolen the final loneliness is not only an extension of suffering when she feels she has already suffered and recovered, but a suggestion that her tragic nurture is still incomplete. It is expressed in terms of her egoism, in terms of her innocence in the world of action and great causes (to which Daniel belongs), and in terms of her superstitious fear, which has been kept in our minds throughout the book. There is even the backward glance at her early casual anti-Semitism, when she dismisses the Jew dealers as unscrupulous. Her discovery is made slowly: 'I hope there is nothing to make you mind. *You* are just the same as if you were not a Jew.' Then he tells her that he is glad of the discovery, and his words inspire her 'with a dreadful presentiment of mountainous travel for her mind before it could reach Deronda's'. When he explains his political mission, she undergoes the equivalent of Rosamond's experience when forced by Will's anger to see the world outside herself. Gwendolen thinks that she has suffered in her marriage, and she thinks she has learnt a tragic lesson, but her egoism is to meet another violent shock. It has been prepared for not only by our knowledge of Daniel's commitment but our knowledge of her careless ignorance of 'the great movements of the world':

There comes a terrible moment to many souls when the great movements of the world, the larger destinies of mankind, which have lain aloof in newspapers and other neglected reading, enter like an earthquake into their own lives. . . .
She was for the first time feeling the pressure of a vast mysterious movement, for the first time being dislodged from her supremacy in her own world, and getting a sense that her horizon was but a dipping onwards of an existence with which her own was revolving. All the troubles of her wifehood and widowhood had still left her with the implicit impression which had accompanied her from childhood, that whatever surrounded her was somehow specially for her, and it was because of this that no personal jealousy had been roused in her in relation to Deronda: she could not spontaneously think of him as rightfully belonging to others more than to her. (ch. lxix)

This is still before she knows that Daniel is going to marry Mirah. Her reaction to 'I am going to marry' is done entirely from the outside, from Daniel's point of view and from the tense dialogue. There is no return to Gwendolen's consciousness—in fact the only return to her in any way is in her short letter to Daniel on his marriage. Her shock is presented partly by the long elaborate exposition describing her reaction to Daniel's vocation, and by the contrasting absence of any commentary on her reaction to his love and marriage. We are abruptly shut off from her responses.

The novel has an open ending, in very marked contrast to the closed conclusions of death and marriage in the earlier books, and in particularly marked contrast to the end of *Middlemarch*, where the moral direction of each set of characters is established, and their future lives briefly and definitely surveyed. In this way *Daniel Deronda*, for all its flaws, is an experiment in realism.

This openness must not be exaggerated. As far as Daniel Deronda's Zionist mission is concerned, silence is plainly as necessary as it is at the end of *The Family Reunion*. But as far as Gwendolen's future is concerned, the novel is as functionally non-committal as the end of *The Portrait of a Lady*. It is true there is a moral conclusion: Gwendolen is 'redeemed'—as George Eliot had promised Blackwood when he began to read the book—and her letter to Daniel has a moral finality. It is also true that there is a very faint and tactful and almost unobtrusive suggestion of a possibility that appeared at the beginning of the novel. When George Eliot first presents Rex and Gwendolen in the imagery of youth and nature with the pathetic wish that they could pledge themselves 'then and there' she makes some preparation for Hans Meyrick's suggestion. This is only a hint (one taken, by the way, by Henry James's Theodora), and it is carefully placed in the prejudiced speech of a character. Hans says: 'I understand now why Gascoigne talks of making the law his mistress and remaining a bachelor. But these are green resolves. Since the duke did not get himself drowned for your sake, it may turn out to be for my friend Rex's sake. Who knows?' (ch. lx).

Speculation is checked by Daniel, whose reaction (a well-observed mixture of guilt and disapproval) reminds the reader that 'Hans's success in constructing her fortunes hitherto had not been enough to warrant a new attempt', and by Rex him-

self, who suppresses his first reaction—the 'egoistic escapes of
the imagination'—to the news of Grandcourt's death by
saying to himself 'She would not have me on any terms, and
I would not ask her. It is a meanness to be thinking about it
now—no better than lurking about the battle-field to strip
the dead . . .' (ch. lviii). But the question has at least arisen,
and Rex is brought back into our interest, briefly but sharply
after a long absence. It remains as almost less than a possibility, and George Eliot's own voice says nothing. The novel
expands through its open ending, an ending rare in its century though common enough in ours, where the openness
is sometimes organic or sometimes an inconclusive playing at
slice-of-life realism. A striking illustration of the rareness of
this kind of ending is found in the objection, made by the
reviewer in *The Westminster Review* of April 1859, that even
the ending of *Adam Bede* was 'abrupt':

The reader longs to know somewhat of the fate of Hetty during
those dreary years of transportation, as well as the circumstances of
her death. It would also be a satisfaction to him to be informed of the
chief events of Arthur Donnithorne's life after his return to Hayslope.

For Gwendolen and for Isabel Archer the unfinished ending
has genuine thematic significance. Dr Leavis does not mention
this resemblance, but it strengthens his comparison of the
two novels. For both Gwendolen and Isabel the blank future has
its moral import, but in *The Portrait of a Lady* Isabel returns
to the world she has left, while Gwendolen's is the isolation of
a new beginning. Isabel is left without her other possible
worlds, all of which she rejects in favour of the undesired
return to Gilbert and her promise to Pansy. Gwendolen is
free from her imprisoning marriage, but she is now without
Daniel, and the ending gives us the imaginative equivalent of
the shock of space confronting a narrow and protected vision
for the first time. There is perhaps the slight invitation to
speculate, but it is vague. The very openness checks speculation by its lack of cues. Blackwood wrote to her on 12 July
1876 after finishing the book: 'There will I know be disappointment at not hearing more of the failure of Gwendolen
and the mysterious destiny of Deronda, but I am sure you are
right to leave all grand and vague' (Haight, vi, p. 272).

CHAPTER VIII

The Author's Voice:
Intimate, Prophetic, and Dramatic

(i)

I HAVE already said something about George Eliot's direct appeal to the reader. This can take the form of direct interpretation of characters who have been deliberately deprived of an articulate voice of their own. It can also take the form of a gloss or a generalization made from an apparently detached viewpoint. The author's 'voice' is itself a formal constituent: it shifts the point of view, it frames and underlines characters or groups or actions, and it often gives us an explicit clue to the oblique statements made by pattern or imagery. But this voice is not static and unchanging. It is a voice with different tones, and it is also a voice whose significance lies in silence as well as speech.

George Eliot's voice is sometimes a fictitious one, like the professional voice of the author in Scott and Thackeray and Conrad, though it is never presented with the status of a dramatically conceived personality like a Pendennis or a Marlow. To begin with, in *Scenes of Clerical Life* and *Adam Bede*, the voice is masculine. It is the voice of the pseudonym,[1] and its tone and reference are often elaborate and pointed reminders of the author's assumed masculinity, as self-conscious as Meredith's assumption of the feminine voice for Dame Gossip's interventions in *The Amazing Marriage*. There is more than a reminder of masculinity: there is also an extended quasi-autobiographical reference which speaks directly for George Eliot's exploration of her early life as well as having the important function of making a special context for the characters, a context of intimacy and familiarity. The voice

[1] This was first used in a letter to William Blackwood (Haight, ii, p. 292) and appeared as a formal pseudonym when the *Scenes* were published in volume form.

of the story-teller in *Scenes of Clerical Life* is the voice of someone remembering, and the memory gives us the impression
of someone who has—even if very slightly—a stake in the
story.

It is this voice of personal knowledge and recollection, for
instance, which introduces the story of *The Sad Fortunes of
Amos Barton* by establishing the place and the period. The
period is that of 'five-and-twenty years ago' and it is the voice
of memory which acts as a calendar:

> Mine, I fear, is not a well-regulated mind: it has an occasional
> tenderness for old abuses; it lingers with a certain fondness over the
> days of the nasal clerks and topbooted parsons, and has a sigh for
> the departed shades of vulgar errors. So it is not surprising that I
> recall with a fond sadness Shepperton Church as it was in the
> old days. . . . (ch. i)

There are of course excellent reasons for the casting-back in
time. George Eliot seems to have needed the feeling of distance and understanding, as a creative condition. Her past
experience is recollected in tranquillity as she works back
through the layers of experience (her metaphor) and achieves
detachment and confidence and a sense of a period and place
framed and formulated by the passing of time. Moreover the
gradual fading-out from present to past is an excellent introduction to a story, which she uses again in *Mr Gilfil's Love-
Story* and *The Mill on the Floss*. It combines the presentation
of the author as character with the necessary historical exposition. The voice here is nostalgic, possessive, and personal.
Such things as historical or topographical detail are fused with
the reminiscences of touring memory.

It is this nostalgic and reminiscent voice which presents
the characters of the story—at this stage, also taken from
actual recollection—and these characters are presented in the
context of familiar knowledge and attachment. It is an
affectionate voice which makes the introduction, and the stake
in the real past gives the necessary excuse for the lingering
affectionateness. Pity itself is given the excuse of nostalgia:
this happened long ago, and the people are dead, or old, or
changed. In *Amos Barton*, we hear of George Eliot as a little
'boy', being given bread-and-butter in church by his nurse.

In *Mr Gilfil's Love-Story* 'he' talks to people about the past, and tells it from his memory and knowledge. In *Janet's Repentance* 'he' gives a brief detail of being present at the confirmation service, as 'an unimaginative boy'. In *Adam Bede*, as we have seen, 'he'—though the sexual reminders have ceased to be persistent—holds a conversation with Adam Bede about Mr Irwine. This kind of anecdotic comment goes beyond the bare need of choric appeal and generalization, but it creates a context where the choric comment becomes personal and dramatic, and is not the sharply distinct voice of the author making his story. The story is told as the thing remembered, not the thing invented, and this dramatic use of memory, strong in the early stories, leaves its traces to the last.

The familiarity of tone extends to the reader as well as the characters. The characters are people she, or 'he', has known; the 'dear reader' is as present as the vividly silent listener in Browning's monologues. He is a reader sometimes particularized as male or female, sometimes reproved for his literary taste and reading habits, sometimes rejected as unsympathetic, sometimes apologized to with disarming irony. The address is sometimes heavy in its archness, sometimes surprisingly effective as a dramatic means of smooth transition or effortless introduction. In *Adam Bede*, for instance, the reader is presented with a description by being invited to follow a conducted tour. When characters are presented for the first time the reader may be treated as an actual though invisible presence, as he is in the Chapter called 'The Rector':

Let me take you into that dining-room. . . . We will enter very softly . . . the walls, you see, are new. . . . He will perhaps turn round by-and-by, and in the mean time we can look at that stately old lady. . . . (ch. v)

It is the convention of the reader's presence and the author's limitations. The polite pretence is that neither reader nor author knows whether that character is going to turn round, nor what will happen when he does. Its function, I suppose, is that of making an introduction immediate and visually precise while keeping it fairly formal. It is not a device which she labours and it can be easily dropped for another convention, as indeed it is later in this same chapter, when we are being introduced to Arthur Donnithorne: 'If you want to know more particularly how he looked, call to your remembrance some tawny-whiskered, brown-locked, clear-complexioned young Englishman whom you have met with in a foreign town.' As an introduction this is equally direct and immediate, and has the additional function—important to our reception of Arthur as a character—of inviting us to give him a place in our own generalization. This kind of device may also be the result of George Eliot's visual habits: there is a marked precision in her descriptions which often extends to the author's visible or invisible stance in the scene. The point of view, in the literal sense of the term, is usually precisely placed.

Visual habits are perhaps less important here than the insistence on personal knowledge. The tone is personal: it is the tone of voice in which the author tells a story about remembered people. It is also the tone in which she addresses a living reader. There are many places even in the early stories where the intimate chatting voice is apparently felt to be inappropriate and is dropped in favour of a more neutral and impersonal tragic reflection, but the sense of the reader and the intimacy of the author makes itself felt as part of the whole fabric of narrative. It may well have been of great importance in George Eliot's practical scene-shifting, and it is a technical device which is bound to strike many modern readers as offensively cosy, but it is more than a mere device: it is part of the tone of familiarity which George Eliot, from the beginning of her writing life to the end, diffused through her novels. It presents her, knowing, watching, and pitying, untroubled by the creative contradiction that the author is destiny but must deplore the destiny, that the author is omnipotent but must appear to be merely omnipresent.

In *Scenes of Clerical Life* the archness of the familiar voice is probably more irritating than in the later novels because it is the prevailing tone. Moreover the tone of voice here has a fairly small range, and the range could be indicated, without too much simplification, as extending from arch irony to extreme pathos. But it begins to enlarge its range as early as *Adam Bede*—in fact, as soon as George Eliot embarks on a long novel, her tone of voice becomes much more mobile and varied. Irony comes in now in the author's presentation of her characters, not merely in her critical rebuke to her reader. The voice which speaks of Hetty, for instance, can speak with sympathy and pathos and also with harsh irony: 'Ah, what a prize the man gets who wins a sweet bride like Hetty! How the men envy him who come to the wedding breakfast, and see her hanging on his arm in her white lace and orange blossoms. The dear young, round, soft, flexible thing!' (ch. xv). Here the overloaded sweetness is the first half of an ironical reversal in an image which recapitulates the sweetness and softness and roundness but revalues the qualities by putting them in a new context: 'No: people who love downy peaches are apt not to think of the stone, and sometimes jar their teeth terribly against it.' Here the author's voice is confirmed by another voice within the story, for Mrs Poyser gives a faint but clear echo of the image when she is reported, later in the chapter, as saying, 'It's my belief her heart's as hard as a pibble'.

There is genuine unironical warmth and pathos in some of George Eliot's comments on Hetty—in her account of Adam's response to Hetty's beauty, for instance, as a good and natural thing. The harsh irony which classifies Hetty with the peach can give way to a calmer tone. It is still stern but without exclamatoriness or violence:

Does any sweet or sad memory mingle with this dream of the future—any loving thought of her second parents—of the children she had helped to tend—of any youthful companion, any pet animal, any relic of her childhood even? Not one. There are some plants that have hardly any roots. . . . (ch. xv)

It is a quiet rhetoric, a question elaborated lingeringly and extenuatingly, then answered with brief certainty. It is this stern calm which is the prevailing tone of *Adam Bede*, just as excited pathetic demand is the prevailing tone of *Scenes of Clerical Life*—which is not meant to suggest that either is a narrative delivered in a single tone. The emotional canvassing of *Scenes of Clerical Life* is more peremptory and at the same time implicitly superior in its sensibility and intelligence. As

I have already suggested, in *Adam Bede* the gap between character and author narrows, and though the tone of the narration is still maternal, it is calmer, gravely reconciled to the limitations it mourns, gravely joyful in the possibilities it applauds. Adam and Dinah, with all their simplicity—in social status, or in religious belief—are presented as equals:

> For Adam, though you see him quite master of himself, working hard and delighting in his work after his inborn inalienable nature, had not outlived his sorrow—had not felt it slip from him as a temporary burthen, and leave him the same man again. Do any of us? God forbid. (ch. 1)

The fictitious mask is no longer necessary. This is the voice of George Eliot or Marian Evans at its calmest and most intense, without disguise, exaggeration, or arch humour.

From *Adam Bede* onwards this undisguised voice is heard. In *The Mill on the Floss* there is a continued sorrowful affectionateness, but it has very little of the overflowing pathos of the early pleading for Amos Barton. Maggie can represent and recognize tragic endurance as Janet could not, though there is still a protectiveness in the author's sorrow and affection which comes out strongly as it regards the unprotected female plight. For all her sensibility and wit, Maggie is more defenceless than Adam Bede, and George Eliot's pitying voice accompanies her through all the stages of her tragic history, darkening even the apparent brightness of the early scenes. In Maggie's childhood the author's voice laments the end of childhood, and as Maggie grows up the pity increases in intensity. It is not always the omniscient glance ahead which casts the shadow. It is sometimes the intensifying movement from the case of Maggie to the human generalization. When the Tullivers lose their money and Mr Tulliver is sick and humiliated, Maggie is forced into loneliness and apathy. Tom can go out to redeem the family pride and fortune, she can only look at her lost enchantments. The author's voice moves away from Maggie, with the wisdom of maturity pitying youth:

> There is no hopelessness so sad as that of early youth, when the soul is made up of wants, and has no long memories, no super-added life in the life of others; though we who look on think

lightly of such premature despair, as if our vision of the future lightened the blind sufferer's present. (bk. III, ch. v)

Here there is no condescension: the personal voice puts the author—and the reader—inside the experience and not above it or outside it. There is more reflection and less lyrical pathos than we find even in *Adam Bede*, though passion is often present in the compression of metaphor rather than in the direct statement:

It is the moment when our resolution seems about to become irrevocable—when the fatal iron gates are about to close upon us— that tests our strength. Then, after hours of clear reasoning and firm conviction, we snatch at any sophistry that will nullify our long struggles, and bring us the defeat we love better than victory. (bk. v, ch. iii)

These are the words used to describe Maggie's recoiling resolution after she first tells Philip that friendship with him is impossible, and must be denied both on the grounds of family loyalty and her private effort to 'subdue her will'. The author's generalization is a passing of judgement, but it is made in the warm and tolerant tones of shared experience. It is not a sententious comment: the reflective judgement is warmed by the passionate image which retains something of the urgency of Marvell's original use, though here the gates are prison gates and cannot be challenged by exhilaration. The very contrast has something of the irony of inappropriate allusion. Maggie is a long way from *The Coy Mistress* though the situations are not wholly unlike.

This oblique way of combining the author's warmth and sympathy with the calmer or dryer tones of reflective comment continues throughout the later novels. Alexander Main, in an unpublished letter[1] (21 August 1872), notices the increase in generalization in the style from *Romola* onwards, though he insists that there is also an increase in emotional intensity and certainly no accompanying loss of dramatic life. Henry James's Constantius, on the contrary, notices the same change but with disapproval:

Her spontaneous part is to observe life and to feel it—to feel it

[1] National Library of Scotland, Edinburgh.

with admirable depth. Contemplation, sympathy, and faith—
something like that, I should say, would have been her natural
scale. . . . But she has chosen to go into criticism, and to the
critics she addresses her work; I mean the critics of the universe.

The following examples, taken at random, demonstrate the reflective commentary, though they are—by accident—amongst
the more directly emotional appeals to the reader in the last
four novels and therefore not quite representative. But they all
combine the reflective tone with the bid for sympathy:

With the sinking of high human trust, the dignity of life sinks
too; we cease to believe in our own better self, since that also is
part of the common human nature which is degraded in our
thought; and all the finer impulses of the soul are dulled. Romola
felt even the springs of her once active pity drying up, and leaving
her to barren egoistic complaining. (*Romola*, ch. lxi)

Why was it, when the birds were singing, when the fields were a
garden, and when we were clasping another little hand just larger
than our own, there was somebody who found it hard to smile?
Esther had got far beyond that childhood to a time and circumstances when this daily presence of elderly dissatisfaction amidst
such outward things as she had always thought must greatly help
to satisfy, awaked, not merely vague questioning emotion, but
strong determining thought. (*Felix Holt*, ch. xlix)

Not that this inward amazement of Dorothea's was anything very
exceptional: many souls in their young nudity are tumbled out
among incongruities and left 'to find their feet' among them, while
their elders go about their business. Nor can I suppose that when
Mrs Casaubon is discovered in a fit of weeping six weeks after her
wedding, the situation will be regarded as tragic. . . . That element
of tragedy which lies in the very fact of frequency, has not yet
wrought itself into the coarse emotion of mankind; and perhaps
our frames could hardly bear much of it. If we had a keen vision
and feeling of all ordinary human life, it would be like hearing the
grass grow and the squirrel's heart beat, and we should die of that
roar which lies on the other side of silence. (*Middlemarch*, ch. xx)

Could there be a slenderer, more insignificant thread in human
history than this consciousness of a girl, busy with her small inferences of the way in which she could make her life pleasant?—in
a time, too, when ideas were with fresh vigour making armies of
themselves, and the universal kinship was declaring itself fiercely.
(*Daniel Deronda*, ch. xi)

Intimate, Prophetic and Dramatic

The first three extracts are reflective commentaries which present shrewd observations about the mind and conduct of her characters. All four passages make the characteristic shift from particular to general. This constant movement away from the actual case before us is itself the reminder of 'that element of tragedy which lies in the very fact of frequency', but it is a special kind of generalization, one made with a vigour of feeling which makes it more than an academic admission. The voice is still personal though the tone is quiet and calm, without intense solicitation. The quality we may call 'personal' is hard to pinpoint in style: it seems to come from such things as colloquial language, the inclusive use of 'we', the questioning address, and—almost always—the poetic image which lights the reflective passage. The direct appeal still appears from time to time—it is there in the second extract above, from *Felix Holt*, and less pathetic, but still direct, in the last extract, from *Daniel Deronda*, but the intense soliciting voice of *Scenes of Clerical Life* has in general become quieter, more neutral, and more reasonable.

The compassion never dies out of George Eliot's commentary. Even when this commentary takes the form of explanation and analysis it still makes a context of brooding solicitude which surrounds the characters. But it is not unreservedly compassionate, and even though there are very few characters who do not move in the medium of their author's considerate sympathy, there are many occasions when the accompanying tone changes from sympathy to impatience and highly critical irony. We have already seen one crude and early instance of George Eliot's scathing irony in her description of Hetty, where exaggeration is followed by harsh deflation—the most blatant form of the ironical habit of saying the opposite of what you mean. In later novels the irony is less harsh and less explicit: the reader is left to translate the exaggeration into the truth for himself. There is a good example in the passages which introduce Dorothea in *Middlemarch*, though here the irony comes into the *oratio obliqua* which is only grammatically the author's commentary, and is in all important senses the revelation of the character's consciousness. We first see Dorothea, innocent and confident in her inexperience. There is vigorous irony, and it is not directed, as Dr Leavis suggests, only to the environment. Dorothea's sensibility and 'views' are mocked in these brief hits:

> Riding was an indulgence which she allowed herself in spite of conscientious qualms; she felt that she enjoyed it in a pagan sensuous way, and always looked forward to renouncing it. (ch. i)

> The really delightful marriage must be that where your husband was a sort of father, and could teach you even Hebrew, if you wished it. (ch. i)

In many comments of this kind, and in several apparently casual episodes such as the conversation with Sir James Chettam about the Maltese puppy which Dorothea suddenly rejects as 'parasitic', her opinion 'forming itself that very moment (as opinions will) under the heat of irritation', there is a strong irony which verges on comedy. But it is true that once Dorothea is embarked on the tragic experience, once she is married to Casaubon, her author seems suddenly to exempt her from irony. There is criticism, but it is both infrequent and gentle, and irony is succeeded by the strong sympathy of direct comment and of romantic and ideal images such as the continual similes of childhood, the image of the Aeolian Harp for her voice, and the suggestions of the 'benignant matron'. I shall say more about this in a later chapter. It is not quite accurate, I think, to suggest that this sentimental bid for sympathy is the prevailing tone: it certainly plays a very large part in the portrayal of Dorothea's relation with Will, but a smaller part than Dr Leavis suggests in the portrait as a whole. There is undoubtedly a certain abruptness—almost a dislocation—about the withdrawal of the strong irony, and I remember feeling this abruptness very strongly on first reading the novel. But irony is not the only corrective to excessive sympathy and pathos, and George Eliot's reflective tone acts throughout the novel as a strong corrective, even when it is used at the same time as a sentimental image. When Dorothea sees Will clasping Rosamond's hands her first reaction is described in these terms:

> It was as if she had drunk a great draught of scorn that stimulated her beyond the susceptibility to other feelings. She had seen

something so far below her belief, that her emotions rushed back from it and made an excited throng without an object. (ch. lxxvii)

This is dramatic exposition: the image has an animation and a movement which fits the reaction it describes and gives life to the psychological observation. After this first reaction of scorn, Dorothea breaks down, and the imagery changes—to some extent—in its nature. It becomes imagery charged with the author's pity, not merely subdued to the appropriateness of the occasion. This is a representative extract:

In that hour she repeated what the merciful eyes of solitude have looked on for ages in the spiritual struggles of man—she besought hardness and coldness and aching weariness to bring her relief from the mysterious incorporeal night of her anguish: she lay on the bare floor and let the night grow cold around her; while her grand woman's frame was shaken by sobs as if she had been a despairing child.

There were two images—two living forms that tore her heart in two, as if it had been the heart of a mother who seems to see her child divided by the sword, and presses one bleeding half to her breast while her gaze goes forth in agony towards the half which is carried away by the lying woman that has never known the mother's pang. (ch. lxxx)

The image of the torn child is dramatic observation, and not the author's lament. The child is Will Ladislaw: 'the bright creature whom she had trusted' and 'the Will Ladislaw who was a changed belief exhausted of hope'. The judgment of Solomon metaphor in the second paragraph is at first sight more appropriate in its physical violence than in its literal content, though it may well carry ironical echoes of Dorothea's sterile marriage and Rosamond's careless miscarriage. But these are undertones—this is the exaggeration which conveys hysteria; in the first paragraph the general comment and the contrast of 'grand woman's frame' and 'despairing child' seem to be placed at a remove from the dramatic impression of Dorothea's emotional state. These phrases convey pitiableness indirectly through the author's pity, while the violent Biblical image is a direct dramatic equivalent. The separation is arbitrary, perhaps, for the dramatic immediacy and the external comment are placed together, but they do appear to me to be two different ways of presenting the situation. After Dorothea begins to recover, the commentary grows more neutral in its observation:

> All the active thought with which she had before been representing to herself the trials of Lydgate's lot, and this young marriage union which, like her own, seemed to have its hidden as well as evident troubles—all this vivid sympathetic experience returned to her now as a power: it asserted itself as acquired knowledge asserts itself and will not let us see as we saw in the day of our ignorance. She said to her own irremediable grief, that it should make her more helpful, instead of driving her back from effort. (ch. lxxx)

Dorothea's tragic catharsis, purging her of self-absorption, depends as much on this calm reflective comment as on the dramatic excitement of the earlier passages. George Eliot's is a voice with many tones, and it is possible to trace their changes within her writing as a whole and within the changing situations and moods of a single novel.

(ii)

But there is a prophetic voice as well as an intimate one, making itself heard, directly and obliquely, in the elaborate pattern of anticipation and retrospect. This pattern binds the novel together, has mnemonic advantages for writer and reader, and has its own special kind of irony which contrasts past and present, author's omniscience and character's innocence.

Most novelists have this concern with unity and tension, though it seldom takes the form of the obsession with dramatic tautness which we find in Henry James. He says in his Preface to the New York edition of *The Tragic Muse*:

> The first half of a fiction insists ever on figuring to me as the stage of the theatre for the second half, and I have in general given so much space to making the theatre propitious that my halves have too often proved strangely unequal.

James's interest in formal premonition probably had its source in his playwriting as well as his habit of serializing. George

Eliot's preoccupation with premonition can sometimes, though certainly not always, be referred to serial publication. The most striking instances of the serial tension are to be found in her first story, and this was very likely written with the serial form in mind. When Lewes writes to Blackwood about *Amos Barton*, he says that it is calculated to be published in two parts in 'Maga', and George Eliot, in her journal for December 1857 (Haight ii, p. 407), describing the writing of this first story, says that it was written with publication in *Blackwood's* in mind. The first chapter of the first instalment of her published fiction ends with the serialist's enigmatic glance ahead:

The thing we look forward to often comes to pass, but never precisely in the way we have imagined to ourselves. The Countess did actually leave Camp Villa before many months were past, but under circumstances which had not at all entered into her contemplation. (*Blackwood's*, January 1857)

When read before the words, *To be continued*,[1] this break has an obvious function, even in a two-part serial. And although the next instalment does not begin with a full recapitulation, its address to the reader is a step backward, before taking a step forward:

The Rev. Amos Barton, whose sad fortunes I have undertaken to relate, was, you perceive, in no respect an ideal or exceptional character, and perhaps I am doing a bold thing to bespeak your sympathy on behalf of a man who was so very far from remarkable. . . . (Part ii, ch. v)

Here the overlap of anticipation and recapitulation may be determined by the serial form, but as I have already said, it is dangerous to make too much of this influence. By no means all George Eliot's serial instalments begin and end so neatly on a rising intonation and a familiar backward glance. By no means all her designed tensions and ironies are there to keep the serial-reader's curiosity alive. The reader of *Mr Gilfil's Love-Story* had to wait for a month after Tina's discovery of Anthony lying in The Rookery—'Anthony, Anthony! speak

---

[1] 'To be continued' does conclude this Part, though the formula is not always used in serials of the time.

to me—it is Tina—speak to me! O God, he is dead!'—but it is very hard to find any comparable curtain-lines in *Romola*, which was, not surprisingly, no great success as a serial, as Blackwood had predicted when he heard that George Eliot had left 'the old colours' for Smith and Elder.

George Eliot's consciousness of the lack of balance in *The Mill on the Floss*, though formulated very differently, testifies to a concern for preparation equal to that of Henry James. It could usually be said of her novels that the first half—four were first published as serials[1]—insists on figuring as the stage for the second. In her case there is a special need for a strong and binding tension. It is less the aesthetic dislike of accidentality, as it is in Henry James, than a moral reliance on the continuity of past and present, comparable (and often compared) with Proust's sense of time and time's landmarks, and also comparable (though less often compared) with Wordsworth's use of nature and memory to bind experience together and keep the past living in the present. Her Don Silva demands 'A Past that lives On through an added Present'. Her own feeling of horror when her rejection of Christianity seemed to dislocate past and present, reason and emotion, is repeated in different forms in most of her heroines, and continuity emerges as a major theme in her novels. There is the practical result that her characters are often looking back, and when they do not, she looks back for them. When they look forward, they are often inaccurate, and their illusion and innocence is given an additional irony by being placed beside a more accurate forecast, either made directly by the author, or by other characters, or by the suggestiveness of imagery and objects. The reader is constantly pushed from the present moment into a future, hazily sketched and half-defined, and not fully forecast except on a few exceptional occasions. It is of course only a few of the hints and forebodings which are apparent on a first reading, and there are a very large number which do no more than contradict the characters' premonitions and hopes, and put the reader in a position of curious and disturbing expectation. There are hints newly noticed on each fresh reading which form part of the

[1] *Scenes of Clerical Life*, *Romola*, *Middlemarch*, and *Daniel Deronda*.

novelist's brooding over the novel as a whole, seeing the first
half as stage for the second, seeing the end in the beginning
and the whole in the parts. Although George Eliot published
some of her novels in parts she did not write hand-to-mouth,
like Dickens, and made relatively few changes[1] (compared say,
with Meredith) after her manuscript had been sent to the
publisher. There is probably a real sense in which our feeling
of continuity comes from her anticipation as she wrote.

The most obvious kind of premonition is the innocent and
casual remark made in the course of dialogue, not revealing its
irony until long after. Even on a first reading we may remember some of these idle hints, because George Eliot often links
them in a chain of recurrence. There are the constant references to death by drowning in *The Mill on the Floss*, ranging
from Mrs Tulliver's maternal fussing to Philip's grave jokes:

'Ah, I thought so—wanderin' up an' down by the water, like a
wild thing: she'll tumble in some day.' (bk. I, ch. ii)

'Maggie, Maggie . . . where's the use o' my telling you to keep
away from the water? You'll tumble in and be drownded some day,
an' then you'll be sorry you didn't do as mother told you.' (bk.
I, ch. ii)

'When I'm a man, I shall make a boat with a wooden house on
the top of it, like Noah's ark. . . . And then if the flood came, you
know, Bob, I shouldn't mind. . . . And I'd take you in, if I saw you
swimming,' he added, in the tone of a benevolent patron. (Tom to
Bob, bk. I, ch. vi)

'There's a story as when the mill changes hands, the river's
angry—I've heard my father say it many a time.' (Mr Tulliver—
bk. III, ch. ix)

'. . . Else she will be selling her soul to that ghostly boatman who
haunts the Floss—only for the sake of being drifted in a boat for
ever.' (bk. VI, ch. xiii)

The individual appearance may be innocent, but there is
a cumulative anticipation, noticeable in varying degrees.
Sometimes the hint is an exact prophecy, like the first two

---

[1] For some examples of her revision, see Professor Haight's notes to
his edition of *Middlemarch*. Some revision was made for the edition of
1874. See also Jerome Beaty's article in *P.M.L.A*, lxxii, (1957), pp.
662–79, 'Visions and Revisions: Chapter LXXXI of *Middlemarch*.'

examples; sometimes an ironical reversal, like the third.
Sometimes the hint depends on its individual prominence
rather than on its place in a series—like Maggie's double-
edged reference to avenging the successes of fair heroines and
the failures of the dark. This comment at first seems to come
true when Maggie takes Lucy's lover, but it is contradicted by
the end of the novel which places her too with 'Rebecca and
Flora MacIvor, and Minna and all the rest of the dark unhappy ones', as well as providing the ironical challenge to
illusion of a reference to characters in fiction by a character in
fiction.

There are dozens of these glances ahead, more or less
memorable, more or less dependent on several readings. Sometimes they are given prominence by being directly presented
as prophecy, like Mr Tulliver's story about the river's anger at
the mill changing hands. Amongst the 'realistic' prophecies
are Philip's, which come out of love and knowledge, and which
are plausibly presented to Maggie when he tries to shape her
future for her:

'It is mere cowardice to seek safety in negations. No character
becomes strong in that way. You will be thrown into the world some
day, and then every rational satisfaction of your nature that you
deny now, will assault you like a savage appetite. (bk. v, ch. iii)

In *Romola* there is a very elaborate use of less realistic
prophecy, shared by Dino, Romola's brother, and Piero di
Cosimo, George Eliot's historical portrait. Dino's prophetic
role is made plausible by his illness and his superstitions. He
tells Romola of his warning dream, saying, 'In visions and
dreams we are passive, and our souls are as an instrument in
the Divine Mind' (ch. xv).

He tells her the dream: of the dead in their shrouds who
make her bridal train, of the stony plain and the bronze and
marble men, the parchments, the blood and the fire, the Great
Tempter, and last, Romola seeking for water, alone. The
dream comes true. After her betrothal comes the *Trionfo della
Morte*, with the Masque of the Hours, the sheeted Dead, and
Time with his scythe. Tito sells Bardo's books, there is war
and famine. Romola drifts in her boat from Florence. The

dream jumbles these fragments: Dino sees Romola looking for water for her father, not for the peasants, but all the implications fit with ease.

The vision is criticized by Romola, for although she feels dread she cannot go with Dino into 'the shadowy region where human souls seek wisdom apart from the human sympathies which are the very life and substance of our wisdom' and she lets Tito shut away the vision with the crucifix in the triptych which Piero di Cosimo paints for him.

Piero's painting has an important function in the novel. It provides a series of prophetic images which also act as a lively extension of Piero's character and are the most imaginative of the historical reconstructions in this novel. When Piero first meets Tito he provides a strong though submerged prophetic parallel. He says to Tito: 'Young man, I am painting a picture of Sinon deceiving old Priam, and I should be glad of your face for my Sinon, if you'd give me a sitting'. (ch. iv).

When Nello protests that this is rather the face of a Bacchus or an Apollo, Piero replies:

'I say not that this young man is a traitor: I mean, he has a face that would make him the more perfect traitor if he had the heart of one, which is saying neither more nor less than that he has a beautiful face, informed with rich young blood, that will be nourished enough by food, and keep its colour without much help of virtue. He may have the heart of a hero along with it; I aver nothing to the contrary.'

The Sinon mirror does not immediately reveal its clear reflection. For the moment there is merely the fact that Tito, like Sinon, is a Greek and a stranger, and looking for shelter in a foreign country, and even these coincidences are left to the reader to find for himself, remembering his Virgil. As the novel proceeds the casual suggestion takes on a more sinister appropriateness. Tito, like Sinon, deceives an old man, and this is only the preliminary to his treachery to Florence. He is a Greek and Greeks were unpopular amongst the Florentines. And—without stretching the correspondence too far, I hope— the gift brought by this Greek is a false and dangerous one: the misleading triptych. Virgil's Sinon is not described in detail, but George Eliot's insistence on Tito's false beauty may owe something to her memory of Shakespeare's Lucrece, who, looking at Sinon's face in the tapestry, first thinks 'It cannot be . . . that so much guile can lurk in such a look,' then, remembering Tarquin, turns her phrase, 'It cannot be, I find, But such a face should bear a wicked mind.' The mirror Lucrece finds in her tapestry repeats itself, in a different context, in *Romola*.

The most prominent of Piero's paintings is the triptych of *Bacchus and Ariadne* which Tito commissions in the chapter called 'The Portrait'. It brings to life Tito's longing for the 'delicious languors such as never seem to come over the "ingenia acerrima Florentina"'. He says to Romola:

'I should like to see you under that southern sun, lying among the flowers, subdued into mere enjoyment, while I bent over you and touched the lute and sang to you some little unconscious strain that seemed all one with the light and the warmth. You have never known that happiness of the nymphs, my Romola.'

It is not a dream wholly alien to Romola, for she sees Tito as 'a sun-god who knows nothing of night', but she rejects it in her answer:

'No Tito, but I have dreamed of it often since you came. I am very thirsty for a deep draught of joy—for a life all bright like you. But we will not think of it now, Tito; it seems to me as if there would always be pale sad faces among the flowers, and eyes that look in vain.' (ch. xvii)

The bright dream is given substance by Piero's painting. The subject is the triumph of Bacchus and Ariadne, Tito supplementing Ovid with the suggestion that Ariadne should be wearing the immortal golden crown which Bacchus gives her. Romola says, 'And I am Ariadne, and you are crowning me! Yes, it is true, Tito; you have crowned my poor life' (ch xx). It is a superb ironical image, used in many ways. It is one of the extensions of Tito's dream of languor and brightness, and he loses his dream just as Romola loses hers. Tessa gives him the sweet sleep amongst flowers and sun, and is nymph to his Hylas, but Romola cannot remain as the crowned Ariadne, and in this story it is her Bacchus, not her Theseus, who abandons her. The triptych and its symbols are among the brilliant associations of her love for Tito, like the sweets which shower on the wedding-gown. Tito presents the little triptych as a symbol:

You will look every day at those pretty symbols of our life together—the ship on the calm sea, and the ivy that never withers, and those Loves that have left off wounding us and shower soft petals that are like our kisses. (ch. xxi)

George Eliot has gone to some trouble to reconstruct a plausible Piero di Cosimo which will act as the appropriate mirror for this situation: it seems to use aspects of several of Piero's paintings, which she would either have seen or read about in Vasari's detailed descriptions. Possible sources in the paintings themselves are the *Ariadne* itself, though here there is no resemblance except in the character of Ariadne, and also the *Mars and Venus and her Loves and Vulcan*, and *Perseus Frees Andromeda*, both of which might give the suggestion for the loves and the strange sea-monsters. And the other details on the triptych—the leopards and tigers and flowers—are all convincing subjects of Piero and familiar attributes of Bacchus. It is the kind of imaginative reconstruction we find later in Henry James. George Eliot took the scene from Ovid's *Metamorphoses*—Tito tells Piero 'A story in Ovid will give you the necessary hints', and if we turn to the Third Book of the *Metamorphoses* we find Ariadne's metamorphosis. In *Romola* her metamorphosis is a different one.

When Piero agrees to do the triptych, he makes two comments. He explains that he wants Bardo and Romola as models for Oedipus[1] and Antigone, and will get them to sit for this and then put 'the likeness into Ariadne'. But 'Antigone' is the name he always gives to Romola, and Romola's resemblance to Antigone is much stronger than her resemblance to the triumphant Ariadne, crowned by Bacchus. Her father is blind, her brother has left him, and she fights for family duty, both against Tito and Savonarola. The

---

[1] There is also the other image of blind Bardo: Teiresias, in the passage from Poliziano which Romola reads to her father. Poliziano is another linking source of allusion, for he supplies Tito's drinking-song.

images correct each other. Piero ironically juxtaposes Bacchus and Antigone, 'my *Bacco trionfante*, who has married the fair Antigone in contradiction to all history and fitness'.

Piero also corrects Tito's image of himself:

'I don't want *your* likeness—I've got it already,' said Piero, 'only I've made you look frightened. I must take the fright out of it for Bacchus.' (ch. xviii)

He shows the painting of Tito 'holding a wine-cup in the attitude of triumphant joy', but his face turned away with 'an expression of . . . intense fear'. Then Piero, whose words are edged with malice, for he does not like Tito, makes his prophecy: 'He's seeing a ghost—that fine young man. I shall finish it some day, when I've settled what sort of a ghost is the most terrible—whether it should look solid, like a dead man come to life, or half transparent, like a mist.'

He does finish the picture, and the ghost becomes the 'dead man come to life'—Baldassare. The imaginary picture, which seems to be in the style of Piero's historical paintings, rather than his fantastic mythological works, grows with the narrative. Piero sees Baldassare clutch Tito, though he knows nothing of their real relationship, and he puts Baldassare in the picture. At each stage it is a prophetic picture: Piero first anticipates the fear, and then the ghost, and the picture itself is almost an exact anticipation of what eventually comes about when Baldassare breaks into the feast in the Rucellai Gardens. Tito is playing the lute, not holding the wine-cup, but they have just called for more flasks of Montepulciano, and Baldassare sees the 'flashing cups' as he looks in at the feast. In the engraving in *The Cornhill*, called 'The Feast in the Rucellai Gardens', Tito is holding a wine-cup as Baldassare watches the feast. Tito is triumphant—filled with 'exaltation at the sudden opening of a new path before him', his game of political power. And he is singing a Bacchic chorus from Poliziano's *Orfeo*:

> 'Ciascun segua, o Bacco, te:
> Bacco, Bacco, evoè, evoè!'

Both the wine-cup and the triumphant joy in the painting are attributes of Tito's image of himself as Bacchus, just as the

Bacchic image is quietly used when Romola first sees him:
'Romola's astonishment could hardly have been greater if
the stranger had worn a panther-skin and carried a thyrsus.'
The Bacchus and the young man frightened by the ghost
merge, and Bacchus, by the way, is also another version of the
Greek carrying gifts. George Eliot keeps all her woven threads
working together in the pattern of anticipation and irony. The
pattern of allusion and analogue in *Romola* is a streak of light
in the dullest of her novels. *Romola* is undoubtedly a book
which it is more interesting to analyse than simply to
read.

The *Bacchus and Ariadne* is revalued by the *Oedipus and
Antigone* and by the unnamed prophetic picture of the ghost at
the feast. It is not merely revalued but flatly contradicted by
the Carnival procession which Tito and Romola meet after
their betrothal, and after they have shut away Dino's prophecy with his crucifix in the triptych which Tito has given
to Romola. Dino's vision comes to life in the *Miserere* with its
masked procession of Time and the mourners. The crucifix
cannot be hidden so easily: 'It is still there—it is only hidden',
says Romola after she shrinks in horror from the masque. The
masque itself is Piero's work. Tito says, 'Doubtless this is an
invention of Piero di Cosimo, who loves such grim merriment',
and this is not a reconstruction by George Eliot, for Vasari
describes in detail the *Trionfo della Morte*, devised by Piero
in 1511.

There is another work of Piero's, which passes almost unobserved at first sight because it is a part of Nello's conducted
tour of Florence. The tour itself is full of suggestiveness:
Tito does not respond to Giotto's *campanile*, which 'seemed a
prophetic symbol, telling that human life must somehow and
some time shape itself into accord with that pure aspiring
beauty', but he admires Ghiberti's Baptistery Gates—'these
heads in high relief speak of a human mind within them'.
At last they come to Nello's barber-shop, and go into the small
room where the *eruditi* meet. Nello shows him a sketch of three
masks. It is another 'fancy of Piero di Cosimo's, a strange
freakish painter, who says he saw it by long looking at a
mouldy wall' (the 'mouldy wall' is a detail from Vasari):

The sketch Nello pointed to represented three masks—one a drunken laughing Satyr, another a sorrowing Magdalen, and the third, which lay between them, the rigid, cold face of a Stoic: the masks rested obliquely on the lap of a little child, whose cherub features rose above them with something of the supernal promise in the gaze which painters had by that time learned to give to the Divine Infant. (ch. iii)

Tito attempts an interpretation, not too seriously, touching a lute while he speaks, and Nello comments: 'Ah! everybody has his own interpretation for that picture.'

There is no need to press the interpretation made by the story: Tito speaks of 'the gross, the sad, and the severe'. Tito is no satyr, Romola is no Magdalen, Savonarola no Stoic, but the three masks, with the child, are a faint image of the three faces of Tito, Romola, and Savonarola: the child, the hope, and the Golden Age are there at the end, when Romola tells Tito's children about Savonarola and Tito, and the emblem is made good.

This very elaborate and oblique kind of forecasting has a much smaller place in *Felix Holt* and *Middlemarch* though both novels are full of ironical anticipations of a more simple kind. But they contain very few visions—the dreams people dream in Treby Magna and Middlemarch are illusory or impossible, not to be exploited as a source of fantastic narrative premonition. There is one prophetic comment in *Felix Holt*, when Felix says to Esther:

I do believe in you; but I want you to have such a vision of the future that you may never lose your best self. Some charm or other may be flung about you—some of your atta-of-rose fascinations—and nothing but a good strong terrible vision will save you. (ch. xxvii)

It is not until *Daniel Deronda* that we return to the continued and elaborate method of *Romola*. The anticipation—which I have mentioned already in Chapter VI, for, like *Romola*, this is a novel where coincidence and anticipation work together—depends on a kind of fantasy. The dead face in the picture is very like Piero's painting of Tito and Baldassare. Gwendolen's confident pleasure and poise both dissolve when her sister opens the panel: 'The opened panel had disclosed the picture of an upturned dead face, from which an obscure figure seemed to be fleeing with outstretched arms' (ch. iii). Her terror is repeated later when the panel flies open in the middle of Gwendolen's performance as Hermione, and 'she looked like a statue into which a soul of Fear had entered'. The dead face, the image of the Furies, Grandcourt's 'feyness', Daniel's feeling of exile and Mordecai's vision of the bridge and the disciple are fused in the interwoven destinies, and the conclusion brings all the premonitions together in a climax which gains much of its impact from these preparatory tensions.

(iii)

The narrative medium is composed of many voices. There is the direct speech of the author's pity, both for her own creatures and extending in generalization to lament and admiration for all humanity. There is the more detached voice of irony and analysis. There is the omniscient warning, veiled and unveiled, working in the interests of aesthetic unity and dramatic irony. At times—though I believe these occasions to be rare— we may resent the absence of dramatic isolation and feel, as some readers certainly have in the case of Dorothea, that the author's solicitude stands between us and the character, blurring the sharp edges of the clear portrait, softening, idealizing, or sentimentalizing. But such blurred effects are not the consequence of the author's inability to withdraw her own commentary. There are some very powerful instances of her sense of a dramatic decorum which demands just such a withdrawal, and both the voice of maternal pity, and the voice of ironical wisdom, can be stilled in favour of a dramatic method which presents the character in its nakedness. When this happens the very change in convention has its own effect of isolation and constriction. This is what happens as early as *Adam Bede*, in the section describing Hetty's flight from Hayslope, her search for Arthur, and her terror and panic which ends—though not for the direct view of the reader—in the birth of her child and its murder. This account, though grammatically presented in *oratio obliqua*, is restricted to Hetty's

177

sensibility and experience. It is as if George Eliot had expended both pity and irony and, at the moment of crisis, let the character present itself.

This account begins with the author's point of view. George Eliot comments on Hetty's sorrow and fear and the uncaring natural beauty around her:

> A long, lonely journey, with sadness in the heart; away from the familiar to the strange: that is a hard and dreary thing even to the rich, the strong, the instructed: a hard thing, even when we are called by duty, not urged by dread. (ch. xxxvi)

This is gradually converted into an ungeneralized and unreflective commentary which is in all essentials—vocabulary, syntax and reference, in fact everything except the third-person form—the flight as it is experienced by Hetty. There is little or no margin for the author's sensibility. The words are short and simple, the sentences short and broken, there are many questions and repetitions. If we compare this episode with the first-person account given by Hetty to Dinah in prison there is little difference. The first-person account is ungrammatical, and the extracts below are a kind of linguistic compromise: grammatical accuracy alone gives the superficial adherence to the third-person narration, but the sophisticated narrator is, to all intents and purposes, absent:

> What *could* she do? She would go away from Windsor—travel again as she had done the last week, and get among the flat green fields with the high hedges round them, where nobody could see her or know her; and there, perhaps, when there was nothing else she could do, she should get courage to drown herself in some pond like that in the Scantlands. . . . (ch. xxxvii)

Later in the same chapter:

> The pool had its wintry depth now: by the time it got shallow, as she remembered the pools did at Hayslope, in the summer, no one could find out that it was her body. But then there was her basket—she must hide that too: she must throw it into the water—make it heavy with stones first, and then throw it in. She got up to look about for stones, and soon brought five or six, which she laid down beside her basket, and then sat down again. There was no need to hurry—there was all the night to drown herself in. She

sat leaning her elbow on the basket. She was weary, hungry. There were some buns in her basket—three, which she had supplied herself with at the place where she ate her dinner. She took them out now, and ate them eagerly, and then sat still, looking at the pool. (ch. xxxvii)

Compare this with Hetty's direct statement:

And I walked on and on, and I hardly felt the ground I trod on; and it got lighter, for there came the moon—O Dinah, it frightened me when it first looked at me out o' the clouds—it never looked so before; and I turned out o' the roads into the fields, for I was afraid o' meeting anybody with the moon shining on me. And I came to a haystack, where I thought I could lie down and keep myself warm all night. (ch. xlv)

This goes on for more than six pages of faltering simplicity. The similarities between it and the account of the journey are striking: *oratio recta* and *oratio obliqua* alike have the same simplicity of words and sentences: there is no periodic elaboration or surview, but a sentence-by-sentence, step-by-step absorption in the present. The style is abrupt and jerky, and the details are given flatly, with an extraordinary impression of practical and precise care. It is a childlike practical absorption which makes a terrifying impression in the moments of crisis: the very absence of emotional language and the presence of practical detail is almost unbearable when Hetty is planning her suicide, thinking of the discovery of her body, or covering up her baby in the wood. It is dramatic narrative reminiscent of the naïve practical detail of *The Ancient Mariner* or *The Idiot Boy*. The pointed exclusion of the author's sensibility has its own kind of heightening effect, in no way dependent on heightened language or generalization. Indeed, all generalization is shut off here: Hetty is incapable of it. We are face to face with her 'narrow imagination' which cannot anticipate. She plans unemotionally, and only recoils from death when she is about to jump into the pond. Instead of imagination we have the flat references to her actual experience—to the woman and baby who came to Hayslope, nearly dead with cold and hunger, to the pond in the Scantlands: this is the unimaginative mind which thought of Arthur's love in terms of finery. George Eliot speaks of 'the narrow circle of her imagination' and this is exactly demonstrated in the account of her flight. It is done in terms of sensation not of sensibility, of practical memory not of generalization, of careful matter-of-fact planning not of terrified anticipation.

This is perhaps the most striking examples of the dramatic ability to present a limited consciousness, and it is sustained, in the account of Hetty's flight, for many pages. But there are many other examples of George Eliot's refusal to present character in the frame of her own thought and feeling: there is the presentation of Tito's process of rational argument, limiting his sensibility as it accelerates. There is the account of Casaubon's surprise at the disappointing quality of his own ardour. There is the elated description of Will's walk across the fields to see Dorothea at church, blinkered by love and sunlight. There is the survey of Gwendolen, oscillating between intention and desire.

Quick, quick, like pictures in a book beaten open with a sense of hurry, came back vividly, yet in fragments, all that she had gone through in relation to Grandcourt—the allurements, the vacillations, the resolve to accede, the final repulsion; the incisive face of that dark-eyed lady with the lovely boy; her own pledge (was it a pledge not to marry him?)—the new disbelief in the worth of men and things for which that scene of disclosure had become a symbol. That unalterable experience made a vision at which in the first agitated moment, before tempering reflections could suggest themselves, her native terror shrank.

Where was the good of choice coming again? What did she wish? Anything different? No! and yet in the dark seed-growths of consciousness a new wish was forming itself—'I wish I had never known it!' (ch. xxvi)

It was perhaps this dramatic immediacy which the reviewer of *Felix Holt* in *The Westminster Review*, July 1866, had in mind when he made this not altogether fair contrast of Jane Austen with George Eliot:

Whilst Miss Austen makes you feel that you are in the next room to the speakers, and can overhear them, George Eliot, that you are in the room with them. Jane Austen gives you the idea that her characters are all members of the Established Church, George Eliot, that they have souls.

There are some occasions when the dramatic presentation depends on a slightly different version of this absence of comment. The crudest example is the account of Dunsey Cass on the night of his death when he robs Silas Marner. We do not know what has happened to Dunsey until Raveloe knows, but if we look back we find that George Eliot has played fair. The last word about Dunsey is ambiguous: 'So he stepped forward into the darkness.' It is, in one sense, the last word that can be said about him, and the withdrawal from his narrative, essential for the plot, has a literal necessity.

In *Romola* there is something similar. It also involves a refusal to use the omniscient commentary; it interrupts George Eliot's normal method and makes a kind of hiatus in time. To begin with, we do not know much about Tito, except that he has a special sensibility to certain references:

'Anybody might say the saints had sent *you* a dead body; but if you took the jewels, I hope you buried him—and you can afford a mass or two for him into the bargain.' (ch. i)
'Young man, I am painting a picture of Sinon deceiving old Priam, and I should be glad of your face for my Sinon, if you'd give me a sitting.' (ch. iv)
'Ah, then, they are fine intagli,' said Bardo. 'Five hundred ducats! Ah, more than a man's ransom!' (ch. vi)

There is also the deliberate question accompanying Tito, as it introduces Gwendolen at the beginning of the novel. Bratti scents a mystery:

'I picked up a stranger this morning as I was coming in from Rovezzano, and I can spell him out no better than I can the letters on that scarf I bought from the French cavalier.'
'But the riddle about him is—' (ch. i)

But there is the deliberate refusal either to describe Tito's character or to reveal his secret in any other way until chapter ix. Then we return to the phrase Bardo used in innocence, and at last Tito's inner conflict appears, together with the guilty secret of his abandoned foster-father:

'A man's ransom!'—who was it that had said five hundred florins was more than a man's ransom? If now, under this mid-day sun, on some hot coast far away, a man somewhat stricken in years —a man not without high thoughts and with the most passionate heart—a man who long years ago had rescued a little boy from a life of beggary, filth, and cruel wrong, had reared him tenderly, and had been to him as a father—if that man were now under this summer sun toiling as a slave, hewing wood and drawing water, perhaps being smitten and buffeted because he was not deft and active? (ch. ix)

This suspension may seem at first to be a mere device for creating mystery and tension at the beginning, but it is an unusually long mystery for George Eliot, who usually gives the necessary data about her characters at an early stage in the process of introduction. A little later we are given the reason:

This was his first real colloquy with himself: he had gone on following the impulses of the moment, and one of those impulses had been to conceal half the fact; he had never considered this part of his conduct long enough to face the consciousness of his motives for the concealment.

George Eliot has moved a long way from her affectionate exposition of character in *Scenes of Clerical Life* and *Adam Bede*—here she fits exposition to character, and Tito's past is withheld from us until he ceases to withhold it from his own consciousness. It is a decorous subduing of author's commentary to the process of character, so that the two seem to move together.

There is something like this in the portrayal of Bulstrode in *Middlemarch*, where once more there is the question of facing the problem within the mind. Bulstrode is at first presented externally, almost flatly, like Raffles or Rigg. Then George Eliot, refusing to make flat characters, explores his consciousness, and once more we see villainy from the inside.

This inside view of egoism often shows a terrifying and unexpected innocence. We turn back to Bulstrode's past rather as we might in a play by Ibsen, because we are forced to, because the fuse laid in the past has led to the explosion in the present:

Even without memory, the life is bound into one by a zone of dependence in growth and decay; but intense memory forces a man to open his own blameworthy past. With memory set smarting like a reopened wound, a man's past is not simply a dead history, an outworn preparation of the present: it is not a repented error shaken loose from the past: it is a still quivering part of himself, bringing shudders and bitter flavours and the tinglings of a merited shame.

Into this second life Bulstrode's past had now risen, only the pleasures of it seeming to have lost their quality. Night and day, without interruption save of brief sleep which only wove retrospect and fear into a fantastic present, he felt the scenes of his earlier life coming between him and everything else, as obstinately as, when we look through the window from a lighted room, the objects we turn our backs on are still before us, instead of the grass and the trees. . . .

Once more he saw himself the young banker's clerk. . . . (ch. lxi)

He does not turn back, we do not turn back, until memory has been 'set smarting like a reopened wound' by Raffles's threats. He faces the past only when he is forced to, and it is not until then that the reader moves back in time with him.

Bulstrode, like Casaubon, is trapped by necessity, but in his case the process from bad to worse took place in the past. It is presented, necessarily and organically, as past haunts present, in retrospect. It may look like the haunting of guilt, and yet it presents a kind of innocence. What is innocent is Bulstrode's fear—he is afraid of the past only as something which might be discovered. Set in counterpoint against George Eliot's insistence that he is what the past has made him, is his hope that he is free, except from being found out.

There is another dramatic evasion of this kind, this time not leading up to disclosure. On the night of Raffles's death, there is Bulstrode's version of Tito's refusal to face his consciousness, shown in the conflict of words and images. This is the hypocrite at prayer:

Whatever prayers he might lift up, whatever statements he might inwardly make of this man's wretched spiritual condition, and the duty he himself was under to submit to the punishment divinely appointed for him rather than to wish for evil to another —through all this effort to condense words into a solid mental state, there pierced and spread with irresistible vividness the images of the events he desired. (ch. lxx)

There is no account of the moment of decision. We are given the process, the sleight-of-hand which Bulstrode performs in his 'indirect' and verbally innocuous prayers, and then comes Mrs Abel's fatal suggestion of brandy. This is dealt with from her point of view—like her, the reader is outside Bulstrode's door, only hearing the silences and the husky voice. Bulstrode gives her the key of the wine-cooler. This is George Eliot's comment:

Early in the morning—about six—Mr Bulstrode rose and spent some time in prayer. Does any one suppose that private prayer is necessarily candid—necessarily goes to the roots of action? Private prayer is inaudible speech, and speech is representative: who can represent himself just as he is, even in his own reflections? Bulstrode had not yet unravelled in his thought the confused promptings of the last four-and-twenty hours.

When we are expecting her to continue her commentary on what goes on in Bulstrode, she withdraws. There is a gap in explanation because there is a gap in the consciousness. Bulstrode, like Tito, is withdrawn from our view, and the convention of omniscience suspended. The voice is as expressive in its absence as in its presence.

CHAPTER IX

The Scene as Image

(i)

GEORGE ELIOT'S scenic method is as varied as her other means of presenting character and developing action. The scene can serve the double purpose of narrative and theme, often providing a visual resting-place which may cover a subterranean movement of the action. Her scenes are of course not all scenes of crisis, though it is the status of the scene as symbol which I am concerned with here. In most of the novels there are a large number of domestic scenes which are not even essential to the development of plot, but which familiarize us with character before character is set in tragic action. They are there also, as in all successful novels, to give the essential illusion that the action is rooted in normal space and time. The one novel which has very few of these 'free' scenes is *Romola*, and the result is the disastrous absence of normality. In *Romola* George Eliot attempts various laboured naturalistic scenes of Florentine life, like the episode of the practical joke played on the doctor, which she explained was there for accuracy of background and not for comic relief. There are no private scenes in *Romola* which are not scenes of crisis. We never see Tito and Romola together in a scene free from the tension of development, and it is the static domestic scene which is free from crisis that George Eliot uses to solidify and stabilize her novels.

There is all the richness of detail of the Hall Farm scenes in *Adam Bede*, for instance, and of the childhood scenes in *The Mill on the Floss* and of the later scenes in the Red Deeps or in Lucy's drawing-room, where the plot moves, but not so fast or so intensely that we lack the sense of resting in ordinary life. There are a few such scenes in *Felix Holt*, in Mr Lyon's drawing-room, where Felix knocks down the works of Byron, or in Transome Court where Job Tudge and Harold's son and Mrs Holt make their comic contribution. This kind of scene

185

of course need not be comic, although it is often used to give room for the digressions and reliefs of comedy.

Perhaps the best example is the opening scene in *Middlemarch*, the only opening scene, with the exception of the first scene in the carpenter's shop in *Adam Bede*, which does not introduce the plot in a moment of crisis. The first scene is usually both demonstration of character and a plot-impetus, but here it is only a calm and revealing scene free from anticipation or crisis, though, like the first chapter of *Adam Bede*, it has its skeleton of debate. It is the kind of domestic beginning which D. H. Lawrence manages so well: the dividing of the jewels. It presents the self-righteousness and egoism of Dorothea and Celia, and establishes their social background. It gives us the quality of Dorothea's ardour as well as her Puritanical and theoretic superiority:

'How very beautiful these gems are!' said Dorothea, under a new current of feeling, as sudden as the gleam. 'It is strange how deeply colours seem to penetrate one, like scent. . . .' (ch. i)

We see with irony and sympathy her attempt 'to justify her delight in the colours by merging them in her mystic religious joy'.

Then there is her 'scorching quality' which sears Celia for the moment when she shows her surprise at Dorothea's susceptibility to the jewels. This scorn is to be an essential quality in her gradual discovery of Casaubon, and in her immediate reaction when she finds Will with Rosamund. This is a scene which shows character in a domestic interlude, and it, and many like it, are important not because they add to the dramatic display of character, and alleviate the omniscient exposition, but because their cumulative effect leaves an impression of the flow of real and ordinary life. They present character in the atmosphere of normality, and even where careful preparation for the action may be at work, or where the very normality is an ironical prelude to tragedy, as it is in the early scenes in the Hall Farm in *Adam Bede*, they have the essential function of giving the novel the substance and motion of life. Where it is missing, as in the deliberately 'ideal' Romola, tragedy is in danger of becoming theatrical.

The Scene as Image

There is also another kind of scene, apart from the main flow of plot, but an essential part of it, which presents character in a special way. It is the scene of solitude which expands and solidifies the inner reverie or conflict given elsewhere in a more analytical form. The characters talk to themselves, and both the content and the manner of their talk are revealing. But the talk is accompanied by the careful use of scenes which localize—sometimes with symbolic appropriateness, sometimes not—the process and growth of the characters. These scenes have a visual intensity which marks the crisis. The description short-circuits the slow presentation of gradual change, and has a sacramental decisiveness. There are some simple examples in the early books. In *Janet's Repentance*, for instance, after Janet has found a brandy bottle, flung it from her in fear of backsliding, and gone to Tryan, there is a quiet scene of solitude. She walks home in the 'dewy starlight' where she feels the sense of a protective presence and temptation quietens into confidence:

That walk in the dewy starlight remained for ever in Janet's memory as one of those baptismal epochs, when the soul, dipped in the sacred waters of joy and peace, rises from them with new energies, with more unalterable longings. (ch. xxv)

In *Adam Bede* and *Silas Marner* the 'baptismal moment' is spread out in time, and not shown in a single vivid scene. In *The Mill on the Floss* there is the scene where Maggie meets disenchantment by self-abnegation, taking her impetus from Thomas à Kempis. She is alone, reading 'till the sun went down behind the willows', and she makes her 'plans of self-humiliation and entire devotedness' in 'the deepening twilight'.

In later novels the scene of decision grows more elaborate in its visual equivalent of the state of mind. There is Romola's solitude, interrupted by Savonarola: 'The bare wintry morning, the chill air, were welcome in their severity: the leafless trees, the sombre hills, were not haunted by the gods of beauty and joy,[1] whose worship she had forsaken for ever' (ch. xxxvii).

[1] The painting on the triptych is a source of many images in Romola: here we have 'the gods of beauty and joy', earlier we have had Romola's

The Scene as Image

The landscape contradicts Tito's triptych, with its vines
and roses, just as Romola 'discrowns' Ariadne by putting on
the grey mantle and cowl. There is breadth, 'the sky would be
broad above her', and a sudden burst of light, which sharpens
her solitude by casting 'the long shadow of herself that was
not to be escaped' and by its suggestion of 'a divine presence
stirring all those inarticulate sensibilities which are our deepest
life'. She sits under a cypress, we return to Tito for two
chapters, and then the decisive debate with Savonarola sends
her back. As she waits, the visual detail makes its insistence:

> All things conspired to give her the sense of freedom and solitude:
> her escape from the accustomed walls and streets; the widening
> distance from her husband . . . the great dip of ground on the road-
> side making a gulf between her and the stony calm of the mountains.
> For the first time in her life she felt alone in the presence of the
> earth and sky, with no human presence interposing and making a
> law for her. (ch. xl)

The natural symbol is illusory, for Savonarola disturbs the
sense of freedom and solitude and reinterprets the inescapable
golden light and her own shadow. The visual detail fixes the
scene as a vivid crisis in the novel, and also makes some play
with visual suggestion, rather like the appropriate scenes in
Adam Bede, where Dinah is associated with the bare hills
on the Stonyshire side, Adam with the strong oaks, Hetty
and Arthur's love with the enervating suggestions of the
larches. It is too tactfully and gently managed to be called
symbolic, but has the force of temporary symbol which gives
a decisive scene a memorable gravity.

These scenes are not exactly symbolic but act as temporary
visual flashes which make crisis stand out, and which at the
same time, by their intensity, persuade us of the possibility
of sudden change. There is Dorothea's image of St Peter's,
which is associated with the 'stupendous fragmentariness' with
which she sees Rome, and here, as elsewhere, George Eliot
analyses while she presents the visual detail, explaining the
first impression of Tito stated in terms of the Bacchic emblems of
panther-skin and thyrsus, and at the end when Romola 'has lost her
crown' we hear the echo of Ariadne's golden crown. The Greek and
Christian references play against each other throughout. Love makes a
god of Tito for Romola as it does of Will for Dorothea.

persistence of visual association and rationalizing Dorothea's symbolic scenes:

> Our moods are apt to bring with them images which succeed each other like the magic-lantern pictures of a doze; and in certain states of dull forlornness Dorothea all her life continued to see the vastness of St. Peter's, the huge bronze canopy, the excited intention in the attitudes and garments of the prophets and evangelists in the mosaics above, and the red drapery which was being hung for Christmas spreading itself everywhere like a disease of the retina. (ch. xx)

And there is the other scene of solitude which recurs in changing lights, Dorothea's boudoir:

> Nothing had been outwardly altered there; but while the summer had gradually advanced over the western fields beyond the avenue of elms, the bare room had gathered within it those memories of an inward life which fill the air as with a cloud of good or bad angels, the invisible yet active forms of our spiritual triumphs or our spiritual falls. (ch. xxxvii)

(ii)

This is George Eliot's dramatic use of scenery, often carefully rationalized by the general explanation which makes the visual association appear as the natural act of the character's mind, but at the same time chosen with feeling for the appropriate lights and properties. It is much briefer and quieter than the scene-setting of Dickens, or Meredith, or even of Henry James, but it is a recurring way of presenting character and crisis, not too obviously a delegation of the omniscient commentary. But in order to look closely at her scenic method, it is best to choose a group of similar scenes which recur throughout the novels. I do not suggest that this is the only group of recurring scenes—it is not—but it is a significant group.

The sacramental or symbolic scene cannot be entirely separated from George Eliot's use of imagery. Scene and image reinforce each other. In almost all the novels, for instance, there is a crisis of disenchantment described in images which echo, more or less closely, a passage in one of her letters. On 4 June 1848 she wrote to Sara Hennell:

The Scene as Image

Alas for the fate of poor mortals which condemns them to wake up some fine morning and find all the poetry in which their world was bathed only the evening before utterly gone—the hard angular world of chairs and tables and looking-glasses staring at them in all its naked prose. (Haight, i, p. 264)

This disenchanted day-lit room is one of her most important recurring scenes of crisis. It first returns in *Janet's Repentance* though in a context very different from that of George Eliot's lament. Janet's cold, hard vision of reality is no result of waking from a dream: it summarizes and freezes a disenchantment with which she has long been living without fully admitting it:

The daylight changes the aspect of misery to us, as of everything else. In the night it presses on our imagination—the forms it takes are false, fitful, exaggerated; in broad day it sickens our sense with the dreary persistence of definite measurable reality. . . . That moment of intensest depression was come to Janet, when the daylight which showed her the walls, and chairs, and tables, and all the commonplace reality that surrounded her, seemed to lay bare the future too, and bring out into oppressive distinctness all the details of a weary life to be lived from day to day. . . . (ch. xvi)

The clear light on the objects in a room, the definiteness and dreariness, and the suggestion of a prosaic present stretching into an unchanging prosaic future are the unmistakable links with the first image in the letter and many later repetitions.

With Hetty Sorrel in *Adam Bede* it is the second look at a very new loss of enchantment which makes her feel 'that dry-eyed morning misery, which is worse than the first shock, because it has the future in it as well as the present' (ch. xxxi), and so it is with Adam, on whom George Eliot bestows her own image of the well-lit charmless room:

Now that by the light of this new morning he was come back to his home, and surrounded by the familiar objects that seemed for ever robbed of their charm, the reality—the hard, inevitable reality of his troubles pressed upon him with a new weight. (ch. xxxviii)

This also echoes faintly the desolation of his mother, Lisbeth Bede, when after her husband's death 'the bright afternoon's sun shone dismally' in her kitchen. But for Lisbeth this is no disenchantment marking or making growth, while for Adam, as for Janet, the hard impact of reality is a crisis in nurture. It is also a crisis which corresponds to Hetty's and thus brings the two into oblique but organic relation. His joyless vision of the world in which there is 'no margin of dreams beyond the daylight reality' recapitulates the common unromantic daylight which drove her, ironically, to him. The dreamless daylight makes the challenge which he accepts, propelled as he is by the strong inseparable combination of his character and his vocation, and which Hetty rejects in panic.

In *The Lifted Veil*, the story published in *Blackwood's*, July 1859, the scene is compressed into an image. The lighted room is the metaphor which stamps the crisis, though the crisis itself is less one of disenchantment than one of discovery. It is rather a melodramatic use of the image, partly because it *is* a metaphor and one not very closely in keeping with the actual pressure of the seen world within the story, mainly because of the feverish fantasy of the narrative as a whole:

The terrible moment of complete illumination had come to me, and I saw that the darkness had hidden no landscape from me, but only a blank prosaic wall: from that evening forth, through the sickening years which followed, I saw all round the narrow room of this woman's soul.

Here is the first appearance of the antithetical image of space which in the later novels puts extra emphasis on the narrowness of the room; but this is the only instance I know where the narrow room is the woman's soul itself and not the soul's oppressive environment. Here the woman is a villain, not a victim.

Maggie Tulliver's awakening from her dream, in *The Mill on the Floss*, has enormous causal significance. It prepares her for her second dream, made up of an unrealistic renunciation which is both self-abnegation and self-indulgence, but it also prepares the last and real awakening, when the revival of her old dream of life and beauty in her meeting with Stephen leads first to the drifting with the stream and then to the genuine renunciation.

The immediate causes of Maggie's disenchantment are close

to the causes of George Eliot's: family trouble, especially her father's illness, a lasting feeling of separation, and a sense of impotence and aspiration. Here, although there is the emphasis of the dull and heavy prosaic routine, we move away from the autobiographical images of light and common objects:

> She could make dream-worlds of her own—but no dream-world would satisfy her now. She wanted some explanation of this hard, real life: the unhappy-looking father, seated at the dull breakfast table; the childish, bewildered mother; the little sordid tasks that filled the hours, or the more oppressive emptiness of weary, joyless leisure. (bk. iv, ch. iii)

In *Romola* the images of light return, though not the common objects. Romola's disenchanting illumination is something more dramatic than the cold light of morning, as we might expect from the novel which contains almost nothing of George Eliot's characteristic understatement of event and character. Like Arnold's Empedocles, Romola looks at the stars. She loses her dream, the dream of human fellowship and service, and she shrinks from 'the light of the stars, which seemed to her like the hard light of eyes that looked at her without seeing her' (ch. lxi). Like the common daylight in the other books the significance of the light is that it forces her to see the indifferent life outside the self.

Here too the image is repeated, and the repetition emphasizes a coincidence of character. Similar light falls on Savonarola, the parallel and the contrast to Romola. When he asks for a sign from Heaven there is a sudden stream of sunlight which lights his face and satisfies the crowd. The effect is a temporary one:

> But when the Frate had disappeared, and the sunlight seemed no longer to have anything special in its illumination, but was spreading itself impartially over all things clean and unclean, there began, along with the general movement of the crowd, a confusion of voices. (ch. lxii)

Two chapters further on the images of light are repeated. There is the light of common day in Savonarola's cell in San Marco contrasted with the colour and radiance of Fra Angelico's frescoes, and especially his Madonna's 'radiant glory', which catch Tito's eye as he goes along the corridors. Savonarola's cell has no frescoes: 'The light through the narrow windows looked in on nothing but bare walls, and the hard pallet, and the crucifix.'

But this contrast between the glory and the hard reality exists for the reader rather than the characters. In the next chapter, Savonarola himself sees the light, after he has evaded the trial by fire. It is the disenchanting light which was the image of the crowd's disillusion and which returns now as the image of his own doubt:

> But there seemed no glory in the light that fell on him now, no smile of heaven: it was only that light which shines on, patiently and impartially, justifying or condemning by simply showing all things in the slow history of their ripening.

The images of light in *Romola* stand apart from those in the other books but they are still images of the light which shows a dreamless or unresponsive world outside the self.

In *Felix Holt* the description of brightly lit despair is put into the motto which prefaces chapter xliv:

> I'm sick at heart. The eye of day,[1]
> The insistent summer noon, seems pitiless,
> Shining in all the barren crevices
> Of weary life, leaving no shade, no dark,
> Where I may dream that hidden waters lie.

This fragment introduces Esther's endurance of the dream which comes true, in a different sense, 'that state of disenchantment belonging to the actual presence of things which have long dwelt in the imagination with all the factitious charms of arbitrary arrangement' (ch. xliv). There is no place here for the dull and common room. Esther has to feel the oppression of spaciousness, of 'a life of middling delights, overhung with the languorous haziness of motiveless ease, where poetry was only literature' (ibid.) and the light which shines too brilliantly for her is one she can put out: 'she put out the wax lights that she might get rid of the oppressive urgency of walls

[1] This is a quotation from *The Spanish Gypsy*, though George Eliot gives no reference here.

and upholstery and that portrait smiling with deluded brightness' (ch. xlix). Once more the correspondences of character
are underlined by the linking imagery. Both a cause and a
symbol of Esther's disenchantment is the disenchanted face,
in the portrait and outside it, of Mrs Transome, and Mrs
Transome's unbearable reality is also fixed in two images of
light. We are shown the tragic desolation which is more violent
than the awakening to prose reality:

All around her, where there had once been brightness and
warmth, there were white ashes, and the sunshine looked dreary as
it fell on them. (ch. ix)

And there is the duller impact too, though again the visual
impression is strengthened by metaphor:

Here she moved to and fro amongst the rose-coloured satin of
chairs and curtains . . . dull obscurity everywhere, except where the
keen light feel on the narrow track of her own lot, wide only for a
woman's anguish. (ch. xxxiv)

In the last novels we come back to the double image of light
and common objects. Dorothea's disenchanted room, in
Middlemarch, is of course the boudoir with the bow-window
and the faded blue chairs. She comes back to it after her wedding journey to find a changed aspect.

The distant flat shrank in uniform whiteness and low-hanging
uniformity of cloud. The very furniture in the room seemed to have
shrunk since she saw it before: the stag in the tapestry looked more
like a ghost in his ghostly blue-green world; the volumes of polite
literature in the bookcase looked more like immovable imitations of
books. The bright fire of dry oak-boughs burning on the dogs
seemed an incongruous renewal of life and glow. (ch. xxviii)

The emphasis is on disenchantment—'Each remembered
thing in the room was disenchanted, was deadened as an un-
lit transparency'—but the objects recede and grow small
rather than strike the vision with their dullness or their hardness. The strong and precise simile deprives the objects of
light. The image presents a dim light not a brilliant one, both
here and even in a scene of actual bright sunlight in a later
scene in the same room. She is sitting in 'the dazzling sun-rays'
but the metaphor dims the light:

194

'And just as clearly in the miserable light she saw her own and her husband's solitude—how they walked apart so that she was obliged to survey him.' (ch. xlii)

When Gwendolen, in *Daniel Deronda*, first meets the unmistakable impact from outside which breaks her steady dream of potential brilliance, she comes to realize the shock in a dull room. Klesmer has put an end to her wild schemes of making a fortune on the stage or as a singer. The disenchanted scene is described in a way which takes us back to the images used in the original letter to Sara Hennell:

The noonday only brought into more dreary clearness the absence of interest from her life. All memories, all objects, the pieces of music displayed, the open piano—the very reflection of herself in the glass—seemed no better than the packed-up shows of a departing fair. (ch. xxiii)

And a little later:

But this general disenchantment with the world—nay, with herself, since it appeared that she was not made for easy pre-eminence—only intensified her sense of forlornness: it was a visibly sterile distance enclosing the dreary path at her feet. (ch. xxvi)

There is some interest in following the course of an image which suggested itself in experience or in imagination nine years before George Eliot began to write novels, and the persistent recurrence suggests both the impact of the first experience and the common thematic thread which runs from novel to novel. In order to look more clearly at the common element in these scenes of disenchantment—they are not the only examples but probably the most important—it is necessary to go back to the letter to Sara Hennell. After describing the awakening in the disenchanted room George Eliot continues:

It is so in all the stages of life—the poetry of girlhood goes—the poetry of love and marriage—the poetry of maternity—and at last the very poetry of duty forsakes us for a season and we see ourselves and all about us as nothing more than miserable agglomerations of atoms—poor tentative efforts of the Natur Princep to mould a personality. (Haight, i, p. 264)

This disappearance of glamour is an essential part of the process of every novel, and this letter is almost a forecast of

195

what she was to write: the poetry of girlhood vanishes for
Janet and Maggie, the poetry of love and marriage for Gilfil,
Hetty, Adam, Silas, the poetry of maternity for Mrs Transome,
and the poetry of duty for Romola. Moreover, each conversion
of poetry into prose depends on the dispelling of a dream. This
lost 'poetry' is usually not seen as a lost glory, as it is in Wordsworth and Coleridge. George Eliot emphasizes the departed
illusion rather than the departed joy. It is a poetry erected on
a dream, a dream in which the dreamer occupies the centre,
and disenchantment is the waking which forces the dreamer
to look painfully at a reality which puts him in his place.
Janet, Adam, Maggie, Esther, Romola, and Dorothea all move
out of their different dreams into the same clearly lit world
where they have to do without the dreamer's drug. The crisis
is one of the oblique demonstrations of George Eliot's precept, enunciated as the positivist's challenge to Christianity:
'The "highest calling and election" is *to do without opium.*'[1]
George Eliot does not show anything very like her own renunciation of opiate, but she shows opiates as various as
alcohol, daydream, literature, love, and inexperienced idealism.
Most of her heroines need only one disenchantment, though
Hetty and Gwendolen withdraw from their disenchanted
worlds to find some other temporary opiate. Their failure to
find nurture in despair is as significant as the success of Dorothea. George Eliot sees maturity as the ability to live without
illusion; her moral is the opposite of that of *The Wild Duck* and
The Iceman Cometh.

'Nothing more than miscrable agglomerations of atoms'—
the sense of dislocation within the personality was something
which George Eliot felt as strongly as Wordsworth and
Coleridge had before her. Her metamorphosis, as she called it,
was indeed like Wordsworth's in more ways than one. They
were both haunted by a double sense of disintegration: by the
break between past and present, and by the break between the
heart and the reason.

It is the first break, the loss of continuity in time, the sense
of an isolated present snapped off from the past, which she

---

[1] I have listed these images of opium in a note in *Notes and Queries,*
November 1957.

emphasizes most vigorously in the novels. In their very different ways Maggie, Silas, Esther, Dorothea, and Gwendolen all share with their creator this feeling of fragmentariness and unreality. In their lives, as in hers, it was a stage in the metamorphosis. For most of them the break with the past is a break with an opiate, with the exception of Silas, whose opiate was provided by the very isolation of the present. For him exile in place and hence in time was desirable:

Minds that have been unhinged from their old faith and love, have perhaps sought this Lethean influence of exile, in which the past becomes dreamy because its symbols have all vanished, and the present too is dreamy because it is linked with no memories. (ch. ii)

George Eliot too had rejected the symbols of her past, and her fear of emotional isolation from the past and from her family is retold, with a difference, in the progress of Silas.

Silas is perhaps not strictly relevant to this discussion since he is one of the very few characters who is not absorbed in the dream of self. This is why his disintegration is a pleasantly unreal state, whereas most of the disenchanted heroines feel clearly and harshly aware of a reality which blocks past from present. It is a blocking which ends the dream of self, which marks the rude and salutary awakening to the world where self is reduced. Gwendolen's awakening stands alone in this respect for it is a slow process, not fairly simply identified with the awakening disenchantment which alters both past and present. Even in her disenchanted moment she is preoccupied with self, and she has to go far before her dread of solitude becomes an acceptance of solitude. The process is given unity by the repeated images.[1]

For Gwendolen, and for many of the others, disenchantment works, slowly or quickly, towards 'the state of prostration—the self-abnegation through which the soul must go', as George Eliot described it in the letter to Sara Hennell quoted at the beginning. Gwendolen even shares with George Eliot the sense of physical shrinking. Gwendolen felt that she was reduced to a 'speck'; George Eliot says in this same letter:

[1] See Chapter XI below.

The Scene as Image

I feel a sort of madness growing upon me—just the opposite of the delirium which makes people fancy that their bodies are filling the room. It seems to me as if I were shrinking into that mathematical abstraction, a point—so entirely am I destitute of contact that I am unconscious of length or breadth. (Haight, i, p. 264)

In the feeling of self-annihilation George Eliot is closer to Keats than to Wordsworth or Coleridge.

Whether or not they are reduced to a point, her heroines are certainly forced from the centre to the periphery, from the dream of self which filled the world to a reduced consciousness. The place of the oppressive room in this process is plain. For all the heroines the forcible reduction is in part at least the realization of the woman's lot, and the image of the room is the appropriate feminine image of the daily round and the shut-in life. The hard reality of the common objects is the only furnishing for the social trap portrayed in *The Mill on the Floss*, *Middlemarch* (perhaps to a lesser extent), and *Daniel Deronda*.

Not that these scenes and images are only a plea for the imprisoned woman. They can present Adam Bede's despair of himself and his world, and indeed any crisis in the development of the egoist—and all her characters are egoists—in which self shrinks and vision expands. Three weeks after she wrote to Sara Hennell describing her disenchantment, she wrote, with a backward glance: 'All creatures about to moult or to cast off an old skin, or enter on any new metamorphosis have sickly feelings. It was so with me, but now I am set free from the irritating worn-out integument' (Haight, i, p. 269).

This is the important thing. The disenchantment marks a stage in metamorphosis: it is the well-lit day which makes George Eliot's dark night of the soul. It is a test and a prelude to change. The idealists, Adam, Romola, and Dorothea, are forced to recognize the egoism in their ideal. The egoists who are successfully nurtured, Maggie and Esther, are forced to abdicate their splendid dreams. But classification is too rough a process. There is all the difference in the world between Maggie's reaction to disenchantment and Esther's: Maggie's prosaic shock leads her into a new dream of theoretical renunciation, Esther's leads her to accept as bitter what had been sweet in the dream. Maggie is roused by the twin shocks of sympathy and helplessness, Esther by the ironical solidifying of her romantic dream. There is also Hetty, caught in the 'narrow circle of her imagination' able to do nothing but run desperately from the unbearable daylight. There is Gwendolen, who has to endure a triple disenchantment before she abandons the place of the princess. The pattern remains, the people change. To point to a common image which links character and theme is merely to point to a constant which throws all the variations into relief. George Eliot used the landmarks of her own way of the soul—and this may be one reason why she is sometimes said to use one heroine many times—but it is only the landmarks which are unchanging.

Even the landmarks change in details. The disenchanted objects change. Janet sees ordinary chairs and tables, as George Eliot did, but Adam sees the dressing-table he made for Hetty. Esther sees richer furniture, and Mrs Transome's portrait, while Dorothea sees the tapestry she had welcomed because it belonged to Casaubon's mother, and, as the one living object, the portrait of Ladislaw's grandmother. Gwendolen, the aspiring amateur rebuked by Klesmer, the beauty whose face is her fatal fortune, sees the piano and the mirror.

What is more, for Esther and Dorothea and Gwendolen there is the movement away from the image of the narrow room. Gwendolen's sense of space has terror in it, but in its implications it is not so very different from the triumph in space which is found in *Felix Holt* and *Middlemarch*. Esther and Dorothea look away from the dead objects and see people: they look at a light which has some promise. Esther wanted 'the largeness of the world to help her thought' (ch. xlix) and she turns from the room to the window. Dorothea does the same. She 'could see figures moving. . . . Far off in the bending sky was the pearly light; and she felt the largeness of the world and the manifold wakings of men to labour and endurance' (ch. lxxx). What was a single image becomes a significant antithesis. The narrow room marks one stage in metamorphosis, the open window another. Just as metaphors and characters seem inseparable in *Timon of Athens*, for instance, where the images of gold and sex get body from the real gold

and real harlots, and the properties and characters are given
a symbolic status by their relation with the metaphors, so in
George Eliot the scenic method is inseparable from the habit
of metaphor. The interplay between scene and image fixes a
symbolic frame around the scene and gives visual intensity to
the imagery.

CHAPTER X

The Pathetic Image

(i)

THE imagery has many functions in George Eliot's novels. Imagery, for instance, provides a continuing source of pathos. Both the content of the image and the method of presentation make a part of the author's special plea for her characters. In the early stories, as we have seen, it is a plea made necessary by her choice of ordinary unexciting human material. The lack of excitement lies in the characters rather than the situations, for after *Amos Barton*, where both characters and events are unsensational, she relies on a fair amount of melodrama and coincidence. But from the beginning to the end of her writing, though with varying emphasis, as we have seen, she draws on a certain kind of human material which is pathetic as distinct from tragic. It may be unattractive, like Amos Barton, or weak, like Caterina, or limited in sensibility and passion, like Hetty: we must learn to accommodate ourselves to the discovery that some of those 'cunningly-fashioned instruments called human souls have only a very limited range of music, and will not vibrate in the least under a touch that fills others with tremulous rapture or quivering agony' (*Adam Bede*, ch. ix). Such characters, who play a decreasingly conspicuous part as the novels develop, lack complexity, passion, growth—all the equipment which makes the tragic hero rise in some or other way to his tragic occasion. The pathos of such characters lies—to follow her own formula—in pity rather than admiration. Since neither their tragic adventure nor their own awareness will arouse the interest of tragedy, George Eliot provides a supplementary appeal on behalf of their very inadequacy. The appeal is made in various ways, and imagery is one. It is possible to trace several pathetic images which recur throughout the novels, often in similar contexts, but changing as George Eliot's concept of tragedy—and her style—changes.

The Pathetic Image

There are three prominent pathetic images which are repeated: the image of the wounded animal, the image of the plant, and the image of the child. It is at first tempting to put too much stress on the force of the associations of these images. While it is true that they exploit the associations of nature and childhood with a romantic nostalgia which is a source of pathos, the pathos itself can vary in kind even where the content of the image is unchanged. While it is true that all these images are diminutive—all appealing with the pathetic defencelessness of little things, it is also true that the diminution varies: at times there is a lasting reduction of adult or even of human sympathy which may or may not be felt to be in character, at times this reduction is only a temporary shift in the point of view, and makes a special and generalizing appeal which does not diminish the stature of the characters. As one traces the progress of the image it becomes increasingly difficult to generalize about George Eliot's use of pathos.

The small wounded animal makes its first appearance in *Scenes of Clerical Life*. Caterina, the pathetic heroine of *Mr Gilfil's Love-Story* is described naturally enough as a small singing-bird—she is small and she sings. Perhaps the most noticeable thing about this image is its indiscriminate use. Wybrow, her false lover, calls her his 'little singing-bird' (ch. ii). The image then becomes part of the fabric of the author's commentary. In chapter iii we are told, still in the author's voice, 'The poor bird was beginning to flutter and vainly dash its soft breast against the hard iron bars of the inevitable' and later she is 'a humming-bird'. The image is elaborated in the next chapter:

Indeed, in the long monotonous leisure of that great country-house, you may be sure that there was always some one who had nothing better to do than to play with Tina. So that the little southern bird had its northern nest lined with tenderness, and caresses, and pretty things.

Then, in the same chapter, the old gardener picks up the author's endearment:

'She's as nesh an' dilicate as a paich-blossom—welly laike a linnet, wi' on'y joost body anoof to hold her voice.'

The Pathetic Image

In chapter v Sir Christopher tells her 'You must not be dressed in russet, though you are a singing-bird'. The image is taken up later by the author's generalization:

> Caterina, who had passed her life as a little unobtrusive singing-bird, nestling so fondly under the wings that were outstretched for her, her heart beating only to the peaceful rhythm of love, or fluttering with some easily stifled fear, had begun to know the fierce palpitations of triumph and hatred. (ch. v)

While this poor little heart was being bruised with a weight too heavy for it, Nature was holding on her calm inexorable way, in unmoved and terrible beauty. The stars were rushing in their eternal courses; the tides swelled to the level of the last expectant weed; the sun was making brilliant day to busy nations on the other side of the swift earth. . . . What were our little Tina and her trouble in this mighty torrent, rushing from one awful unknown to another? Lighter than the smallest centre of quivering life in the water-drop, hidden and uncared for as the pulse of anguish in the breast of the tiniest bird that has fluttered down to its nest with the long-sought food, and has found the nest torn and empty. (ch. v)

The image next shifts from bird to leveret, because in this passage birds are needed for another purpose, that of pathetic contrast. It is an effect rather like that of Coleridge's 'Dejection' where the very denial of the pathetic fallacy has its pathetic force:

> The golden sunlight beamed through the dripping boughs like a Shechinah, or visible divine presence, and the birds were chirping and trilling their new autumnal songs so sweetly, it seemed as if their throats, as well as the air, were all the clearer for the rain; but Caterina moved through all this joy and beauty like a poor wounded leveret painfully dragging its little body through the sweet clover-tufts—for it, sweet in vain. (ch. vii)

Here there is the double appeal of the harsh realistic rejection of the natural parallel and its oblique association within the simile. The bird image goes on in Sir Christopher's affectionate condescension: he calls her 'bird' and 'monkey' and the child-like endearments point ironically to the adult passions. Even here, in this early story, the apparently sentimental image has a complex effect. It is muted by the appropriateness which gives it a nickname status, and it is sometimes used with an

apparently ironical recognition of its inadequacy. When
Sir Christopher knows the whole story it is perhaps significant
that for the first time he does not pet her with his usual images
but merely says 'that poor thing' and 'poor little dear one',
pathetic comments of a different kind. On the other hand there
is a certain sense of inconsistency of tone for the image is also
used with the opposite of irony in the excessive pathos of
Gilfil's love and the author's sympathy. It is this uncertainty
and excess which gives the story an occasional sentimentality
not wholly in keeping with the psychological study of Caterina's
jealousy. This is an interesting first version of the treatment
of Gwendolen's 'murderous thought' but blurred and softened
by the excessive pathos.

In *Adam Bede* the pathetic images delineate Hetty, though
their appeal is modified by irony: Hetty's portrait is sharply
critical but far from being unsympathetic, and the diminutive images used of Caterina recur again, though with strong
Biblical associations. Each recurrence of the image is to some
extent coloured by context, and just as Caterina's story gave
rise to the bird image, so the character of Dinah and her relation to Hetty turn the small wounded creature into the lost
sheep. It makes its first appearance in Dinah's prescient
reverie:

By the time Dinah had undressed and put on her nightgown,
this feeling about Hetty had gathered a painful intensity; her
imagination had created a thorny thicket of sin and sorrow, in
which she saw the poor thing struggling torn and bleeding, looking
with tears for rescue and finding none. (ch. xv)

It is repeated in a scene of natural contrast very like that
in *Mr Gilfil's Love-Story*, introducing another desperate
journey:

There are no leaves on the trees and hedgerows, but how green
all the grassy fields are! and the dark purplish brown of the ploughed
earth and the bare branches, is beautiful too. What a glad world
this looks like, as one drives or rides along the valleys and over the
hills! I have often thought so when, in foreign countries, where the
fields and woods have looked to me like our English Loamshire—
the rich land tilled with just as much care, the woods rolling down

the gentle slopes to the green meadows—I have come on something
by the roadside which has reminded me that I am not in Loamshire:
an image of a great agony—the agony of the Cross. It has stood
perhaps by the clustering apple-blossoms, or in the broad sunshine
by the cornfield, or at a turning by the wood where a clear brook
was gurgling below; and surely, if there came a traveller to this
world who knew nothing of the story of man's life upon it, this
image of agony would seem to him strangely out of place in the
midst of this joyous nature. He would not know that hidden behind
the apple-blossoms, or among the golden corn, or under the shroud-
ing boughs of the wood, there might be a human heart beating
heavily with anguish; perhaps a young blooming girl, not knowing
where to turn for refuge from swift-advancing shame; understanding no more of this life of ours than a foolish lost lamb wandering
farther and farther in the nightfall on the lonely heath; yet tasting
the bitterest of life's bitterness. (ch. xxxv)

The animal image recurs in snatches—Hetty is compared
to 'a bright-eyed spaniel with a thorn in her foot', 'a round,
soft-coated animal' and 'the hunted wounded brute', but the
two prominent images, used in Dinah's anticipation and in
George Eliot's more elaborated generalization, make a pathetic
appeal which corrects the stern irony used elsewhere.

The image returns with the next pathetic childish heroine—
Tessa, in *Romola*. Here it is only a glimpse of possibility, fixing
Tito's character and Tessa's situation:

That future necessity of grieving Tessa could be scarcely more
to him than the far-off cry of some little suffering animal buried in
the thicket, to a merry cavalcade in the sunny plain. (ch. xx)

Next, it describes Mrs Transome in *Felix Holt*, where it is
used for the first time to send a startling shaft of pathos into
our reaction to a character who is neither small nor defenceless. It is the first pathetic image used, perhaps with deliberate
inappropriateness, to penetrate a character not presented as
pathetic. It is effective pathos for the moment, not part of a
full attempt to identify character and image:

They never said anything like the full truth about her, or divined
what was hidden under that outward life—a woman's keen sensibility and dread, which lay screened behind all her petty habits
and narrow notions, as some quivering thing with eyes and
throbbing heart may lie crouching behind withered rubbish. (ch. i)

The moment of pathos here helps to emphasize the parallelism of Mrs Transome and Esther, and is indeed an echo of another image, powerfully presented at the end of the Introduction:

The poets have told us of a dolorous enchanted forest in the under world. The thorn-bushes there, and the thick-barked stems, have human histories hidden in them; the power of unuttered cries dwells in the passionless-seeming branches, and the red warm blood is darkly feeding the quivering nerves of a sleepless memory that watches through them. These things are a parable.

It is, I think, a parable which is clearer in the light of this repeated image of the hidden animal, though there is more than pathos in the imprisoned humanity in the enchanted forest.

The image returns once more to generalize the pathos of Mirah when Daniel Deronda first sees her:

His mind glanced over the girl-tragedies that are going on in the world, hidden, unheeded, as if they were but tragedies of the copse or hedgerow, where the helpless drag wounded wings forsakenly, and streak the shadowed moss with the red moment-hand of their own death. (ch. xvi)

Daniel thinks of Mirah as 'a half-reared linnet, bruised and lost by the wayside' (ch. xxxii), and later sees Gwendolen in terms of a splendidly appropriate image, 'like a lost, weary, storm-beaten white doe, unable to rise and pursue its unguided way' (ch. lxi).

The common element in this group of images is plain, but the treatment varies remarkably: the associations of the small animal and its unobserved tragedy are continued but the tone moves from cosy and undignified endearment, to a more detached and observed natural image. It is generally, but not always, used as part of an attempt to create an inadequate, simple, pathetic character.

(ii)

The image of the flower makes its first appearance with the bird-images in *Mr Gilfil's Love-Story*. Mr Bates the gardener,

The Pathetic Image

with a not too convincing vocational excuse, compares Caterina to a peach-blossom and cyclamens. Later, when she turns to Gilfil, we are told 'The delicate-tendrilled plant must have something to cling to', and in the conclusion the image has a new pathetic extension:

But it is with men as with trees: if you lop off their finest branches, into which they were pouring their young life-juice, the wounds will be healed over with some rough boss, some odd excrescence; and what might have been a grand tree expanding into liberal shade, is but a whimsical misshapen trunk. (Epilogue)

In *Janet's Repentance* the image recurs in order to emphasize the theme of growth and regeneration. It acts as a recurrent demand for pathos and approval. Its recurrence acts as a triumphant religious praise. Restoration is miraculous: 'We reap what we sow, but Nature has love over and above that justice':

Was it for this you looked proudly at her when she came back to you in her rich pale beauty, like a tall white arum that has just ·unfolded its grand pure curves to the sun? (ch. iv)

She was too like the cistus flowers in the little garden before the window, that, with the shades of evening, might lie with the delicate white and glossy dark of their petals trampled in the roadside dust. (ch. v)

She tried to have hope and trust, though it was hard to believe that the future would be anything else than the harvest of the seed that was being sown before her eyes. But always there is seed being sown silently and unseen, and everywhere there come sweet flowers without our foresight or labour. We reap what we sow, but Nature has love over and above that justice, and gives us shadow and blossom and fruit that spring from no planting of ours. (ch. v)

How hard it is to kill the deep-down fibrous roots of human love and goodness. (ch. vii)

Blessed influence of one true loving human soul on another! Not calculable by algebra, not deducible by logic, but mysterious, effectual, mighty as the hidden process by which the tiny seed is quickened, and bursts forth into tall stems and broad leaf, and glowing tasseled flower. (ch. xix)

For a delicious hope—the hope of purification and inward peace—had entered into Janet's soul, and made it spring-time there as well as in the outer world. (ch. xx)

His words come to me like rain on the parched ground. (ch. xx)

If the adjectives are omitted little is lost in association, though a certain amount in insistence: the adjectives are warm with praise: 'clear, shining rain', 'delicious hope', 'soft rains of heaven'. They are also pathetic in their diminutives: 'tender leaf-buds', 'tiny seed' and 'little garden'.

The image is used more precisely of Hetty, to make a point about character and environment which George Eliot thought important. Here the pathos is only part of a total effect. In fact, the first appearance of the flower image is an ironical revaluation of the blossom and bud image used of Caterina— its irony is a violent one:

. . . Those eyelids delicate as petals . . . long lashes curled like the stamen of a flower. . . . How she will dote on her children! She is almost a child herself, and the little pink round things will hang about her like florets round the central flower. (ch. xv)

The irony of 'how she will dote' is one of context—there is nothing in the excessive softness and prettiness of the images which we do not find in other places where we are far from irony, and even here the stab beneath the deceptive soft imagery does not make itself felt on the first innocent reading. The precision comes on a later page when the image is used very differently: 'There are some plants that have hardly any roots: you may tear them from their native nook of rock or wall, and just lay them over your ornamental flower-pot, and they blossom none the worse.' A related image forecasts the tragedy in an apparently innocent piece of natural description of harvest, the introduction to Adam's discovery of Arthur and Hetty amongst the 'enervating' beeches and limes: 'If only the corn were not ripe enough to be blown out of the husk and scattered as untimely seed!' (ch. xxvii).

This image is used many times, both casually and emphatically, startlingly and conventionally, intensely and quietly. It appears in *Felix Holt*, again for the joint purposes of making appealing pathos and of underlining the theme of Esther's nurture: 'In our spring-time every day has its hidden growths in the mind, as it has in the earth when the little folded blades are getting ready to pierce the ground' (ch. xviii). Other slight comments on growth and roots throughout the novel become livelier and more noticeable after the introduction of this precise and affectionate image.

In *Daniel Deronda* we find another image generating the author's warmth and pity for a character elsewhere unexempted from sharp irony. The final chapter-heading is 'Fruit and Seed' (in *The Mill on the Floss*, Book v, for similar reasons, is headed 'Wheat and Tares'). Gwendolen, in that turn back in time which has succeeded our first view of her at the roulette-table, is presented in this image:

Goodness is a large, often a prospective word; like harvest, which at one stage when we talk of it lies all underground, with an indeterminate future: is the germ prospering in the darkness? at another, it has put forth delicate green blades, and by-and-by the trembling blossoms are ready to be dashed off by an hour of rough wind or rain. Each stage has its peculiar blight, and may have the healthy life choked out of it by a particular action of the foul land which rears or neighbours it, or by damage brought from foulness afar. (ch. vii)

The image is echoed by Daniel when he speaks to her after Grandcourt's death: 'You will find your life growing like a plant' and 'This sorrow, which has cut down to the root . . . ' (ch. lxv).

There is also the seed-image used of Mirah, again used softly and pathetically but with more restraint and more force of natural observation than the earliest examples: 'And she had grown up in her simplicity and truthfulness like a little flower-seed that absorbs the chance confusion of its surroundings into its own definite mould of beauty' (ch. xx). There are diminutive images used of Mirah—the water-nixy, for instance, and the repeated adjective 'dear', used both by Mordecai and the author. Even though the tone may be sober and restrained, as it is in the last example of the seed, it still fails, I think, to avoid sentimentality. The affectionate tone is unrelieved in Mirah's case. Unlike Maggie and Dorothea, she is a completely idealized and diminutive portrait, never at any time subjected to irony or criticism. The effect of the imagery depends on its context. The strong and iridescent character of Gwendolen can stand such moments of sober pathos, the character of Mirah is damagingly softened by them.

The Pathetic Image

Lastly, there is the image of the child, again a spring of pathetic association. On the whole, George Eliot does not sentimentalize children as characters—'Childhood is only the beautiful and happy time in contemplation and retrospect' she wrote to Sara Hennell on 3 March 1844. Eppie is presented explanatorily, as the restoration of the past and the maker of human contact, in an intellectual commentary which gives stiffening to the story. But the image of childhood as the golden time does recur at least three times, together with many pathetic images. The three images which can be included in this group play on the nostalgia of the lost childhood. There is a certain ambivalence here for, as I have already said, George Eliot is too interested in psychology not to anticipate her tragedies in childhood, and we have both the realistic treatment of childhood and the exploitation of some of its romantic qualities.

The first intensely pathetic image of this kind comes in *Adam Bede*. It is an image with some irony—choosing childhood as much for its lack of social complication as for its purity and simplicity. Here is childhood the Leveller:

Poor things! It was a pity they were not in that golden age of childhood when they would have stood face to face, eyeing each other with timid liking, then given each other a little butterfly kiss, and toddled off to play together. Arthur would have gone home to his silk-curtained cot, and Hetty to her homespun pillow, and both would have slept without dreams, and tomorrow would have been a life hardly conscious of a yesterday. (ch. xii)

In *The Mill on the Floss* the image is presented differently. We are there in the golden age—in a selected golden day—and we look forward instead of back. But the function is the same:

It was one of their happy mornings. They trotted along and sat down together, with no thought that life would ever change for them: they would only get bigger and not go to school, and it would always be like the holidays; they would always live together and be fond of each other. . . .

Life did change for Tom and Maggie. . . . (bk. I, ch. v)

Here the pathos is accompanied by the reflection that in a sense the eternity of childhood does last:

We could never have loved the earth so well if we had had no childhood in it,—if it were not the earth where the same flowers come up again every spring that we used to gather with our tiny fingers as we sat lisping to ourselves on the grass. . . .

The third image comes in *Daniel Deronda*. Gwendolen and Rex are riding:

It was an exquisite January morning in which there was no threat of rain, but a grey sky making the calmest background for the charms of a mild winter scene:—the grassy borders of the lanes, the hedgerows sprinkled with red berries and haunted with low twitterings, the purple bareness of the elms, the rich brown of the furrows. The horses' hoofs made a musical chime, accompanying their young voices. She was laughing at his equipment, for he was the reverse of a dandy, and he was enjoying her laughter: the freshness of the morning mingled with the freshness of their youth; and every sound that came from their clear throats, every glance they gave each other, was the bubbling outflow from a spring of joy. It was all morning to them, within and without. And thinking of them in these moments one[1] is tempted to that futile sort of wishing—if only things could have been a little otherwise then, so as to have been greatly otherwise after!—if only these two beautiful young creatures could have pledged themselves to each other then and there, and never through life have swerved from that pledge! (ch. vii)

Although this is an image of youth, not of childhood, it is close to the scene in *The Mill on the Floss* in its romantic appeal and its combination of the appropriate natural scene with the moment of youth and joy. It brings together too the exaltation of the moment and the shadow of the future. And its evasive 'then and there' and 'never through life' may perhaps make some contribution to the possibilities that haunt the end of the novel.

These are scenes, not metaphors, it is true, but their force is pathetic with something of the pathos of the images of animal and flower, and their contribution to the novel is similar. Their

---

[1] This 'one' would almost certainly have been 'I' or 'we' in an early novel.

visual appeal groups them with the use of imagery: in the
scene from *Adam Bede* the adult scene fades and the glamour
of childhood is superimposed, and in the other instances the
reverse takes place, the shadow of the adult tragedy falls on
the image of youth. The tone is affectionate, nostalgic, re-
signed. Once more the scene and the image have the same kind
of function.

There are also many ordinary images of the child which
carry the same kind of pathos—sometimes ironical, sometimes
straightforwardly pathetic. George Eliot's omniscient affection expresses itself maternally, often calls its creatures
'child' and 'poor child'. The endearment is often present as an
image, used with irony, pathos, and rebuking gravity. Hetty,
also called child and childish, is compared—in Dinah's
reverie—to 'A child hugging its toys in the beginning of a
long toilsome journey, in which it will have to bear hunger
and cold and unsheltered darkness' (ch. xv). This is of course
an image which exactly anticipates Hetty's 'Journey in
Despair'. Maggie is also 'poor child' and the force of her childhood scenes colours the whole novel. Dorothea is often presented in terms of the child: she speaks to Will 'with the simple
sincerity of an unhappy child, visited at school', and looks at
him, in the same scene, while he tells her about his mother,
'with serious intentness before her, like a child seeing a drama
for the first time' (ch. xxxvii). She speaks 'in a voice as clear
and unhesitating as a young chorister chanting a *credo*' and
she and Will look 'at each other like two fond children who
were talking confidentially of birds' (ch. xxxix). In the final
scene where they come together 'they stood, with their hands
clasped, like two children, looking out on the storm' and the
scene ends with Dorothea speaking of their future 'in a sobbing
childlike way' (ch. lxxxiv). Such images are too frequent to
list in full. It is worth noticing Esther (always 'child' to her
father) and Felix, in the scene in prison. Their love, like
Dorothea's and Will's, is presented in an image of children:
'He smiled, and took her two hands between his, pressed together as children hold them up in prayer' (ch. xlv). And later
she 'went towards him with the swift movement of a frightened
child towards its protection'. In *Daniel Deronda*, the first book

is called 'The Spoiled Child'. Gwendolen is often called 'child', 'poor child' and 'poor spoiled child'. Mirah shares the image, and their peculiar relation of plot-parallel and moral anti-thesis (both 'Maidens Choosing') is given a further emphasis. Mirah 'submitted like a tired child' (ch. xvii). Lydia Glasher 'kept hold of her purpose as a child might tighten its hand over a small stolen thing, crying and denying all the while' (ch. xxx). Daniel thinks of Mirah as a child: 'It was, a delight to have rescued this child acquainted with sorrow' (ch. xxxii). Gwendolen's 'belief in her power, with her other dreams before marriage, had often to be thrust aside now like the toys of a sick child, which it looks at with dull eyes, and has no heart to play with, however it may try' (ch. xxxv) and this is repeated later in the same chapter: 'For the reasons by which she had justified herself when the marriage had tempted her, and all her easy arrangement of her future power over her husband to make him do better than he might be inclined to do, were now as futile as the burnt-out lights which set off a child's pageant'. Daniel 'took one of her hands, and clasped it as if they were going to walk together like two children' (ch lvi). Later, 'she cried as the child cries whose little feet have fallen backward—cried to be taken by the hand, lest she should lose herself' (ch. lxv) and when she eventually knows that she has to stand alone, like Mirah at the beginning, 'She submitted like a half-soothed child' (ch. lxix).

These are not the only pathetic images in George Eliot, but they are the most prominent, though their effect is often a cumulative one, and strengthened by many other isolated endearments, metaphors and epithets. There does seem to be a development in their use: the images come to be expressed more coolly and an effect of distance is achieved by an in-creased observation and precision within the image itself. But this only applies to some of the images, and it will not do to correlate the growth in dignity in the image with the growth in complexity of the human material. There is at times a possible correlation, but there are still many pathetic images used in the last novels as sentimentally as they are used in the first. Indeed, these pathetic images may in part account for what has been called George Eliot's identification with some of her heroines. If one inspects the personality with which she endows Maggie and Dorothea, it seems plain that this is no biographical projection. It is rather her affectionate pity for her characters, a pity diffused through many images, which may account for a certain softness in her presentation. Will and Dorothea are in places reduced, as Dr Leavis says, by the pathetic image which George Eliot uses for several of her love-scenes, and this kind of reduction to childish sweetness and innocence is often a weakness in her treatment of sex. The images of light and flowers and childhood which accompany the commentary on their relationship (Dorothea is presented as a child most often in the scenes with Will) give them an exaggerated air of innocence and simplicity and an unnecessary pathos. We may not always tolerate the diminutive images and endearments which make up part of the author's commentary, for the sentiment appealing for Amos Barton and Caterina is not always appropriate for Dorothea and Gwendolen. But it does not do to dismiss them as sentimental: these pathetic images are usually part of a deliberate demand which is there to control the reader's response, and their recurrence reveals something of her method and her themes.

CHAPTER XI

The Ironical Image

(i)

PATHOS is plainly not the chief effect of George Eliot's use of recurring and insistent images. The recurrence itself has many functions. It is perhaps worth suggesting that the more elaborate structure of the last two novels, *Middlemarch* and *Daniel Deronda*, seems to have brought with it, perhaps deliberately, a Shakespearean use of running images. The recurrence of the pathetic image is fairly obvious, once we think of following its track, even if the characters it images are sometimes modified in less predictable ways. But in the last two novels, though also in *The Mill on the Floss* and *Romola*, we find single images and clusters of images which recur throughout the long narratives, acting as a mnemonic which helps author and reader to see and remember the book as a whole, binding past and present by anticipations and echoes, weaving the separate actions by clear or oblique cross-reference. Like Shakespeare's images, or like Wagner's motifs, these repetitions also have the function of thematic emphasis, and I would suggest that this is a function which George Eliot seems increasingly to delegate to such indirect methods rather than to the open generalization in her own voice which is blatant and unashamed—and usually successful—in the earlier novels. As we have seen, her own voice is still heard, and heard extensively, in the last novels, but it is sometimes silent where it might not have been in an earlier work, and in this silence imagery speaks for her. This may be the result of using more complex forms, and it may even be a result of her increasing interest in verse, in which case it is pleasant to find the novel benefiting from an interest which can hardly be said to have contributed to poetry.

The early novels are full of images. They are sometimes there to heighten an emotional appeal, either by repetition as

215

well as association, like the images of the little animal and
the plant, or by a strong single appearance, like the day-lit
room or the open window. They are sometimes there to
brighten a moral generalization, often, especially when they
are artistic and scientific images, used with a tone of wit
or ingenuity or jocularity, sometimes confident, sometimes
heavy, which carries over from her early essays and reviews.
Where there is a sustained use of imagery it is simpler than
the later patterns. Daniel Deneau, writing in *The Victorian
Newsletter* (Autumn 1957), rightly suggested that in the
article which was an earlier version of this chapter I had
laid too much stress on the naïve nature of the imagery in
the early novels. There are two kinds of imagery which I
should still like to describe as different from the ironical
images of the last two novels. One kind is very plainly naïve
in content because it is used in the mouth of simple characters.
Here the naïvety is both the author's and the characters',
for this is a simple matter of narrative decorum. Adam Bede
thinks in terms of images drawn from the carpenter's shop,
and he is sometimes speaking restrictedly, in terms of the
life and laws he knows and understands, sometimes apparently
making a more sophisticated attempt to look on life at large
in terms of good carpentry. Silas Marner's fumbling equation
of the lost gold and the golden hair is of this same kind. In
these cases, George Eliot, far from using imagery in a subtle
way of generalization, is making her plea for her characters'
simplicity by showing their imagery as a struggle to generalize
in the terms of their own particulars. It is not so very different, if I dare make the suggestion, from Henry James's use
of his golden bowl. He uses his characters' interpretation
of the bowl in order to demonstrate their distinct points of
view—exploiting their wit and agility, true, and not their
intellectual limitations—but in each case, we are conscious
of the characters, deliberately and appropriately choosing
the metaphor. He sometimes takes their imagery over, in
The Wings of a Dove and *The Golden Bowl*, where he has
chosen images some of whose associations (the Blake echo
in the 'golden bowl', for instance) the characters seem unaware of, and then his imagery takes on the kind of irony

we find in *Middlemarch* and *Daniel Deronda*, where there is a converse in imagery between author and reader which circumvents even those characters in whose mouth the image is placed.

There is also another kind of imagery—the borderline case of some of the repeated images in *The Mill on the Floss* and *Romola*. The metaphors of river and music in the one, and of Greek and Christian myth in the other, go underground and recur in a growing resonance. But they are images which take their glow from the strong symbols which have a real existence and reinforce the verbal reference: from Maggie's love of music, and the voices of Philip and Stephen, from the Floss, from the painting of Piero di Cosimo. There are sometimes images made both by characters and author, like the musical images, the imagery of the river in both novels, and the suggestions, thrown out by the antique-dealer and Romola, and underlined in the chapter-heading, 'The Garment of Fear', which make Tito's light armour take on a varied symbolic life. This is thematic imagery which takes its colour from real events and objects whose significance is plain in the action, and it is most conspicuous, I believe, in the neighbourhood of these events and objects. Perhaps it would be more accurate to call it simpler, rather than more naïve, than the imagery of the last novels.

This third use of imagery, which we find most extensively in the last two novels, and which I want to call ironical, also depends almost always on a literal source. These images too are taken from objects which have an actual presence in the novel. This literal existence, this almost casual air of metaphor picked up from the surface of life, seems to free the author's tone from the tone of forced ingenuity which often accompanies her clever and unexpected comparisons in her early writing. This casual air of freedom is something we find as early as *Adam Bede*. But in *Middlemarch* and *Daniel Deronda*, existing at the same time as the large and emphatic symbols like Jewish exile or Jewish unity, which carry the weight of their reference outside the context of fiction, there is the slow and minutely growing impression of repeated images which are often not related to any vital or traditional symbol either

217

inside the novel or outside it. They make something like a symbolic impression by the sheer weight of their repetitions, and also—the main source of their irony—by their movement from one character to another. They are often still spoken or thought by the characters. They are usually still reflecting real events and objects. But they do not rely for their strength on the neighbourhood of these events and objects, and their main function seems to be that of gradually creating a private ironical understanding between the author and the reader. Of course this understanding depends on more than a single or a casual reading. I can only say that the patterns I want to discuss have seemed to me to present themselves conspicuously, naturally, and illuminatingly, after several readings.

(ii)

There is an ironical converse between the author and the reader who is willing to return to the novel. It is one of the chief narrative equivalents of dramatic irony. The characters in these two novels are usually unaware of the significance of the images they use. They are not part of the characters' deliberate musing and commentary but part of an elaborate chain which binds character, unknowingly, with character.

This is what happens in *Middlemarch*. Here two important themes, the theme of egoism and the theme of frustration, have their signatory images which move on from character to character. There are three important repeated images, the image of the water, the image of the dark or narrow place, and the image of the mirror.

The image of the water is repeated with variations. It is also repeated in different tones: comic, critical, and highly serious. We meet it first in conjunction with the image of the mirror and the image of the labyrinth. Dorothea is learning to know her future husband, and imagery here has a highly critical function:

Dorothea by this time had looked deep into the ungauged reservoir of Mr Casaubon's mind, seeing reflected there in vague labyrinthine extension every quality she herself brought (ch. iii).

The Ironical Image

Next the image is put into Dorothea's own words, and the shift in viewpoint brings its irony:

'He thinks with me,' said Dorothea to herself, 'or rather, he thinks a whole world of which my thought is but a poor twopenny mirror. And his feelings too, his whole experience—what a lake compared with my little pool.' (ch. iii)

We next meet the image in Casaubon's mind, where it is echoed with accumulated irony in his metaphor of water:

Hence he determined to abandon himself to the stream of feeling, and perhaps was surprised to find what an exceedingly shallow rill it was. As in droughty regions baptism by immersion could only be performed symbolically, so Mr Casaubon found that sprinkling was the utmost approach to a plunge which his stream would afford him. (ch. vii)

It recurs again, for Dorothea, after her marriage:

In this way, the early months of marriage often are times of critical tumult—whether that of a shrimp-pool or of deeper waters —which afterwards subsides into cheerful peace.' (ch. xx)

And a little later we read:

Having once embarked on your marital voyage, it is impossible not to be aware that you make no way and that the sea is not within sight—that, in fact, you are exploring an enclosed basin. (ch. xx)

Later images reduce even the enclosed basin; we hear of 'the cloudy, damp despondency of uneasy egoism' (ch. xxi), of 'the swampy ground' where his soul was hatched (ch. xxix), and of his 'passionate longings' which 'clung low and mist-like in very shady places' (ch. xlii).

Then, as far as the Casaubons are concerned, the image of water, after its significant reduction from the fountain and the sea to the bathetic basin and suggestions of swamp, is discontinued. It has done its work and the vision of frustrated enclosure is developed in other images. But we have not done with the image of water.

It turns up again in the parallel disillusionment of Lydgate. His lake, however, is a reality: 'Rosamond's presence at that moment was perhaps no more than a spoonful brought to the lake'[1] (ch. xlv).

It is echoed when his agility and power, like Dorothea's desires, are deprived of their element:

Lydgate was much worried, and conscious of new elements in his life as noxious to him as an inlet of mud to a creature that has been used to breathe and bathe and dart after its illuminated prey in the clearest of waters. (ch. lviii)

Then the image of the mud obliquely revalues the romantic images of flowers which he has associated with Rosamund, and which her name keeps in our minds:

He could not succeed in keeping out of his mind for long together that he was every day getting deeper into that swamp, which tempts men towards it with such a pretty covering of flowers and verdure. (ch. lviii)

Here the associations with mermaids and sirens which are played on so differently by Lydgate and Farebrother are also put in their place. These images are not startlingly original in content, but in their echoing process they establish an ironical harking-back to the past, and also they underline the contrast and parallel which links Dorothea's story with Lydgate's. They also pick up an image which was used in the Prelude to *Middlemarch*, justifying the Wagnerian comparison. George Eliot began by saying: 'Here and there a cygnet is reared uneasily among the ducklings in the brown pond, and never finds the living stream in fellowship with its own oary-footed kind.'

The contrast between the great stretch of water and the shallow pond or swamp may also owe something to Bunyan's symbolic landscape. On 3 November 1842, George Eliot wrote to Sara Hennell of her 'slough of despond' which she described as 'the shallowest, muddiest, most unblessing stream' (Haight, i, p. 150). In a later letter, December 1848, she spoke of being 'left entangled among slimy weeds' and

[1] There is a joking version of this kind of contrast in a letter she wrote to Charles Bray, June 1848: 'Judge of me as men judge of their divinities —what you feel in your little half-drained puddle of a soul, I feel in my great Atlantic.' (Haight, i, p. 268)

hearing the distant 'rushing of the blessed torrent' (Haight, 1, p. 274). The slough turns up again in *The Mill on the Floss*, amongst the more conspicuous river-symbolism there, and has some influence on the shifting images in *Middlemarch*.

There is another recurring image of frustration, this time one of the images caught up from the actual surface of life. This is the image of the tomb or the labyrinth. We have met Dorothea's vision of Casaubon's 'labyrinthine extension' of her own qualities and the mocking 'labyrinthine extent' of his work. The labyrinth begins as a compliment to unknown knowledge and turns into an image of imprisonment. Casaubon's antiquarian researches provide the source for the image, and the first doubt comes for Dorothea when he diverts the talk from the improvements in village cottages 'to the extremely narrow accommodation which was to be had in the dwellings of the ancient Egyptians' (ch. iii)—a splendid example of comic satire and tragic preparation going hand-in-hand. We first meet this image of frustration in George Eliot's general comment on Dorothea's social imprisonment:

> With such a nature, struggling in the bands of a narrow teaching, hemmed in by a social life which seemed nothing but a labyrinth of petty courses, a walled-in maze of small paths that led no wither, the outcome was sure to strike others as at once exaggeration and inconsistency. (ch. iii)

She turns to Casaubon who walks in 'vaults, taper in hand' (ch. x) as an escape from this walled-in maze, and the image returns ironically to mark her vicious circle:

> But she was gradually ceasing to expect with her former delightful confidence that she should see any wide opening where she followed him. Poor Mr Casaubon himself was lost among small closets and winding stairs. . . . With his taper stuck before him he forgot the absence of windows, and in bitter manuscript remarks on other men's notions about the solar deities, he had become indifferent to the sunlight. (ch. xx)

We have already seen something of the significant use of the window in George Eliot and here we have 'the absence of windows'. Brief allusions and images gradually accumulate weight until Will's fury at Dorothea's 'tomb' and 'stone prison', the description of Casaubon's memory as a 'dark closet', classical associations, and even Tantripp's wish that the books in the library might be made into a 'caticom' for Casaubon, all make their contribution to the image of darkness and narrowness.[1] The images reach a climax just before Casaubon tries to pass on his cramped researches as a legacy to Dorothea. Here Ladislaw participates in the natural imagery of sun and rain—the character of the man has to live up to an apotheosis in imagery:

> She longed for work which would be directly beneficent like the sunshine and the rain, and now it appeared that she was to live more and more in a virtual tomb, where there was the apparatus of a ghastly labour producing what would never see the light. Today she had stood at the door of the tomb and seen Will Ladislaw receding into the distant world of warm activity and fellowship—turning his face towards her as he went. (ch. xlviii)

And the image returns, with what must be deliberate recapitulation, when Dorothea doubts Will and thinks of him as 'the spirit of morning visiting the dim vault where she sat' (ch. lxxx).

One of the reasons why Will's character may seem inadequate or unsatisfactory is the highly emphatic force of this imagery. Will has to live up to the powerful images of space and light which fix him, in Dorothea's desire, as the antithesis to the 'rayless' Casaubon. The images of space are also associated with her urge away from self. The tomb and the labyrinth are the narrowness and restriction of a woman's lot, irradiated only by feeling, but they are also the enclosed and enclosing egoism of Casaubon's world, that 'mental estate mapped out a quarter of a century before, . . . sensibilities thus fenced in' (ch. xxix), the world described in images drawn from its own research. Will is 'a lunette opened in the wall of her prison' (ch. xxxviii) and when she knows that he loves her the sensation is described in terms of space and warmth: 'It was as if some hard icy pressure had melted, and her con-

---

[1] There is a striking resemblance between the images used of Dorothea's oppressive marriage to Casaubon and those used of Isabel Archer's marriage to Gilbert Osmond in *The Portrait of a Lady*: Isabel associates Gilbert with metaphors of darkness and enclosure.

sciousness had room to expand: her past was come back to her with larger interpretation' (ch. lxii).

Again the images have been faintly anticipated in the Prelude, which speaks of 'dim lights and tangled circumstances' and again George Eliot uses the image in a letter (June 1848), speaking of herself, 'groping' in 'this dark, damp vault' (Haight, i, p. 265).

When we first met the word 'labyrinthine' as it was used to suggest the vast unknown possibilities of Casaubon's thought and feeling it was combined with the third prominent thematic image of *Middlemarch*, the image of the mirror. When Dorothea saw herself reflected in the waters of the reservoir, she saw a distorting mirror reflecting herself, not showing through clear glass a true image. This use of the mirror to express the in-turned vision runs through the book. Dorothea, like the cruder egoists, has to learn that each self is his own centre, and it is significant that she begins by looking at her own image in Casaubon, but ends, in her scene of renunciation where she decides to go to Rosamond, by looking away from self through a window. The enclosure of the single point of view, the Narcissus gaze, one of George Eliot's recurring themes from *Amos Barton* onwards, finds its metaphor in the mirror.

Middlemarch is, amongst other things, a novel about distorted vision, and this image of the mirror[1] moves from character to character, making its generalization in different contexts. Dorothea's vision is distorted by illusion (as well as by actual short-sightedness), but there are other sources of error. George Eliot briefly surveys various views of Casaubon—Mrs Cadwallader's, Sir James Chettam's, Mr Brooke's, and Celia's and comments in her caustic comic tone:

I am not sure that the greatest man of his age,[2] if ever that solitary superlative existed, could escape these unfavourable reflections of himself in various small mirrors; and even Milton, looking for his portrait in a spoon, must submit to have the facial angle of a bumpkin. (ch. x)

[1] George Eliot uses the image of the mirror ('doubtless defective') in her discussion of the novelist's vision in ch. xvii of *Adam Bede*.
[2] Perhaps a tilt at Ruskin's discussion of 'great men' in *Modern Painters*.

It is not only other people's view of Casaubon which interests her, and she looks also at his vision of the world outside himself. His impediment is egoism: 'Will not a tiny speck very close to our vision blot out the glory of the world, and leave only a margin by which we see the blot? I know no speck so troublesome as self' (ch. xlii).

But to return to the mirror. The fullest statement of this theme of the shifting and separate centres of vision is the elaborate image of the pier-glass, at the beginning of chapter xxvii. This turns, after some characteristic generalization, to Rosamond, but it echoes what we have already heard of Casaubon, that Dorothea came gradually to realize

With that distinctness which is no longer reflection but feeling—an idea wrought back to the directness of sense, like the solidity of objects—that he had an equivalent centre of self, whence the lights and shadows must always fall with a certain difference. (ch. xxi)

This seems rather a mysterious metaphor, with self presumably conceived of as a source of light, until we find the repetition and a possible explanation in the image of the pier-glass. Like Rosamond, Casaubon is the light reflected in the mirror:

Your pier-glass or extensive surface of polished steel made to be rubbed by a housemaid, will be minutely and multitudinously scratched in all directions; but place now against it a lighted candle as a centre of illumination, and lo! the scratches will seem to arrange themselves in a fine series of concentric circles round that little sun. It is demonstrable that the scratches are going everywhere impartially, and it is only your candle which produces the flattering illusion of a concentric arrangement, its light falling with an exclusive optical selection. These things are a parable. The scratches are events, and the candle is the egoism of any person now absent—of Miss Vincy, for example. (ch. xxvii)

There are many other images of distorted or inadequate vision, from the double image of telescope and microscope applied to an examination of Mrs Cadwallader's motives, to the calm and illusionless vision of Mary Garth, contemplating other people's egocentric illusion, which 'made their own lies opaque while everyone else's were transparent, making themselves exceptions to everything, as if when all the world looked yellow under a lamp they alone were rosy' (ch. xxxiii). But the favourite image for vision is the reflection. There are two powerful images—one comic, one tragic—of Bulstrode's reflection. The first comes in his interview with his brother-in-law Vincy:

> This was not the first time that Mr Bulstrode had begun by admonishing Mr Vincy, and had ended by seeing a very unsatisfactory reflection of himself in the coarse unflattering mirror which that manufacturer's mind presented to the subtler lights and shadows of his fellow-men; and perhaps his experience ought to have warned him how the scene would end. But a full-fed fountain will be generous with its waters even in the rain, when they are worse than useless; and a fine fount of admonition is apt to be equally irrepressible. (ch. xiii)

Here is an interesting example of the combination of the images of water and mirror, which seems to bear a resemblance to some Shakespearean clusters. Although elsewhere each image has a similar function—both dealing with reflection, or both with contrast between fact and illusion—here the combination seems to be an accidental association. And indeed the repetition may often be unconscious, though even if it is, the sign of thematic obsession could still be there.

Bulstrode's second unwanted reflection shows his futile attempt to escape from memory, reinforcing Garth's comment that we cannot escape our deeds:

> Night and day, without interruption save of brief sleep which only wove retrospect and fear into a fantastic present, he felt the scenes of his earlier life coming between him and everything else, as obstinately as, when we look through the window from a lighted room, the objects we turn our backs on are still before us, instead of the grass and the trees. (ch. lxi)

Another related image comes in the motto heading chapter lxxii, where Dorothea's belief in Lydgate is generalized in the lines:

> Full souls are double mirrors, making still
> An endless vista of fair things before,
> Repeating things behind.

The Ironical Image

The last appearance of the mirror image makes it an image of generous but undistorting vision—the gap between the supposed reflection in the 'reservoir' and the double mirror is filled by Dorothea's progress.

Connected with this metaphor is another, that of the crystal, which appears obliquely in *Romola*. In *Middlemarch* the crystal is related rather to the group of mirror and lens images, which George Eliot uses with scientific precision and emotional urgency. This image too she uses in her letters. She writes to Sara Hennell in September 1861, 'I hope you have some agreeable lens through which you can look at circumstances,' (Haight, iii, p. 450), and just as Dorothea sees Will as the lunette in her prison, so he sees her as 'the crystal that you want to see the light through' (ch. xxxviii). When the image recurs George Eliot seems to expect the reader to be conscious of the echo, for she says 'Will, we know, could not bear the thought of any flaw appearing in his crystal' (ch. xlvii).

Just as the images of flowers make an ironical link between Will's vision of Dorothea and Lydgate's vision of Rosamond, so does this image of the crystal. Will's image is Lydgate's also: 'It was as if a fracture in delicate crystal had begun, and he was afraid of any movement that might make it fatal' (ch. lxiv).

The image is used later in chapter lxxxi of Dorothea, with the same new suggestion of fragility: 'nervous exaltation which made her frame as dangerously responsive as a bit of finest Venetian crystal'.

There is another small group of images in *Middlemarch* which is plainly linked with a similar group in *Daniel Deronda*. This is a group of animal images which have a dehumanizing effect—again, they are sometimes used with deadly seriousness, sometimes with unequivocal or deceptive humour. The swamps and vaults are of course images which help to create character, but they have a wider thematic function as well. The animal images are used to build the portraits of those grim egoists, Rosamond and Grandcourt. Rosamond has a 'torpedo contact' (ch. lxiv) and possesses 'pincers' (chs. lxv, lxxviii) and Grandcourt in *Daniel Deronda* is a masculine version of Rosamond.

The Ironical Image

(iii)

Before Gwendolen meets Grandcourt she jokes to her mother about a dream in which she is 'looking at the face of a magnified insect' (ch. ix). The image of her pretended dream finds its echo. When she has met him there is a new animal comparison, still made fairly lightly:

Grandcourt after all was formidable—a handsome lizard of a hitherto unknown species, not of the lively, darting kind. But Gwendolen knew hardly anything about lizards, and ignorance gives one a large range of probabilities. This splendid specimen was probably gentle, suitable as a boudoir pet: what may not a lizard be, if you know nothing to the contrary? (ch. xiii)

Two chapters later, the lizard has become 'an alligator' in the mind of Lush, who knows him rather better than Gwendolen. Later he is compared to a 'sleepy-eyed animal on the watch for prey' (ch. xxxv) and, in this same chapter, with a torpedo, a crab and a boa-constrictor. Like Rosamond's, his is the egoism which grasps, encloses, and paralyses. The lizard recurs, together with the pincers (ch. xlviii), and the last inhuman image comes just before Grandcourt's death, when the animal is 'a dangerous serpent ornamentally coiled in her cabin' (ch. liv). The original joke is far out of sight.

This is running imagery of a different kind from the snow-ball accretions of the water and the tomb. These images depend on a much simpler kind of repetition. The villain is called animal names so often that the names transform him, though there is also the ironical movement from past to present. But there is another recurring image in *Daniel Deronda* which is of the ironical stuff of the central images of *Middlemarch*. It is also an animal image, though this time it is taken from an animal which has a real existence within the novel. This is the image of the horse or the chariot drawn by horses. Katherine Mansfield noticed the passionate effect of Stephen's panting horse in *The Mill on the Floss*, and the images in *Daniel Deronda* were also anticipated by one image in *Felix Holt*, where Esther, a Gwendolen who escapes her Grandcourt, has her possible fate described by Mrs Transome, who speaks with authority: 'This girl has a fine spirit—plenty of fire and

pride and wit. Men like such captives, as they like horses that
champ the bit and paw the ground: they feel more triumph in
their mastery' (ch. xxxix).

This image is repeated, with ironical flexibility, throughout *Daniel Deronda*. Its source within the novel is obvious and
appropriate, for Gwendolen's imperious egoism, her ruthless-
ness, and her love of splendour are all shown, carefully and
separately, in some episode concerned with riding or horses.
The princess in exile, she demands a fine horse. She rides to
hounds and leaves Rex to ride after her, for a fall. Her courtship by Grandcourt is almost entirely equestrian. When she
has accepted him they go to the window to see the horse
Criterion:

> They could see the two horses being taken slowly round the
> sweep, and the beautiful creatures, in their fine grooming, sent a
> thrill of exultation through Gwendolen. They were the symbols
> of command and luxury, in delightful contrast with the ugliness of
> poverty and humiliation at which she had lately been looking
> close. (ch. xxvii)

This is the suggestive object in literal existence, but the
horse has another life in metaphor. What Gwendolen does in
fact she plays with in imagination, and the modulation from
the real horses to the horses in imagery seems hardly noticeable. When she is first considering marriage with Grandcourt:
'Gwendolen wished to mount the chariot and drive the plung-
ing horses herself, with a spouse by her side who would fold
his arms and give her his countenance without looking ridi-
culous' (ch. xiii). The image recurs just before she accepts
Grandcourt, when she moves in mind from one alternative to
another: 'Meanwhile, the thought that he was coming to be
refused was inspiriting: she had the white reins in her hands
again' (ch. xxvii). It comes again in the following chapter,
after Gwendolen's sleepless night. Grandcourt has come and
she has not refused him. She is disturbed but quietens her
doubts, 'with a determination to do as she would do if she
had started on horseback, and go on with spirit'. But when
we next meet the image of the horse it is with a difference,
for it is now the image in Grandcourt's fantasy, where it
has a violent existence: 'She had been brought to accept

him in spite of everything—brought to kneel down like a
horse under training for the arena, though she might have an
objection to it all the while' (ch. xxviii). The clash of the
separated images has its own tension, and gives life to Grandcourt's desire, which is no mere sadistic desire for mastery,
but an urge to master the woman who would have liked to
master him, and who would have been capable of mastering
another man. The coincidence of the images makes an oblique
statement to the effect that two can play at metaphors.
Gwendolen's image of mastering horses turns into Grandcourt's vision of her as a mastered horse. The clash of images
continues, Gwendolen is forced to change hers: 'It was as if
she had consented to mount a chariot where another held the
reins: and it was not in her nature to leap out in the eyes of
the world' (ch. xxix). And, six pages later in the same chapter:
'The horses in the chariot she had mounted were going at full
speed.'

This is before her marriage. Afterwards, the images fall off,
existing, like the contrast between fountain and pond, to
make an ironical contrast which ends with the heroine's
awakening. Grandcourt comes to observe that she answered
to the rein (ch. xxxv): not only is she not holding the reins,[1]
but she is being driven, and towards the end Grandcourt feels
'perfectly satisfied that he held his wife with bit and bridle'
(ch. liv). This silent struggle in imagery is joined only once
by another character—Deronda seems to hear Gwendolen's
trust call out 'as if it had been the retreating cry of a creature
snatched and carried out of his reach by swift horsemen'
(ch. l). This is not the only image of Grandcourt's grasping
egoism. There are also many metaphors and suggestions of
political and military power which have their part to play
in the total impression of his character, but the image of the
horse has a special local irony as well as its violent physical
impact. It owes much of its physical effect to the careful observations of Grandcourt's sadistic treatment of his dogs.

---

[1] Daniel also observes 'I have my hands on the reins now . . . and I will
not drop them' when he decides to arm himself against falling in love
with Mirah (ch. xxxii) but this seems to stand outside the cumulative
irony of the other horse images.

Deronda and Gwendolen share another image. This is again an experience with literal existence, the experience of wide space, which has the dual life of fact and metaphor. We meet it first in a metaphor so familiar that it is unremarkable. Klesmer is attacking Gwendolen's choice of Bellini—'woman was dear to him, but music was dearer':

'It is a form of melody which expresses a puerile state of culture —a dandling, canting, see-saw kind of stuff—the passion and thought of people without any breadth of horizon. There is a sort of self-satisfied folly about every phrase of such melody: no cries of deep, mysterious passion—no conflict—no sense of the universal. It makes men small as they listen to it. Sing now something larger. And I shall see.'

'Oh, not now. By-and-by,' said Gwendolen, with a sinking of heart at the sudden width of horizon. . . . (ch. v)

Klesmer's rebuke is the first affront to Gwendolen's self-satisfaction, and her fear of the widening horizon is shown as a peculiarity of her sensibility. This special dread is also the natural reaction of the spoilt princess who finds that space and solitude take her out of 'her usual world in which her will was of some avail':

Solitude in any wide scene impressed her with an undefined feeling of immeasurable existence aloof from her, in the midst of which she was helplessly incapable of asserting herself. The little astronomy taught her at school used sometimes to set her imagination at work in a way that made her tremble: but always when some one joined her she recovered her indifference to the vastness in which she seemed an exile. (ch. vi)

The relation between Deronda and Gwendolen depends very much, I believe, on our acceptance of the prominence of this theme, which establishes, in imagery and in actual landscape, the difference between the two, the need Gwendolen has for dependence, and the measure of her final solitude. Deronda, like Klesmer, attacks her narrowness, tries to make her understand the possibility of non-attachment, and behind the flatness of precept is his experience. He delights in the broad view, independent of an insistent centre of self:

He chose a spot in the bend of the river just opposite Kew Gardens, where he had a great breadth of water before him reflecting the glory of the sky, while he himself was in shadow. He lay with his hands behind his head propped on a level with the boat's edge, so that he could see all around him, but could not be seen by any one at a few yards' distance; and for a long while he never turned his eyes from the view right in front of him. He was forgetting everything else in a half-speculative, half-involuntary identification of himself with the objects he was looking at, thinking how far it might be possible habitually to shift his centre till his own personality would be no less outside him than the landscape. (ch. xvii)

There is a link here with Mordecai, whose 'imagination spontaneously planted him on some spot where he had a far-stretching scene; his thought went on in wide spaces' (ch. xxxviii). This delight in wide spaces is made suggestive of the breadth of vision, the altruist's out-turned look. It is, on a larger scale, Esther and Dorothea's gaze through the window. And what is triumph for them is also triumph for Gwendolen, though for her it is the tragic and cathartic shock. Just as her vision of the insect face and the dead face in the picture came to have an actual presence, like Mordecai's vision of the bridge, so her terror in wide spaces becomes an actual nightmare. This is the last image which, in its echo of what we have heard before, completes the fantasy and fixes the moral:

There was a long silence between them. The world seemed getting larger round poor Gwendolen, and she more solitary and helpless in the midst. The thought that he might come back after going to the East, sank before the bewildering vision of these wide-stretching purposes in which she felt herself reduced to a mere speck. . . .
She was for the first time feeling the pressure of a vast mysterious movement, for the first time being dislodged from her supremacy in her own world, and getting a sense that her horizon was but a dipping onward of an existence with which her own was revolving. (ch. lxix)

I began by emphasizing the unity built by these repeated images. Perhaps I should end by emphasizing their effect of inevitability, seen nowhere so clearly as in *Daniel Deronda*. George Eliot is clearly working away from a full use of omniscient commentary, skilfully managed though this is in her novels, towards the indirect methods of hinting images. Once we find the trail the purpose is clear though the hints are often embedded in passages which we probably read more carelessly than we read the conversations or spotlighted action. *Middlemarch* and *Daniel Deronda* depend for their full effect on the kind of slow and repeated attentiveness to detail which we are more willing to give to the medium of poetry than to the medium of the prose narrative. The pattern of events and character is inseparable from a pattern of images as elaborate, if much less conspicuous, as the patterns in the novels of Henry James.

Conclusion

GEORGE ELIOT'S formal subtlety is something which places her in a special relation to the writing of our own century, not because it is different in kind and in complexity from the art of Dickens and Thackeray and Meredith,[1] but because it finds an expression for themes which are close to the themes of novelists and poets of our time. Her elaborate narrative pattern, composed of many elements, is not only very close to the formal experiments of later writers, but is used in the service of a very similar human picture. She succeeds, as all good novelists must, in making that intense particularization for the moment, which engages our imagination. Many of the superficial attitudes and appearances of characters and society—and some of the narrative conventions, though not many—have become a part of history, but beneath their remoteness lies the questioning and the sympathy of a humanism which speaks warmly and directly to this century and even to this decade.

Like so many later writers, George Eliot is concerned with the problem of a humanity without a providence. She turned from her deeply emotional attachment to Christianity for intellectual reasons common in her time and ours, but eventually, after a painful interval, brought her early faith and fervour to her new humanism. Basil Willey has suggested that, like Feuerbach, whom she translated, she turned from God to Reason, and from Reason to Man. Mrs Joan Bennett has suggested that, like Spinoza, whom she also translated, she took from Christianity 'the precept of neighbourly love'. Humanity was piteous, and pity plays a central part in the tragedy she writes, but she saw within the human condition the possibilities of a humanity which could be its own providence, and this honest and tentative faith which she called meliorism even extended to a human equivalent for her lost belief in immortality.

The social impulse could act as miraculously as the lost

---

[1] Many of Meredith's formal devices are very like George Eliot's.

angels, as she tells us in *Silas Marner*, and the little act can be
perpetuated beyond the vision and the immediate influence of
the unheroic hero. She insists on her precept of neighbourly
love in many ways, simple and less simple. It is present in a
slight poem like 'Brother and Sister':

> The nobler mastery learned
> Where inward vision over impulse reigns
> Widening its life with separate life discerned,

and, more elaborately, in *The Spanish Gypsy*, where there is
the theme, diffused through all the characters, but concentrated in Fedalma and Don Silva, of 'union deeper than division'. For the social impulse is not shown as an arrow pointed
happily towards the future, it is controlled by self-regard, its
opposite. The power of union is shown in its opposition to the
powers of division. Theophrastus Such says, 'I had the strug-
ling action of a myriad lives around me, each single life as
dear to itself as mine to me', but although he speaks for many
of her characters when he insists that each man must recognize his place within 'the common lot', the progress of her
souls, as we have seen, is never an easy passage from self-
regard to social love.

Apart from Daniel Deronda's Zionism, there are no political
extensions of the precept of love, and Deronda's has been
turned by the irony of history into an ill-chosen symbol for
love and union. But where she comes very close to the writers
of our time is in her attempt to show the strength of social
love in ordinary human relations—passionate or casual, permanent or fleeting. Her ethical and social generalizations, like
her muted optimism, emerge more strongly from her diffused
and covert statement of theme than they would from strongly
explicit and stereotyped character and event. Her generalizations are themselves tentative and are expressed in an appropriate form. Like Joyce, Virginia Woolf, E. M. Forster, and
some of the poets of the thirties, she uses her art to recreate
what appears to her as hope dispersed in fragments in a world
where individuals and communities blindly or wittingly make
their affirmations of love and integrity, their negations of self-
regard and division. Like Marx, she sees that 'otherworld-

liness' may be an opium, and believes that man must live un-
drugged. Like Freud, she has her Eros and her Thanatos, and
sees their powers of integration and negation in human relations and in the life of societies.

The human tragedy is always placed in a precisely defined
social context, where classes are graded and work brought
to life. Like Tolstoy and Zola, though in a less spectacular way,
she tries to measure the individual life against the flow of
history, showing society as shaping and being shaped by each
of its human units. The first idea she seems to have had for a
novel had its germ in the prospect of a rural society, and when
she eventually came to write *Scenes of Clerical Life* she re-
hearsed her skills in social delineation by starting with the
small rural community. Gradually she masters the difficulties.
She learns, her subtlety growing, to make background and
foreground fade in and out, and move in significant contrast.
She makes the social scene live in dialogue and brilliantly
animated technical detail. She combines dramatic display
and professional description. In *The Mill on the Floss* she
brings in the whole sweep of provincial life in one of the most
successful studies ever written of human beings in a social
medium—it has satire and sympathy. Then in *Middlemarch*
she presents with magnificent confidence an even wider social
scene. The community is shown with precision in most of the
novels: there are no vague sketches of weaver and carpenter
and surveyor, but men at work. We feel that we are moving
from square to square as Silas moves in his insect-like agility,
that a door is really being made in *Adam Bede*, that Mrs
Poyser knows about dairy cattle, that dyeing and auctioneer-
ing and medicine are precisely and solidly present in *Middlemarch*. It is a tremendously informed mind which contrives
(except in *Romola*) to suggest its technical accuracy without
overloading the scene with insistent technicalities. It never
becomes Lewes's hated 'detailism'[1] because each technical
detail is carefully placed in the context of character and action.

[1] The amount of technical detail which went into her novels was small
when compared with the research which formed part of the preliminary
work for each novel. See *Quarry for Middlemarch*, ed. Anna Theresa
Kitchel (1950).

Conclusion

A moral debate proceeds while the carpenters are working; Silas's motives and impulses are ticking before us as his fingers move; Fred Vincy's fate is being determined while he helps Caleb Garth with the surveying. And in the last instance, the larger political cause is present too: this is the railway coming to Middlemarch. The Reform Bill or the Beer Acts, trade and war, are sometimes there sounding their roar in the distance, marking the time and the place and the social change, and they are sometimes brought near, with the suddenness of a close-up, to mark the shift of perspective from the human heart to the course of great events.

Within the great event and the large group, she is always interested in individual man, sometimes energetic and powerful, often dwarfed, frustrated, and alone. He is placed in history and in society, given his local colour—in the most precise sense of the term—but emerges primarily as a moral being. The human progress is seen as the movement towards the loneliness and aggressiveness of self-regard, or towards the humane and warm acceptance of one's private case as part of the human lot. The human process at its most hopeful is seen in terms of the tragic education of the egoist. Meredith says at the beginning of *The Egoist*, 'The book of this earth is the book of egoists', but George Eliot uses the word and perhaps shows the case more often than Meredith. She does more than use it as a Comtean term. The tentativeness of her meliorism is something far removed from Comte's dogmatic blueprints for the Positivist society. This is plain when we find her resisting Frederic Harrison's proposal that she might write something in the nature of a Positivist Utopia. She wrote 'Let me join the choir invisible', which was used as a Positivist hymn, but her social analysis was too strongly grounded in the world as it was to write anything as rigidly didactic as Harrison envisaged:

I presume that art must use the 'milieu' before it, and not, except for some special purposes, create a new world fill it and people it with new beings. I suppose an ideal tale relating to [the] state of society which should have subjectively and objectively realized in its completeness a Positive system of life would be, even if an artistic marvel, valuable and intelligible exclusively

Conclusion

(like Bekker's Charicles) to the actual student of Comte; as one might suppose a romance of society in Mars or Venus, with habits and customs of the Martial and Aphrodisian natives might be to an astronomer. I presume no true art is directly didactic or dogmatic. But I can conceive—and forgive me for wearying you with a dream—an ever present dream of mine that the grand features of Comte's world might be sketched in fiction in their normal relations though under the forms of our familiar life. There is nothing in Positive existence which is not in the depths of human nature and civilized society. There is no social force which it uses which is not now in germ or in disuse present around us—no human passion which it supposes absent or which it will not set itself to govern. Now I have imagined the temporal and the spiritual power outlined so in their main functions—the home, the school, the temple, the workroom, the teacher, the ruler, the capitalist, the labourer, the wife, the mother, the child, of the future might be drawn so as to do no violence to our familiar ideas yet consciously standing in their normal place. Types of these all exist about us. All I conceive is a state of society sufficiently favourable for them to develop themselves freely, and hold their natural relations, a surrounding adequate for them to perform normally where for instance the moral and practical forces are sufficiently elevated to control without arousing too strong resistance, and where the good forces are sufficiently strong to show their value by practical results. (Haight, v, p. 286 f.)

This imaginary novel, compared with George Eliot's novels, for all Harrison's insistence on art using the milieu before it, would be a schematic and contracted world where the human relations were adapted to the interests not merely of a parable, but of a rigid political plan. Although George Eliot sometimes speaks of her writing as parable, her honest vision does not allow itself the luxury of a Utopia. She is insistently didactic, but her morally unequivocal world is never a tightly contracted one. 'Aesthetic teaching' she replied to Harrison, must not lapse from 'the picture to the diagram' (Haight, iv, p. 300). She shows all the human variables: the successes as well as the failures, the mixed cases, even the unacted possible lives that haunt all our commitments. The result is moral definiteness, maybe, but it is also human movement. We are left with the impression, after reading one of her novels, that

Conclusion

this is as close as the novelist can get to human multiplicity—
that here form has been given to fluidity and expansiveness.
We can trace the form as we can trace a diagram but the form
is always there in the interest of the human picture.

INDEX

Note. It has not been thought necessary to list references to George Eliot's novels. Readers who wish to refer to the discussion of particular novels will find that they are treated chronologically within chapters or chapter-sections.

Index

Index

Index

Smith and Elder, 168

Spanish Gypsy, The, 116, 137, 168, 193, 234

Stephen, Leslie, *George Eliot*, 54

Stowe, Harriet Beecher, *Uncle Tom's Cabin*, 10, 96

Sue, Eugène, referred to by George Eliot, 16

Taylor, Jeremy, read by Adam Bede and Dorothea Brooke, 49 & n

Teiresias, 173

Tennyson, Alfred, Lord, 9, 89

Thackeray, William Makepeace, 233; author's commentary, 155; *The Newcomes*, 2; *Vanity Fair*, 93, 96

Theophrastus Such, 234

Tillotson, Mrs Kathleen, 5

Tolstoy, Leo, 3, 235; *Anna Karenina*, 8; *War and Peace*, 2, 10, 22, 96

Turner, Joseph Mallord William, 7

Vasari, Giorgio, *Lives of the most eminent Painters*, source for *Romola*, 173, 175

Vermeer, Jan, 15

Victorian Newsletter, The, 216

Virgil, 171–2, 175

Wagner, Wilhelm Richard, 215, 220

Warning to Fair Women, A, 119

Watts-Dunton, Theodore, on George Eliot, 3

Westminster Review, The, 16, 21, 54, 154, 180

Willey, Basil, *Nineteenth Century Studies*, 233

Woolf, Virginia, 4, 15, 22, 29, 234

Wordsworth, William, 168, 196, 198; 'The Idiot Boy', 179; not admired by Mrs Transome, 49; so-called 'Wordsworthian' characters in George Eliot, 15

Zola, Emile, 235; *L'Assommoir*, 23